Understanding Initial Coin Offerings

ELGAR UNDERSTANDING SERIES

This series elucidates fundamental knowledge and foundational research on significant topics and themes across the social sciences. It provides a basis for understanding the key elements of the subject, with expert insight offering a clear and concise exposition.

Illuminating the pertinent issues, each book is authored or edited by a leading scholar in the field, providing clarity and definition, and presenting a comprehensive and authoritative account of the topic. Collectively and individually, these books will advance knowledge and understanding of contemporary issues and challenges.

For a full list of Edward Elgar published titles, including the titles in this series, visit our website at www.e elgar.com.

Understanding Initial Coin Offerings

A New Era of Decentralized Finance

Dmitri Boreiko

Assistant Professor of Corporate Finance, Faculty of Economics and Management, Free University of Bolzano-Bozen, Italy

ELGAR UNDERSTANDING SERIES

Edward **Elgar**
PUBLISHING

Cheltenham, UK • Northampton, MA, USA

Published by
Edward Elgar Publishing Limited
The Lypiatts
15 Lansdown Road
Cheltenham
Glos GL50 2JA
UK

Edward Elgar Publishing, Inc.
William Pratt House
9 Dewey Court
Northampton
Massachusetts 01060
USA

A catalogue record for this book
is available from the British Library

Library of Congress Control Number: 2023952687

This book is available electronically in the **Elgar**online
Economics subject collection
http://dx.doi.org/10.4337/9781803921587

ISBN 978 1 80392 157 0 (cased)
ISBN 978 1 80392 158 7 (eBook)

Printed and bound in Great Britain by
TJ Books Limited, Padstow, Cornwall

To my radiant wife, Lyudmila, who lighted my life many years ago and will continue to do so till our last days.

To my parents, to whom I owe everything; you planted the seeds of curiosity, determination, and grace within me, nurturing them with unwavering support.

To my precious children, Leonardo, Alexander and Olivia, who gave me inspiration, creativity, and immense joy to live this life. Your laughter and wonder breathe life into everything I do and push me to explore new horizons.

To my colleague and good friend Stefano Lombardo, who made me go forward and supported me in the lowest days of my life. Your wisdom, camaraderie, and unwavering faith have been a guiding star, leading me through the dark times.

To my friend and mentor Im Stefano, who taught me how to be strong, brave, and kind. Your lessons have showed me the way to stand tall and compassionate in the face of any adversity.

And to all of my friends, who make an integral part of my life. Your friendships are the threads that weave the rich tapestry of my existence, adding colour, joy, and depth to every single day.

Contents

Figures

Tables

Preface

As a visiting researcher at the London School of Economics in late 2017, I found myself exposed to the world of blockchain technology and Initial Coin Offerings (ICOs). While academic research on the topic was virtually non-existent, the industry was developing rapidly, creating a pressing need for more comprehensive and timely insights into the world of ICOs and blockchain technology. A bustling hub for fintech progress, London's vibrant atmosphere exposed me to this rapidly evolving landscape, and I was instantly captivated. During my time in London, I had the opportunity to attend numerous fintech conferences and events, where I engaged with industry experts, academics, and pioneers in the field. These experiences not only broadened my horizons but also reinforced my passion for exploring the applications and implications of blockchain technology. Furthermore, I realized that my background in computing science and finance, combined with a deep theoretical understanding of corporate financing, provided me with a competitive advantage to study this intriguing phenomenon.

For over 15 years, I have dedicated my research to understanding the intricate world of corporate finance, focusing on capital issues. My industry expertise and the Chartered Financial Analyst (CFA), Chartered Alternative Investment Analyst (CAIA), and Financial Data Professional (FDP) charters under my belt have further honed my ability to analyse and evaluate the nuances of financial markets. As the landscape shifted and crowdfunding emerged as a prominent financing strategy, my focus naturally gravitated towards blockchain technology and ICOs. Over the years, I have written several articles and a book on ICOs, always striving to provide an in-depth analysis and a holistic understanding of this ground-breaking method of financing. This new book represents the culmination of my efforts to offer readers a comprehensive account of the ICO phenomenon.

It is important to note that this book will not delve deeply into the technical intricacies of blockchain technology. The primary focus will be on the ICO phenomenon, providing a unique and valuable perspective for readers. By concentrating on the ICO process, its impact on the financial landscape, and the various actors involved, this book aims to offer a comprehensive understanding of this ground-breaking financing method, rather than an in-depth exploration of the underlying technology. Readers interested in the technical aspects of blockchain technology are encouraged to consult additional resources authored by experts in the field.

In the chapters that follow, I will delve into the complexities of ICOs, exploring their origins, mechanics, and impact on the global financial landscape. I will present and explain the intricacies of the ICO process, examining the roles and interactions of various actors and intermediaries, as well as the regulatory landscape that governed their actions and shaped the development, and the recent demise, of this once-vibrant industry. Drawing from my years of research, experience, and actual investing, I aim to provide a balanced and thorough examination of the ICO landscape, exploring both its potential and its challenges.

As we embark on this journey together, I hope that this book will serve as a valuable resource for anyone seeking to understand the intricacies of ICOs and their place in the world of finance. Whether you are a seasoned professional, an aspiring entrepreneur, or simply an enthusiast, I trust that this book will offer you a comprehensive and insightful overview of the exciting world of ICOs. While it remains uncertain whether the decline of the ICO industry represents the end of the first wave, a cyclical downturn, or a permanent shift in financing trends, the topic continues to hold relevance and interest for both current and future financial landscapes. As a blockchain aficionado, I am certain of its enduring significance.

1. Introduction to Initial Coin Offerings

In the ever-evolving world of startups, the story of the passionate entrepreneur with a brilliant idea is a familiar one. They envision a ground-breaking innovation, one that could potentially change the world, but struggle to secure funding through traditional means. Their own resources are missing; friends and family scorn at their extravagant business ideas; banks, venture capitalists, and angel investors turn them away, leaving their dreams in limbo or, worse, forgotten. This has long been the plight of many entrepreneurs, whose revolutionary ideas face the harsh reality of financial constraints.

For instance, consider the early days of the tech giant Apple. Founders Steve Jobs and Steve Wozniak, initially struggled to secure funding for their innovative computer design back in the 1970s. It was only after they managed to secure a $250 000 investment from angel investor and moneyman Mike Markkula that they could launch Apple as we know it today (O'Grady 2008). Similarly, Jeff Bezos incorporated his online bookstore in 1995 with a $300 000 loan from his parents and a few other investors, whom he could persuade of the potential of the internet channel for selling goods. This modest funding ultimately set the stage for the global e-commerce powerhouse that Amazon has become (Noe and Weber 2019).

These examples illustrate that securing adequate funding is crucial for transforming a brilliant idea into a world-class business. When traditional financing options prove to be out of reach, entrepreneurs must think creatively and embrace alternative methods of fundraising. By doing so, they can bring their innovative ideas to life and change the world for the better. For example, the advent of the internet and the rise of crowdfunding have brought about significant changes to the startup funding landscape. These changes have not only made it easier for entrepreneurs to raise funds, but they have also transformed the way investors approach the financing of new ventures in the early 21st century.

However, all this was true for conventional startups, whereas when funding was sought for projects related to blockchain or Bitcoin, no investors dared risk their money. Bitcoin, envisaged and implemented by anonymous creator(s) under the pseudonym Satoshi Nakamoto, is a digital currency that operates on a decentralized network, allowing for peer-to-peer transactions without the need for intermediaries like banks (Nakamoto 2008). Since the creation (or rather, mining, as the generation process is usually called) of the first bitcoins, crypto-related projects were associated with illegal trade during that early period, as these entities preferred crypto payments due to Bitcoin's anonymity and decentralization. The lack of established market and regulatory frameworks, coupled with the absence of established companies with clear leadership structures from whom to acquire equity, further deterred venture capitalists from investing.

Not surprisingly, it took several years for a young and ambitious innovator named J.R. Willett to understand that he was unable to obtain conventional funding to develop his novel solution that would harness the untapped potential of blockchain technology. Time and again, he was met with scepticism and rejection. With conventional fundraising avenues exhausted, he decided to forge his own path, leveraging the very technology he sought to promote.

Determined to bring his vision to life, Willett began drafting a White paper that detailed his ground-breaking concept: the *Initial Coin Offering*, or *ICO* (Willett 2012). This innovative fundraising method would enable startups and projects to issue their own tokens, representing a stake in the venture. These tokens could then be purchased by investors using other established cryptocurrencies like Bitcoin. As Willett refined his idea, he realized that the best way to demonstrate the potential of ICOs was to launch one himself. Thus, in 2013, he initiated the world's first ICO to raise funds for a project to introduce a new crypto coin that he named *Mastercoin*. The objective of Mastercoin was to create a new layer on top of the Bitcoin protocol that would enable advanced financial features, such as smart contracts and decentralized exchanges.

It took him only one month after publishing a post on the Bitcointalk.org forum website to raise 4740 Bitcoin, which was worth around $500 000 at the time.[1] The Mastercoin ICO garnered significant interest within the cryptocurrency community, as it represented a novel approach to fundraising that did not rely on traditional financial institutions. Without help from professional underwriters, an army of lawyers, an expensive marketing campaign, or venture capitalist involvement, by the end of the fundraising window, Mastercoin had successfully raised the targeted amount, demonstrating the viability and potential of ICOs as a new fundraising mechanism.

The success of the Mastercoin ICO marked a turning point in the world of startup finance. It proved that projects could efficiently raise funds using a decentralized model, attracting the attention of entrepreneurs, investors, and regulators alike. In the years that followed, ICOs gained popularity as a means of raising capital, ushering in a new era of innovation and growth in the cryptocurrency and blockchain industry. By 2018, ICOs experienced a remarkable boom, having collectively raised over $20 billion in funds.[2] The phenomenon of ICOs gained traction as an innovative method of fundraising, allowing blockchain-based projects to bypass traditional venture capital channels and connect directly with potential investors.

The ICO boom in 2017–2018 was fuelled by a combination of factors, including the increasing interest in cryptocurrencies, widespread media coverage, and the promise of high returns on investments (Fromberger and Haffke 2020). This led to a surge in both the number of projects and the funds raised, as investors and entrepreneurs sought to capitalize on the opportunity. However, the rapid growth of ICOs was not without its pitfalls. Many projects failed to deliver on their promises, resulting in substantial losses for investors. The lack of regulation and oversight in the space made it ripe for fraudulent activities and scams (Hornuf et al. 2022).

Back then, the regulatory environment for ICOs was relatively lax, with little to no oversight from authorities, putting investors at risk and undermining the legitimacy of the ICO market. As ICOs gained more attention, regulatory bodies across the globe began to take notice and implement measures to protect investors and bring order to the market. One of the most prominent steps taken was in July of 2017 when the US Securities and Exchange Commission (SEC) issued a report stating that tokens issued through ICOs could be considered securities under US law.[3] This effectively brought ICOs under the purview of securities regulations, requiring projects to comply with registration and disclosure requirements. Following this, many countries started to develop their own regulations and guidelines for ICOs, with some opting for a more restrictive approach, while others chose to encourage innovation through a balanced regulatory framework (Bellavitis et al. 2021).

The increased scrutiny and regulatory actions resulted in a decline in the number of ICOs and a shift towards more compliant fundraising methods, such as Security Token Offerings (STOs), Initial Exchange Offerings (IEOs), and later Initial DEX Offerings (IDOs) (Fromberger and Haffke 2021). STOs involved the issuance of security tokens, which were digital assets representing ownership in real-world assets, such as stocks, bonds, or real estate. These tokens were subject to securities regulations, providing a more compliant and secure approach for both projects seeking funding and investors (Lambert et al. 2022).

IEOs were conducted on cryptocurrency exchange platforms, which acted as intermediaries between the project developers and the investors. IEOs provided a higher level of trust and security for investors compared to ICOs. The exchange platform typically conducted due diligence on the projects and ensured compliance with regulatory requirements, along with immediate liquidity of the issued tokens. By utilizing the established infrastructure and user base of the exchange, IEOs offered a more streamlined and secure fundraising process for both project developers and investors (Anson 2021).

IDOs, on the other hand, were conducted on Decentralized Exchanges (DEXs) and allowed blockchain projects to raise capital by issuing tokens directly to investors. IDOs offered a fast, transparent, and decentralized way for projects to gain funding while providing investors with an opportunity to acquire new tokens early in their development (Chitsaz and Bigdeli 2021). They also provided instant liquidity, as the tokens were listed on the DEX immediately after the offering.

These DEXs later assumed a much wider role in the crypto ecosystem and, at roughly the same time as ICOs began to decline due to increased regulatory scrutiny and concerns about fraudulent activities, Decentralized Finance (DeFi) gained traction as a new evolutionary venue to raise funds for start-ups. DeFi, as an ecosystem of decentralized financial applications, provided a more transparent and accessible way for projects to raise capital. Various DeFi platforms enabled startups to leverage decentralized lending, liquidity pools, and yield farming as new methods of fundraising that eliminated the need for intermediaries and increased trust among investors. DeFi also offered improved risk management and compliance, as many platforms integrated Know-Your-Customer (KYC) and Anti-Money Laundering (AML) checks, which addressed some of the concerns that arose during the ICO boom.

Non-Fungible Tokens (NFTs) also emerged as a unique way for projects to raise funds by tapping into the growing interest in digital assets with distinct properties. NFTs allowed startups to create and sell unique digital assets tied to their projects, offering investors a more tangible and verifiable value proposition. The uniqueness and provable scarcity of NFTs also helped address some of the concerns around fraud and trust that plagued the ICO market (Borri et al. 2022).

By 2023, the blockchain financing industry had significantly matured, carving out a distinct niche within the realm of startup financing. In the forthcoming chapters, this book delves deeply into the multifaceted ICO phenomenon, aiming to present a comprehensive and exhaustive examination of the subject matter. Our exploration will encompass the historical development of ICOs, the various regulatory approaches, the role of various parties involved, and the evolution of the fundraising landscape, all while shedding light on the successes, pitfalls, and lessons learned throughout this transformative period in the blockchain and cryptocurrency space. Through this analysis, the author hopes to offer valuable insights and guidance for entrepreneurs, investors, and enthusiasts alike, as they navigate the ever-evolving world of blockchain financing.

In Chapter 2, we will explore the origins of ICOs, examining the factors that led to their emergence and the fusion of crowdfunding and blockchain technology. We will also compare ICOs as a funding mechanism with other methods prevalent in the industry.

In Chapter 3, we will systematically explore the development and evolution of ICOs as a primary method for raising capital within the blockchain and cryptocurrency ecosystem. Our discussion will begin with an overview of the early ICO campaigns, highlighting the characteristics that made them appealing to both startups and investors. Furthermore, we will explore the rise of DeFi and NFTs as innovative developments within the blockchain and cryptocurrency space.

Chapter 4 will deal with the economics of ICOs, encompassing the tokenomics and sale structure that play a crucial role in shaping their potential success. The ecosystem surrounding an ICO, involving various stakeholders like founders, investors, intermediaries, and regulators, is also discussed here.

Chapter 5 elucidates the roles and functions of the diverse actors within the ICO ecosystem. The narrative traces the journey from the early, simpler ICOs to the more sophisticated current landscape which necessitates various intermediaries such as advisors, industry experts, exchanges, auditors, and regulatory authorities.

Chapter 6 offers a practical guide to conducting research on ICOs, emphasizing the evolving nature of the field and the methodological challenges it presents. ICO research requires dealing with unstructured big data, a lack of standardized reporting, limited historical data, variable data quality, and significant heterogeneity among ICOs. Given these challenges, a focus on more substantial, confirmed deals and the use of blockchain technology for real-time transaction data are suggested.

Chapter 7 presents an overview of the current academic knowledge about ICOs, emphasizing the contrast between anecdotal industry literature and empirical scientific literature. It highlights the historical delay in academic research on ICOs due to the time-consuming nature of rigorous economic analysis and the recent focus on crowdfunding.

Chapter 8 counters the widespread misconception equating ICOs with scams or fraud. Despite the prevalence of scam-related content in ICO searches, it is crucial to understand that many ICOs are legitimate fundraising tools for startups. We examine the early days of ICOs, characterized by low entry barriers and limited regulation, which attracted fraudsters exploiting the ICO platform. To offer a balanced perspective, we delve into the risks for ICO investors, comparing fraud levels in ICOs with those in conventional finance.

Chapter 9 navigates the evolving landscape of ICO regulation, delving into its complexity and importance. It discusses who should oversee ICOs, establishes rules for this fast-paced market, and maintains a balance between investor protection, market integrity, and innovation. As ICOs evolve towards more structured forms like IEOs and IDOs, the need for a robust regulatory framework is paramount. The chapter traverses global ICO regulation history, regulatory roles, and the challenges they face in this swiftly developing sector.

Chapter 10 explores the evolution of digital asset fundraising, with a focus on STOs and IEOs as significant successors to ICOs. STOs have emerged as a regulated and compliant alternative to ICOs, while IEOs, initiated by cryptocurrency exchanges, provide added credibility and liquidity to investors. We discuss the mechanisms and pros and cons of STOs and IEOs, delve into notable examples, and assess the regulatory environment surrounding these innovations.

In the last chapter, we delve into DeFi and NFTs as emerging mechanisms for blockchain fundraising. We discuss the concept of DeFi, its key components, and how DEXs enable a novel form of blockchain funding, namely, IDOs. Additionally, we investigate NFTs, examining their evolution and diverse applications. The shift from ICOs and IEOs to IDOs and NFTs is analysed, highlighting the increased security, transparency, and flexibility these mechanisms offer.

So, let the odyssey begin!

NOTES

1   bitcointalk.org/index.php?topic=265488.0.
2   As will be evident in the subsequent chapters, general ICO statistics can be inconsistent, making it challenging to precisely identify the total volume and value. Various sources provide differing numbers for ICOs and funds raised, attributable to the inherent nature of the ICO method and discrepancies in data collection methods and timeframes.
3   www.sec.gov/news/press-release/2017-131.

REFERENCES

Anson, M. (2021) 'Initial exchange offerings: The next evolution in cryptocurrencies', *The Journal of Alternative Investments*, 23(4), pp. 110–121.
Bellavitis, C., Fisch, C., and Wiklund, J. (2021) 'A comprehensive review of the global development of Initial Coin Offerings (ICOs) and their regulation', *Journal of Business Venturing Insights*, 15, e00213. Available at: https://www.sciencedirect.com/science/article/abs/pii/S235267342030069X.
Borri, N., Liu, Y., and Tsyvinski, A. (2022) 'The economics of non-fungible tokens', SSRN. Available at: https://ssrn.com/abstract=4052045 (accessed: 1 July 2023).
Chitsaz, E. and Bigdeli, M. (2021) 'Identifying the success factors affecting entrepreneurial finance using Initial Dex Offering', *Journal of Entrepreneurship Development*, 14(2), pp. 221–240.
Fromberger, M. and Haffke, L. (2020) 'ICO market report 2018/2019 – Performance analysis of 2018's Initial Coin Offerings', SSRN. Available at: https://ssrn.com/abstract=3512125 (accessed: 1 July 2023).
Fromberger, M. and Haffke, L. (2021) 'ICO market report 2019/2020 – Performance analysis of 2019's Initial Coin Offerings', SSRN. Available at: https://ssrn.com/abstract=3770793 (accessed: 1 July 2023).
Hornuf, L., Kueck, T., and Schwienbacher, A. (2022) 'Initial coin offerings, information disclosure, and fraud', *Small Business Economics*, 58, pp. 1741–1759.
Lambert, T., Liebau, D., and Roosenboom, P. (2022) 'Security token offerings', *Small Business Economics*, 59, pp. 299–325.

Nakamoto, S. (2008) 'Bitcoin: A peer-to-peer electronic cash system', White Paper. Available at: bitcoin.org/bitcoin.pdf (accessed: 1 July 2023).

Noe, C.F. and Weber, J. (2019) 'Amazon.com, Inc', Case Study no. 17–183, MIT Sloan School of Management. Available at: mitsloan.mit.edu/sites/default/files/2020–03/Amazon.com_.%20Inc.IC_.pdf (accessed: 1 July 2023).

O'Grady, J.D (2008) *Apple Inc.* USA: Bloomsbury Publishing.

Willett, J.R. (2012) 'The second bitcoin whitepaper', White Paper. Available at: drive.google.com/file/d/18iRKDmZy44YDd3jyEtafouT1PA7dEi5e/view (accessed: 1 July 2023).

2. Initial Coin Offerings – how it all started

INTRODUCTION

In this chapter, we delve into the economic and financial environment prevailing in the early 2010s that laid the groundwork for the creation of ICOs, offering a comprehensive understanding of the factors that have shaped this novel approach to fundraising. In the first section, we examine the changing economic environment that has contributed to the rise of Initial Coin Offerings (ICOs). It begins with an analysis of the incumbent financial industry – suffering from a credit crunch brought about by the Great Recession of 2008 – and how traditional institutions have been challenged by the emergence of fintech startups. The section also discusses the shifting regulatory landscape and its implications for the financial sector.

In the second section, the chapter explores traditional funding methods for startups, including bank loans, venture capital, and Initial Public Offerings (IPOs). This discussion provides a basis for understanding the limitations of these conventional financing models, setting the stage for the emergence of alternative funding methods which are briefly analysed in section three. We look at the emergence of crowdfunding as a response to the shortcomings of traditional funding mechanisms. Section three overviews the establishment and growth of crowdfunding platforms and examines various crowdfunding models, while also covering the regulatory developments that have shaped the crowdfunding industry and highlighting notable success stories and challenges that the industry faced at that time.

In section four, the chapter shifts focus to the technological breakthroughs that underpin ICOs – namely, Bitcoin and blockchain technology. The section provides an overview of the key features of these innovations and their implications for the financial industry. Finally, the chapter concludes by summarizing the key findings and offering insights into the economic and financial environment that has led to the creation of ICOs. It emphasizes the importance of understanding these contextual factors in order to grasp the potential of ICOs as an innovative funding mechanism and appreciate their impact on the future of finance.

THE CHANGING ECONOMIC ENVIRONMENT

So, it is the beginning of the 2010s and the world economy is not in very good shape. Virtually all countries still feel the aftermath of the global financial crisis that began in 2007–2008. The crisis, which was largely triggered by a housing market bubble in the United States and the collapse of several large financial institutions, led to a severe and protracted global recession. Whereas the general mood was initially somewhat optimistic about economic recovery and financial conditions at the start of the decade (IMF 2010), later, global recovery was showing signs of further weaknesses (IMF 2012).

Developed economies such as the United States, the European Union, and Japan struggle to regain pre-crisis growth rates and unemployment rates remain elevated and persistent. Governments across the world implement austerity measures to reduce budget deficits and public debt levels. These measures often include spending cuts, tax increases, and reductions in social welfare programmes, which further constrain economic growth. This period is characterized by the escalation of the European sovereign debt crisis, where several European countries, including Greece, Ireland, Portugal, Spain, and Italy, are facing severe fiscal problems. The crisis has led to bailouts, austerity measures, and significant economic turmoil in the Eurozone.

As a result, real-world Gross Domestic Product (GDP) growth rates are far below the pre-crisis levels, hovering around 2.2–2.3 per cent in 2011–2012 (The World Bank 2013a). In response to the slow economic recovery and persistently high unemployment, central banks around the world implement unprecedented monetary policy measures, such as quantitative easing (QE) and near-zero or negative interest rates. These policies aim to stimulate economic growth, reduce unemployment, and prevent deflation – and it seems that they are somewhat effective. However, financial industry, by and large, is still in bad shape.

Incumbent Financial Industry

Following the 2008 financial crisis, in the 2010s the financial industry faces several structural problems that need to be addressed to efficiently function as a lending channel for corporations, small and medium enterprises (SMEs), and startups. The major problems plaguing the industry are as follows (IMF 2013):

1. Excessive reliance on complex financial instruments and high levels of leverage, which make the entire system vulnerable to shocks.
2. Excessive risk-taking due to industry deregulation and complexity of supervising diversified institutions that are lacking transparency.

3. 'Too-big-to-fail' issue, where large financial institutions have become so interconnected and systemically important that their failure would pose a threat to the entire financial system. The global financial crisis demonstrates that governments are often forced to step in and rescue these institutions, which creates moral hazard and distorts market incentives.
4. Stricter capital requirement for banks introduced to avoid their failures and prevent bank runs. As a result, many banks and financial institutions have engaged in downsizing through asset sales, divesting of non-core businesses, and strengthening their balance sheets to meet new capital requirements. This process leads to a shift in focus towards more conservative business practices, as banks seek to reduce risk and improve the quality of their assets. More conservative business practices have led to reduced lending, especially to the higher-risk cohort of borrowers such as SMEs and startups.
5. European sovereign debt crisis. European banks have been heavily exposed to sovereign debt, particularly from peripheral EU countries. As concerns grew over these countries' ability to repay their debts, banks faced significant losses and were forced to deleverage and raise additional capital. The crisis also led to a tightening of credit conditions, which further constrained economic growth and placed additional pressure on the financial industry.

To sum up – as of 2013, the crisis has led to a severe tightening of credit conditions, as banks became more risk-averse and reluctant to lend to consumers and businesses. For example, Ivashina and Scharfstein (2010) documented that, already in the fourth quarter of 2008, the US banks cut new loans to large borrowers by almost half compared to pre-crisis levels. The credit crunch has been even more severe for smaller, high-risk enterprises that often have insufficient collateral (Beck et al. 2010).

This credit crunch has further exacerbated the economic downturn, as reduced access to credit constrained consumption, investment, and overall economic growth. Uncertainty and reduced access to credit during the crisis has led banks and other financial institutions to scale down their investment activities. Additionally, many banks have faced losses from their exposure to toxic assets, which has further limited their ability to invest in new projects or businesses. Moreover, they must deal with higher overhead costs and increased expenditures on risk management and compliance systems. In response, many banks have implemented cost-cutting measures, such as layoffs, branch closures, and divestiture of non-core businesses.

The Shifting Regulatory Landscape

The collapse of Lehman Brothers in 2008 served as a stark warning for regulators about the vulnerabilities in the financial system and the potential consequences of the failure of a large financial institution. With over $600 billion in assets at the time of its collapse, Lehman Brothers was the largest bankruptcy filing in US history up to that point, and it led to widespread panic in financial markets, a dramatic tightening of credit conditions, and a deepening of the global financial crisis (Fernando et al. 2012).

This substantial shock to financial stability has been followed by equally spectacular bankruptcies and failures of large financial institutions such as Washington Mutual in 2008 ($307 billion in assets), Anglo Irish Bank in 2009 (€100 billion), Dexia, a Franco-Belgian bank, in 2011 (€516 billion), Bankia, a Spanish bank, in 2012 (€300 billion) and many smaller banks.

In response, regulators around the world have introduced new regulations, such as the Dodd-Frank Wall Street Reform and Consumer Protection Act in the United States, to increase transparency, limit risk-taking, and strengthen capital and liquidity requirements for banks. These reforms aim to create a more stable and resilient financial system by ensuring that banks are better capitalized and able to withstand future crises. At the same time, these regulations have led to increased red tape and administrative burdens for banks, as well as significantly higher compliance costs. While these measures were necessary to create more stability in the financial system, they also presented challenges for banks as they sought to adapt to the new regulatory environment and to restore profitability.

Emergence of Fintech Startups

Fintech startups emerged as a result of several driving forces and have been able to compete with traditional banks since the 2010s. One key factor contributing to their rise was the technological advancements that occurred during this time. Innovations in the internet, mobile devices, and cloud computing enabled these startups to develop new financial products and services that were more accessible and user-friendly. The global financial crisis of 2008 also played a significant role in the emergence of fintech startups. The crisis led to widespread mistrust in traditional banking systems, creating a demand for alternative financial solutions. As a result, entrepreneurs and investors saw an opportunity to disrupt the financial industry by offering new, innovative services that catered to changing customer preferences.

Fintech startups initially focused on specific niches within the financial industry, such as payments, lending, and personal finance management. By addressing the pain points in these areas, they were able to deliver better customer experiences and to gain traction. For example, they made it easier for people to transfer money, obtain loans, and manage their finances using digital platforms. Another reason fintech startups could compete with traditional banks was their agility and ability to innovate rapidly. These companies tended to have leaner organizational structures, which allowed them to adapt more quickly to market changes and customer needs. Moreover, they were not burdened by the legacy systems and regulatory constraints that often hindered traditional banks.

Furthermore, fintech startups benefited from the rise of a digitally savvy customer base. As more and more people became comfortable with using technology for everyday tasks, they were more open to adopting digital financial services. Fintech startups catered to this shift in consumer behaviour by providing seamless, convenient, and secure services that were often cheaper than those offered by traditional banks.

Lastly, regulatory support also played a role in the growth of fintech startups. Governments around the world recognized the potential of these new financial service providers to improve financial inclusion and stimulate economic growth. As a result, many countries introduced regulatory frameworks that were supportive of fintech innovation, paving the way for the emergence and growth of these startups.

According to Ernst and Young (2016) and Haddad and Hornuf (2019), fintech startups were active in the following nine sectors of the financial industry during the 2010s:

1. Asset management
2. Exchange services
3. Financing
4. Insurance
5. Loyalty programmes
6. Other business
7. Payment
8. Regulatory technology
9. Risk management

Examples of successful fintech stories include firms such as Betterment (betterment.com, USA) and Wealthfront (wealthfront.com, USA) in the asset management sector. Established in 2008, both companies have revolutionized the industry by providing online investment platforms that offer personalized recommendations and automated investment management. In the exchange services niche, Coinbase (coinbase.com, USA), founded in 2012, and Kraken (kraken.com, USA), established in 2011, have emerged as leading digital currency exchange platforms, enabling users to buy, sell, and store cryptocurrencies. In the financing domain, startups such as LendingClub (lendingclub.com, USA) and OnDeck (ondeck.com, USA), both founded in 2006, have gained significant traction by offering innovative lending platforms that connect borrowers with investors and provide small businesses with term loans and lines of credit.

In the insurance industry, Oscar Health (hioscar.com, USA), founded in 2012, and Metromile (metromile.com, USA), established in 2011, have emerged as leaders by using technology to simplify health insurance and offer pay-per-mile car insurance, respectively. In the loyalty programmes space, Belly (bellycard.com, USA), founded in 2011, and Points (points. com, Canada), established in 2000, provide businesses with digital customer loyalty platforms and customizable rewards programmes. Other successful fintech businesses, such as Square (squareup.com, USA), founded in 2009, and Xero (xero.com, New Zealand), established in 2006, offer a range of services such as payment processing, point-of-sale solutions, payroll services, and cloud-based accounting software.

Payment platforms like Stripe (stripe.com, USA), founded in 2010, and Adyen (adyen.com, Netherlands), established in 2006, have become integral to the fintech landscape by enabling businesses to accept and manage online payments in multiple currencies. In the regulatory technology (RegTech) niche, companies like Trulioo (trulioo.com, Canada), founded in 2011, and Chainalysis (chainalysis.com, USA), established in 2014, provide identity verification and blockchain analysis solutions to help businesses prevent fraud, meet regulatory compliance, and assist governments in their investigations. Lastly, in the risk management sector, Credit Karma (creditkarma. com, USA), founded in 2007, and Zest AI (zest.ai, USA), established in 2009 as ZestFinance, empower users with personal finance platforms offering free credit scores, reports, and monitoring, as well as providing lenders with machine learning software to enable better credit decisions and to reduce default risk.

Traditional banks have employed various strategies to compete with fintech startups and adapt to the changing financial landscape. One of these strategies included embracing digital transformation by investing heavily in digital technology to improve their online and mobile banking offerings. Another strategy was instead partnering with, or investing in, fintech companies (Hornuf et al. 2021). By collaborating with these innovative startups, banks could leverage their technology and expertise to develop new products and services. This approach allowed banks to benefit from the agility and innovation of fintech entrants without building everything in-house.

TRADITIONAL FUNDING METHODS FOR STARTUPS

Funding is crucial to startups for several reasons, including fuelling growth, attracting top talent, and staying competitive. Startups require capital to grow and expand their operations, invest in research and development, and to scale their products or services (Stiglitz and Weiss 1981). Obtaining funding allows startups to invest in necessary resources and infrastructure that can lead to increased market share and profitability, enabling them to attract and retain top talent, and proving vital to withstand competitive pressures, invest in marketing efforts, and develop strategic partnerships. Adequate financing can help startups navigate challenges such as economic downturns or increased competition, by providing a financial cushion that allows them to remain operational and provides space for them to continue to innovate (Denis 2004).

While friends, family, and fools (often referred to as the 3Fs) can be a crucial first source of funding for startups, this approach might not be sufficient for long-term growth and success. These initial investors often provide seed capital, which allows entrepreneurs to develop their ideas and start their ventures. However, the amount of funding from this source is usually limited, and the expectations of such investors may not always align with the business's needs.

As startups grow and their financial needs increase, they must explore various other channels for funding. Banks can be a primary source of funding for certain types of business and some startups may seek loans or lines of credit from financial institutions, or even explore alternative financing options such as invoice factoring or revenue-based financing. However, startups often face challenges in securing bank loans due to their risk profile, lack of collateral, and uneven cash flows. As a result, startups usually look everywhere to obtain the money needed for developing their business ideas.

These alternative sources include angel investors, who typically invest in early-stage startups and provide mentorship and guidance; venture capital firms, which invest larger sums of money in exchange for equity in the company; and government grants, which can offer non-dilutive funding for specific research and development projects or industries. Crowdfunding platforms, such as Kickstarter or Indiegogo, have also become popular funding sources, allowing startups to raise capital directly from their potential customers or supporters. Lastly, blockchain financing has emerged as an innovative source of funding for startups, providing new opportunities for raising capital and supporting business growth.

Bank Loans

In a bank-based financial systems, firms predominantly rely on bank loans for their external financing needs rather than capital markets. This is because banks play a central role in such systems, acting as intermediaries between savers and borrowers. As a result, firms in a bank-based financial system often find it more convenient and accessible to obtain financing through bank loans rather than through issuing bonds or stocks in capital markets.

The 2008 financial crisis, also known as the *global financial crisis*, had a profound impact on loan issuance worldwide. The crisis, which originated in the United States due to the collapse of the subprime mortgage market, quickly spread across the global financial system, affecting banks, financial institutions, and economies around the world. Banks, in an effort to mitigate their risk exposure and manage potential losses, have tightened their lending standards, making it more difficult for firms to obtain loans. This credit tightening, as described by Davis and Stone (2004), had a significant impact on the overall economy and businesses seeking financing.

In reality, bank loans may not be the most suitable funding source for startups for several reasons. One significant factor is that banks are generally risk-averse institutions and prefer to lend to established businesses with a proven track record and steady cash flows. Moreover, bank loans typically require collateral, which many startups may not possess. Additionally, the repayment structure of bank loans can be burdensome for startups. Startups may face difficulties in meeting the fixed repayment schedules associated with traditional bank loans and they usually need quick access to capital to seize opportunities and respond to market demands, whereas securing a bank loan may take weeks or even months.

Grants and Other Governmental Support

An alternative to banking resources, the startups may tap into entrepreneurial support programmes such as direct grants, or support through hubs or incubators. Hubs and incubators can be financed by various entities, including governments, private organizations, universities, or a combination of all three. While some business hubs and incubators receive government funding, others are privately funded or sponsored by corporations, foundations, or educational institutions.

In Europe, the United States, and the United Kingdom, during the 2010s, government grants were playing a more crucial role in supporting early-stage startups and innovative projects, especially in sectors such as technology, clean energy, and life sciences, following the credit crunch of bank financing. For instance, in Europe, the European Commission's Horizon 2020 programme has provided billions of euros in funding for research and innovation initiatives. The European Investment Bank (EIB) also offers various financial instruments and support programmes for innovative companies, including grants, loans, and guarantees. Similarly, the United States has programmes like the Small Business Innovation Research (SBIR) and Small Business Technology Transfer (STTR) grants, which provide funding for early-stage technology development and commercialization. In the United Kingdom, agencies like Innovate UK offer grants and other funding opportunities to support innovation across different sectors.

In the United States, the Small Business Administration (SBA) offers various grant and loan programmes tailored to startups and small businesses, but its primary focus is on providing loans and loan guarantees. In the fiscal year 2021, the SBA approved over $36.5 billion of funding (SBA 2022). Additionally, state and local government grant programmes contribute to the overall funding landscape, but their size and scope can vary widely across different regions.

Business Angels and Venture Capital

Equity financing, which can be provided by venture capitalists (VCs) and business angels (BAs), has proven to be an effective alternative source of funding for innovative startups. Equity financing involves raising capital by selling shares or ownership stakes in a company, as opposed to borrowing money through loans. VCs and BAs are more willing to invest in early-stage companies with high growth potential, despite the inherent risks, in exchange for equity in the business (Drover et al. 2017). They often have a higher risk tolerance than banks and are more focused on the potential long-term returns generated by successful startups (Kaplan and Lerner 2017).

VCs typically invest in startups through venture capital funds, pooling resources from various investors and managing the investments on their behalf. Not only do they bring financial resources to the table, but also valuable expertise, industry connections, and strategic guidance to help startups grow and succeed. VCs often invest in multiple startups, creating a diversified portfolio that helps them manage risk, as they anticipate that only a few of these companies will yield substantial returns (Cumming 2012).

Corporate Venture Capital (CVC) financing is an investment approach where established corporations invest in startups or early-stage companies as a means to gain strategic advantages and financial returns. These investments are a form of equity financing, with the investing corporation acquiring shares or ownership stakes in the target company. CVC differs from traditional venture capital in that the investors are established companies rather than venture capital firms or individual investors.

When corporations engage in CVC financing, they often focus on startups operating within the same industry or in complementary sectors. This strategic alignment allows the investing corporation to gain access to innovative technologies, products, or services that can potentially enhance their own offerings or provide a competitive advantage. For startups, CVC financing can be an attractive source of funding, as it may offer more than just capital (Gompers and Lerner 2000, 2001). The investing corporation can provide valuable resources, such as industry expertise, access to distribution channels, and operational support, which can help the startup scale and grow more rapidly. In addition, the endorsement of an established corporation can lend credibility to the startup, making it easier to attract customers, partners, and additional investors (Boreiko 2019).

However, CVC financing also has its potential drawbacks. Startups may face the risk of being overly influenced by the investing corporation's strategic objectives, which could potentially limit their flexibility and independence. Moreover, some corporations may seek to exert control over the startups they invest in, potentially hindering innovation or stifling creativity. For example, Kamepalli et al. (2021) argue that the dominance of major technology platforms, such as Google, Facebook, and Amazon, can create a *kill zone* that stifles innovation and competition. These platforms have the ability to control access to their ecosystems and leverage their market power to either acquire potential competitors or suppress their growth. As a result, startups and innovative companies operating in the kill zone may find it challenging to grow and scale their businesses, leading to reduced innovation and a less competitive market.

BAs, on the other hand, are typically high-net-worth individuals who invest their own money in startups. They tend to have significant business experience and often serve as mentors to the entrepreneurs they invest in, offering guidance and support based on their personal experience and expertise. BAs usually invest in smaller amounts than VCs, making them more accessible to early-stage startups that may not yet be ready for larger investments from venture capital firms. According to Sohl (2015), in 2014 around 73,000 ventures received over $24 billion in angel investments in the US alone and this figure consistently rose to reach $29.1 billion in 2021 (Sohl 2022).

Figure 2.1 illustrates the size of the worldwide VC market by stages. We see that the total funding is high but varies considerably across years. We observe a peak in 2021, followed by a slow decline in subsequent years. Later Stage financing constitutes the largest part, followed by Early Stage funding, with the more mature Seed Stage taking up only a small portion of the total funding.

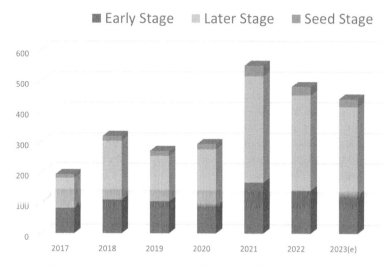

Source: Statista.com and author's calculations. The data for 2023 is an estimation.

Figure 2.1   *Venture capital raised worldwide. The figure shows the value*
of venture capital by stages raised in $US billion worldwide

CROWDFUNDING INNOVATION

With the emergence of the internet, geographical boundaries that once limited
the interaction between financing parties have been eliminated. Many financial institutions have established purely online subsidiaries for private and
corporate customers. A new class of lenders, such as peer-to-peer (P2P) online
lending platforms have also stepped in, assuming the roles of traditional financial institutions by matching assets and liabilities, conducting credit checks,
and monitoring borrowers.

A more revolutionary development emerged in the form of crowdfunding,
which typically involves online platforms that enable entrepreneurs and
companies to raise funds from individual investors by showcasing and promoting their projects. Initially centred around donation- and reward-based
crowdfunding, this approach has evolved into an alternative means of securing
seed capital for entrepreneurs or small firms with limited access to traditional
financing sources. As a result, online platforms have taken on the role of financial intermediaries in the early stages of business development, significantly
reducing costs and expanding the investor base.

What emerged in the early 2000s as a novel, decentralized way for individuals, entrepreneurs, and organizations to raise funds for their projects or

causes, later gained momentum with the launch of platforms like ArtistShare (2003), Kickstarter (2009), and Indiegogo (2008). These platforms made it easy for project creators to showcase their ideas and receive financial support from a broad audience. In its initial stages, crowdfunding mainly focused on donation-based and reward-based models, where contributors donate money without expecting anything in return, or expecting to get products or experiences in exchange for their financial support.

Over time, crowdfunding has evolved and expanded into various forms, such as equity, debt, or real estate crowdfunding, and today it has become a truly global phenomenon with numerous platforms operating across continents, catering to various industries, and supporting diverse funding models. While initial forecasts for the worldwide crowdfunding market in the 2020s projected a size in the range of hundreds of billions of dollars (The World Bank 2013b), more recent estimates paint a different picture. The current data indicates that the market was valued at $13.6 billion in 2021, a more modest figure than previously anticipated.[1] However, the market still demonstrates a strong compound annual growth rate (CAGR) of 11.2 per cent through 2028, reflecting the industry's resilience and potential for continued expansion.

Emergence and Growth of Crowdfunding Platforms

Quasi-crowdfunding examples from the earlier centuries can be traced back to instances where communities or groups pooled resources to support a common cause or project. This form of collective financing laid the groundwork for modern crowdfunding, even though it lacked the technological infrastructure and online platforms that characterize today's crowdfunding industry.

One notable example of an early crowdfunding campaign is the British rock band Marillion's 1997 US tour. Marillion's endeavour was exceptional for its time, as the band raised $60,000 from fans through the internet to fund their tour.[2] This demonstrated the potential of using the internet to connect creators and their supporters directly, paving the way for crowdfunding platforms that would later emerge. Inspired by the success of this novel method of financing, the online platform ArtistShare (artistshare.com) was launched in 2003 as the first dedicated crowdfunding platform. ArtistShare's initial focus was to help musicians fund their projects by connecting them with fans who would contribute money in exchange for exclusive content, such as behind-the-scenes access, updates, and limited-edition releases.

Five years later, other major crowdfunding platforms started to enter the scene, with a broader focus and introducing other forms of crowdfunding. In 2008, Indiegogo (indiegogo.com), offered a more general crowdfunding platform for various types of creative and entrepreneurial projects. A year later, in 2009, Kickstarter (kickstarter.com) launched a platform tailored to creative projects in various categories such as art, music, film, and technology. These early crowdfunding platforms laid the groundwork for the growth and diversification of the industry, enabling creators and entrepreneurs to access alternative funding sources for their projects.

In 2006, LendingClub (lendingclub.com) created a P2P lending platform that enables individuals and businesses to borrow money directly from investors. SeedInvest (seedinvest.com) was the first equity crowdfunding platform that connected startups with investors in 2012, allowing individuals to invest in early-stage companies in exchange for equity shares.

As of 2022, there are approximately 6.5 million crowdfunding campaigns taking place annually worldwide.[3] A significant number of these campaigns can be attributed to the United States, which alone is home to around 1500 active crowdfunding platforms.[4] This demonstrates the growing popularity and reach of crowdfunding as a viable alternative for raising funds across various industries and project types.

Still, despite the global reach of the internet, crowdfunding has primarily remained nationally bounded. This limitation is due to factors such as regulatory frameworks, cross-border financial transactions, and the need to navigate diverse legal, tax, and cultural environments. While some platforms have expanded their services to multiple countries, true global crowdfunding remains a challenge. However, the continued development of financial technologies and efforts to harmonize international regulations could pave the way for a more globally integrated crowdfunding industry in the future. Moreover, as argued by Rossi and Vismara (2018) in order to survive tough competition, the platforms that become de facto financial intermediaries able to offer a wide range of pre- and post-issue services, will be the ones to attract more lenders and investors.

As an example of such a platform, SeedInvest has emerged as a top choice for startups seeking funding to launch their ventures.[5] With a user base of over 700 000 investors, this platform has successfully facilitated funding for more than 250 startups, raising a total of over $465 million in financial support. What sets SeedInvest apart from other crowdfunding platforms is its focus on equity-based financing (discussed below) and its rigorous vetting process that carefully selects high-potential startups, which boosts investor confidence in the quality of projects featured on the platform.

In recent years, the subject of crowdfunding and alternative financing (AF) has garnered significant research interest, resulting in numerous academic papers and even special issues of entrepreneurship journals dedicated to the phenomenon of crowd investing. Scholars such as Agrawal et al. (2014, 2015, 2016) have contributed substantially to the growing body of knowledge on this topic. With access to rich datasets containing information about investors, fund-seekers, and the platforms themselves, researchers have been able to explore various aspects of the investment process and its participants. For a comprehensive overview of the latest literature on this subject, one can refer to the work of Drover et al. (2017).

Crowdfunding Models

In its initial stages, crowdfunding mainly focused on donation-based and reward-based models. In donation-based crowdfunding, contributors donate money without expecting anything in return, while reward-based crowdfunding involves offering incentives, such as products or experiences, to backers in exchange for their financial support. While these were the predominant methods at the start of the crowdfunding epoch, by 2020 these two models, usually grouped together into non-investment crowdfunding, represented only half a per cent of overall crowdfunding volume (Cambridge Centre for Alternative Finance or CCAF 2020).

Even though the other types were conceptually feasible, there was little to no regulation specifically tailored to crowdfunding, as it was a novel concept. Crowdfunding campaigns in the early days were required to comply with existing laws and regulations that varied by country and jurisdiction. Otherwise, they would operate at their own risk and potentially face legal consequences (an example will follow in the next subsection).

Over time, crowdfunding has evolved and expanded into two main alternatives – P2P lending and equity crowdfunding. P2P lending involves individuals or businesses borrowing money from multiple investors, usually through an online platform. In this model, borrowers create loan requests specifying the amount, interest rate, and loan term. Investors then lend money to the borrowers, either in full or as a part of the total loan amount. The borrowers are obligated to repay the loan with interest over a specified period. This crowdfunding method first appeared in 2005 in the US but was regarded by the regulators at that time as unregistered offerings of securities. By 2020, this model accounted for approximately 93 per cent of crowdfunding volume (CCAF 2020).[6]

Equity crowdfunding enables businesses, specifically startups and small enterprises, to raise capital by selling shares or stakes in their company to a collective of investors via an online platform. In this model, investors furnish funds in return for equity in the company. As shareholders, investors may potentially reap benefits from the company's growth and success via capital appreciation and, occasionally, dividends. However, equity crowdfunding bears risks, as investors may lose their investment if the company flounders or underperforms.

Equity crowdfunding models often garner significant attention due to the excitement associated with raising funds from the public. However, with $5 billion raised in 2020 (CCAF 2020), representing only 5.6 per cent of total crowdfunding proceeds (1.6 per cent if China is included), equity models contribute a relatively small portion to the overall funds raised through crowdfunding.

Real estate crowdfunding is a specialized form of crowdfunding that focuses on raising capital for real estate projects or investments. It can be considered a subset of both equity and debt crowdfunding. Investors either lend money that is secured by the real estate property and receive interest payments along with principal repayment at the end of the loan term, or they invest in exchange for ownership shares and may potentially benefit from property value appreciation, rental income, or profits from the sale of the property, which in turn increases the value of their equity stakes.

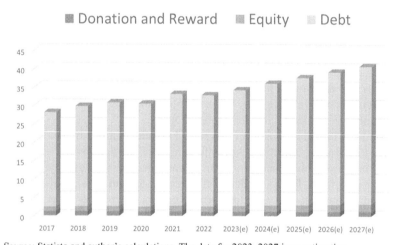

Source: Statista and author's calculations. The data for 2023–2027 is an estimation.

Figure 2.2   *Crowdfunding capital raising worldwide. The figure shows the value of crowdfunded funds by type of campaigns raised in US$ billion worldwide*

Figure 2.2 illustrates the trends and relative sizes of the various types of crowdfunding campaigns over the past six years, as well as projections for the upcoming five years. It is evident that debt crowdfunding dominates the landscape, accounting for more than 90 per cent of the total. The total market is projected to reach $40 billion by 2027, with the majority of this increase attributable to debt crowdfunding, and to a lesser extent, equity crowdfunding.

Donation and reward-based crowdfunding campaigns are expected to maintain their current levels over the next five years.

Regulatory Developments

Since their inception, P2P lending platforms have acted as financial intermediaries and, as a result, have been subject to existing financial regulations and securities laws. Therefore, when Prosper Marketplace (prosper.com, 2005) and LendingClub platforms launched their websites that allowed individuals to lend money to borrowers directly, bypassing traditional financial institutions, they were de facto offering securities (the loan notes) and were supposed (from the legal point of view) to register their offerings with the US Securities and Exchange Commission (SEC) and to adhere to the regulations governing securities. In 2008, the SEC even issued a cease-and-desist order to Prosper, stating that its lending activities constituted the sale of unregistered securities.[7] As a result, Prosper and other P2P lending platforms had to register their loan offerings with the SEC and comply with relevant securities laws which greatly hindered the development of this crowdfunding model.

Before 2012, equity crowdfunding platforms did not exist in the US because the sale of securities to non-accredited investors was prohibited, and equity crowdfunding was undeniably viewed as a form of securities offering. The first significant regulation in the crowdfunding space emerged in the United States with the Jumpstart Our Business Startups (JOBS) Act, signed into law by President Barack Obama in April 2012.[8] The JOBS Act aimed to facilitate access to capital for small businesses and startups, allowing them to raise funds more easily from non-accredited investors through crowdfunding platforms. It did this by easing various securities regulations, such as lifting the ban on general solicitation for certain offerings and raising the limits for how much individuals could invest.

The JOBS Act created a more permissive environment for crowdfunding, leading to an increase in its popularity and usage. In 2015, the SEC adopted the final rules for Title III of the JOBS Act, known as Regulation Crowdfunding (Reg CF). This allowed companies to raise up to $1 million (increased to $5 million in 2021) from non-accredited investors, further opening up the crowdfunding market and providing a push for its growth.[9]

In Europe, the evolution of the regulatory environment for crowdfunding was slower. Different countries introduced their own sets of rules, often with varying levels of rigidity. For instance, in the nascent stages of crowdfunding in the UK, platforms were required to navigate the prevailing regulatory landscape, ensuring compliance with regulations pertaining to securities offerings, investor protection, and anti-money laundering, among others. In certain cases, platforms needed to secure specific permissions or licences from the Financial Conduct Authority (FCA) to operate.

Nevertheless, retail investors were allowed to participate in UK equity crowdfunding even before the introduction of specific crowdfunding regulations in 2014. Dedicated crowdfunding platforms such as Crowdcube (crowdcube.com) and Seedrs (seedrs.com) were subject to existing financial and securities regulations and were opened to non-professional investors. The FCA only published a consultation paper (CP13/13) in October 2013, which outlined their proposed approach to regulating crowdfunding, including both loan-based and investment-based platforms.[10] The paper sought feedback from industry stakeholders and the public.

Surprisingly, it was Italian regulators, and not British ones, that were the first in Europe to address the new crowdfunding activity through the Italian Securities and Exchange Commission (CONSOB), which established specific regulations for equity crowdfunding to support SMEs, and innovative startups by its Regulation No. 18592 (July 2013).[11] This regulation provided a framework for equity crowdfunding, outlining the criteria for the operation of crowdfunding platforms, investor protection, disclosure requirements, and platform management.

The UK followed suit, with the FCA publishing Policy Statement 14/4 (PS14/4) in March 2014, setting out the final rules for regulating crowdfunding platforms.[12] These rules aimed to balance investor protection and financial stability, while also promoting competition in the interest of consumers.

It was only in late 2021 that the EU adopted the European Crowdfunding Service Provider (ECSP) Regulation as a legal framework that governs crowdfunding service providers across the European Union. Effective from 10 November 2021, the regulation aims to create a harmonized environment for crowdfunding platforms, streamlining operations across EU countries and reducing the complexity associated with different national regulations. This makes it easier for businesses and individuals to access crowdfunding opportunities throughout the EU.

One of the main objectives of the ECSP Regulation is to enhance investor protection. This is achieved through measures such as disclosure requirements for crowdfunding projects and platforms, as well as rules to prevent conflicts of interest. The regulation also facilitates cross-border operations by allowing crowdfunding service providers to obtain a 'European Crowdfunding Service Provider' passport, which permits them to operate across the EU under the same set of rules without needing separate authorization from individual countries.

As regards the Asian region, regulatory progress varies widely, with some countries adopting comprehensive frameworks, while others are still in the process of developing their regulations. For example, in China, the government has implemented several regulatory measures, primarily focusing on P2P lending platforms. The China Banking and Insurance Regulatory Commission (CBIRC) has set guidelines to reduce risks, improve transparency, and protect investors. Meanwhile, in India, the Securities and Exchange Board of India (SEBI) released a consultation paper on crowdfunding regulations in 2014, but a comprehensive framework has not yet been implemented. Equity crowdfunding operates in a regulatory grey area, while P2P lending platforms are regulated by the Reserve Bank of India (RBI) under the Non-Banking Financial Company (NBFC) framework.

In contrast, Japan introduced regulations for crowdfunding in 2015, with the Financial Services Agency (FSA) establishing rules for both P2P lending and equity crowdfunding platforms. These regulations focus on investor protection, including disclosure requirements and investment limits for non-accredited investors. Singapore's Monetary Authority of Singapore (MAS) regulates crowdfunding in the country, and in 2016, the MAS simplified the regulatory framework for securities-based crowdfunding. This reduced compliance costs for intermediaries and promoted the growth of crowdfunding platforms. P2P lending platforms are also regulated under the Securities and Futures Act (SFA) and the Financial Advisers Act (FAA). Lastly, South Korea's Financial Services Commission (FSC) implemented a regulatory framework for crowdfunding in 2016, mainly targeting equity crowdfunding platforms. The regulations include investor protection measures, disclosure requirements, and investment limits based on investor types.

Success Stories and Challenges

The crowdfunding landscape has seen numerous platforms rise to success. They have enabled creators to fund their projects and bring innovative products to life by tapping into a community of eager supporters. However, not all platforms have thrived, with, for example, Lending Club shutting its P2P business down due to regulatory issues and declining performance in 2020. Table 2.1 lists the main crowdfunding platforms and some summary statistics of the selected largest players in the market.

Table 2.1   *Largest crowdfunding platforms*

Platform	Country	Year	Model Types	No. of Campaigns	Largest Campaign	Funds raised, US$ billion
Prosper	USA	2005	P2P Lending	1.5m+	Limit of $50k	Over 23
Lending Club	USA	2006	P2P Lending	N/A	Limit of $40k	Over 15
GoFundMe	USA	2010	Donation, Fundraising, Charity	10m+	America's Food Fund – $45m	Over 17
Kickstarter	USA	2009	Reward, Equity, Donation, Lending	500,000+	Pebble Time – $20m	Over 7
Indiegogo	USA	2008	Reward, Equity, Donation, Lending, Charity	800,000+	MATE X – $18m	Over 2
Seedrs	UK	2012	Equity, Lending	1,700+	Revolut – $3m	Over 2
Crowdcube	UK	2011	Equity, P2P Lending	1,000+	Monzo – $24m	Over 1

Source: the data is sourced from platforms' websites, Wikipedia, and various research reports.
Note: Year column refers to the year of establishment of each crowdfunding platform.

Several crowdfunding campaigns have garnered significant attention and success, such as the Pebble Time smartwatch, which raised over $20 million on Kickstarter, and the MATE X, a foldable eBike project, which raised over $18 million on Indiegogo. These campaigns showcased the potential of crowdfunding to not only fund projects but also create massive traction and awareness.

Despite these success stories, there have been instances where famous start-ups secured funding but failed to deliver on their promises. Notable examples include Zano, a mini-drone project that raised $3.5 million on Kickstarter,[13] and Skully, an augmented reality motorcycle helmet that raised $2.4 million on Indiegogo.[14] Both companies faced production and financial challenges, ultimately resulting in their inability to deliver the promised products.

Fraud is not a frequent occurrence in crowdfunding, but it does happen. Even so the reported figures of 10 per cent of all campaigns that misuse the collected funds seem to be an overstatement.[15] More reliable data indicates that fraudulent activities are not so frequent in crowdfunding. The platforms themselves are taking strict measures to ensure the authenticity of campaigns and protect backers by implementing verification processes and terms of use. For example, Cumming et al. (2023) identify only 193 clear fraud cases on Kickstarter which makes up only less than 1 per cent of all campaigns launched on this platform. Nevertheless, it does not mean that backers should not conduct their own due diligence and research projects before supporting crowdfunding projects.

BITCOIN AND BLOCKCHAIN

As crowdfunding platforms gained traction, the traditional financial system, with its intermediaries such as banks, still played a significant role in processing payments. However, the emergence of Bitcoin and decentralized digital currencies marked a paradigm shift, enabling a new way to transact and further disrupting the financial landscape. Prior to Bitcoin's emergence, there were several attempts to create decentralized digital currencies. Examples include David Chaum's DigiCash in the 1990s and Nick Szabo's Bit Gold in the early 2000s. While these early attempts showed promise, they ultimately failed due to factors such as regulatory pressures, lack of widespread adoption, and technical limitations.

Bitcoin in a Nutshell

Bitcoin's introduction in 2008 by the pseudonymous creator Satoshi Nakamoto (Nakamoto 2008) marked a breakthrough in the world of digital currencies. Built on a decentralized network called the blockchain, Bitcoin solved the double-spending problem that plagued previous digital currency attempts. Using cryptographic techniques and a consensus mechanism, Bitcoin eliminated the need for a central authority, fostering trust among participants in the network.

Bitcoin is a decentralized digital currency that enables P2P transactions without the need for intermediaries like banks or other financial institutions. The underlying technology that powers Bitcoin is called blockchain, which is essentially a public, distributed ledger that records every transaction made within the network. The blockchain ensures transparency, security, and immutability, as once a transaction is recorded, it cannot be altered or deleted.

The Bitcoin network is maintained by a group of participants called miners, who use powerful computers to solve complex mathematical problems. These problems are related to validating and adding new transactions to the blockchain, a process known as mining. When miners successfully validate a new block of transactions, they are rewarded with newly minted bitcoins and transaction fees paid by users.

Transactions on the Bitcoin network are secured using cryptography. Each participant has a unique pair of public and private keys, which are used to send and receive bitcoins. The public key acts as an address to which others can send bitcoins, while the private key is required to access and spend the bitcoins held at that address. It is crucial for users to keep their private keys secure, as losing access to them would mean losing their bitcoins permanently.

One of the key innovations of Bitcoin is its solution to the double-spending problem, which refers to the risk of a digital currency being spent more than once. In traditional financial systems, this issue is resolved by relying on central authorities to verify and validate transactions. However, Bitcoin tackles this problem by using a consensus mechanism called *proof-of-work*, where miners compete to solve the mathematical problems and validate transactions. This process ensures that only legitimate transactions are recorded on the blockchain, preventing double-spending without the need for a central authority.

Even though Bitcoin is a decentralized network without any intermediary between the parties willing to use it as a means of payment, it still serves as a form of money, built on new innovative principles. As argued by Martin (2013), throughout human history, various types of money have represented a social contract, implying a collective agreement among numerous parties involved, including sovereigns and bankers, who frequently attempted to change the terms of the bargain to their advantage. The introduction of Bitcoin and other blockchain-based coins or tokens marks one of the first successful attempts to ensure that such an agreement is just, fair, and immutable at all times and for all negotiating parties.

Bitcoin and Illicit Transactions

The advantages offered by Bitcoin include lower transaction fees, faster payment processing, and increased financial privacy. It also provides an alternative for individuals who are disillusioned with central banks and governmental control over monetary policy. However, the anonymity and decentralized nature of Bitcoin has also attracted criminals and tax evaders, who saw it as a means to conduct illicit transactions and evade law enforcement. According to Foley et al. (2019), about one-quarter of Bitcoin users are involved in illicit transactions, with an estimated $76 billion worth of illegal activities conducted through Bitcoin each year. This figure is comparable to the size of the US and European illegal drug markets. Foley et al. also suggest that the illegal share of Bitcoin activity is likely to decrease as mainstream interest in the digital currency grows and more privacy-focused cryptocurrencies emerge.

These findings underscore the double-edged nature of cryptocurrencies. While they offer numerous benefits such as lower transaction fees, faster payments, and increased financial privacy, their decentralized and pseudonymous nature also attracts criminals and those engaged in illegal activities. By enabling 'black e-commerce', cryptocurrencies have the potential to revolutionize black markets in the same way they have transformed legitimate financial transactions.

In the early days of blockchain technology and cryptocurrencies, around the start of the 2010s, the association with black e-commerce and illicit activities deterred many investors from entering the space. As a result, blockchain enthusiasts and early adopters faced significant challenges in securing funding for their projects. Lacking support from traditional investors, these pioneers often had to rely on personal savings, friends, family, and other informal sources of funding.

Coloured Coins

Coloured coins emerged as an early attempt to build upon the success of Bitcoin and expand the use of blockchain technology beyond just a digital currency. The concept of coloured coins involved *colouring* or marking specific Bitcoins to represent other assets, such as real estate, stocks, or commodities. By doing so, coloured coins aimed to enable the creation and transfer of digital tokens that represented these assets on the Bitcoin blockchain, thereby paving the way for more versatile use cases.

Prior to the first ICO of the Mastercoin in 2013, several projects and initiatives sought to implement coloured coins on the Bitcoin blockchain. One of the earliest attempts was the ChromaWallet project, which aimed to create a wallet that supported the management and transfer of coloured coins.[16] Another notable project was the Open Assets Protocol (OAP),[17] which proposed a standard for encoding the issuance and transfer of coloured coins using Bitcoin transactions.

However, these early coloured coin projects faced several challenges, including technical limitations, lack of standardization, and limited scalability. The complexity of implementing coloured coin solutions on the Bitcoin blockchain also made it difficult for developers to create user-friendly applications that could drive widespread adoption.

CONCLUSION

Back in the 1990s, during the time of great experimentation and exploration of emerging internet network, the challenges faced by early internet startups in securing funding from banks were numerous. As the success stories of Amazon, eBay, and other internet giants unfolded, the world witnessed as these once-unlikely ventures transformed into titans of industry. Their rise served as a testament to the importance of embracing innovation and taking risks, a lesson that the traditional banks would eventually learn as undeterred internet entrepreneurs sought alternative means of funding. They turned to the emerging venture capital industry, which was more open to embracing the risk and potential rewards of these ground-breaking endeavours. Angel investors, too, played a significant role in nurturing these digital seeds, providing not only financial support but also mentorship and guidance.

The situation mirrored itself in the 2010s, but this time with startups that were developing blockchain-based projects. What was worse, was that VCs and BAs took a very cautious stance at this time. It is true that VCs are often hesitant to invest in open-source projects due to the unique challenges they present compared to traditional, closed-source business models. One of the primary concerns for them is usually the monetization aspect of open-source projects and their decentralized nature, which often results in greater uncertainty in terms of governance, decision-making, and overall direction of the projects that lack clear business strategies and efficient execution.

At the crossroads of innovation and traditional funding channels, blockchain startups of the 2010s found themselves at an impasse. With regulatory frameworks and incumbent players struggling to keep pace, entrepreneurs needed to find a solution that would both satisfy their financial needs and fuel the progress of their cutting-edge projects. As history has shown, when visionaries encounter obstacles, they have a knack for forging new paths. The limitations posed by conventional funding methods for blockchain startups created a strong demand for an AF approach.

While many developers struggled to develop their business ideas, cut off from any funding source, it was just a question of time before some visionary would offer a long-sought solution. It was 2013 and a developer named J.R. Willett was looking for investors to support his Bitcoin 2.0 idea. Little did he know, his brainchild would eventually lay the groundwork for the first ICO, a ground-breaking mechanism that would forever change the way innovative projects, like his own, raised capital in the digital era. So, it is time to have a closer look at the ICOs.

NOTES

1   www.statista.com/statistics/1078273/global-crowdfunding-market-size.
2   news.bbc.co.uk/2/hi/entertainment/1325340.stm.
3   www.statista.com/outlook/dmo/fintech/digital-capital-raising/worldwide.
4   www.zippia.com/advice/crowdfunding-statistics.
5   Acquired by Circle Inc. in 2019 and divested to another startup fundraising platform, StartEngine, in 2022.
6   Excluding China. If we include China, debt-based crowdfunding makes up 98 per cent of the total volume.
7   www.sec.gov/litigation/admin/2008/33-8984.pdf.
8   www .govinfo .gov/ content/ pkg/ PLAW -112publ106/ pdf/ PLAW -112publ106 .pdf.
9   www.ecfr.gov/current/title-17/chapter-II/part-227.

10 www.fca.org.uk/publication/consultation/cp13-13.pdf.
11 www.consob.it/web/consob-and-its-activities/laws-and-regulations/documenti/english/laws/reg18592e.htm.
12 www.fca.org.uk/your-fca/documents/policy-statements/ps14-04.
13 www.bbc.com/news/technology-35356147.
14 mashable.com/article/skully-motorcycle-helmet-bankrupt.
15 cmr .berkeley .edu/ 2021/ 09/ unveiling -and -brightening -the -dark -side -of -crowdfunding.
16 bitcointalk.org/index.php?topic=106373.0.
17 bitcoinmagazine.com/business/colored-coins-come-life-coinprism-open-assets -1400184072.

REFERENCES

Agrawal, A., Catalini, C., and Goldfarb, A. (2014) 'Some simple economics of crowd-funding', *Innovation Policy and the Economy*, 14(1), pp. 63–97.

Agrawal, A., Catalini, C., and Goldfarb, A. (2015) 'Crowdfunding: Geography, social networks, and the timing of investment decisions', *Journal of Economics and Management Strategy*, 24(2), pp. 253–274.

Agrawal, A., Catalini, C., and Goldfarb, A. (2016) 'Are syndicates the killer app of equity crowdfunding?', *California Management Review*, 58(2), pp. 111–124.

Beck, T., Demirguc-Kunt, A., and Levine, R. (2010) 'Financial institutions and markets across countries and over time: The updated financial development and structure database', *The World Bank Economic Review*, 24(1), pp. 148–170.

Boreiko, D. (2019) *Blockchain-based Financing with Initial Coin Offerings (ICOs): Financial Industry Disruption or Evolution?* Mantova: Universitas Studiorum.

Cambridge Centre for Alternative Finance (2020) The 2nd Global Alternative Finance Market Benchmarking Report.

Cumming, D. (2012) *The Oxford Handbook of Venture Capital*. USA: Oxford University Press.

Cumming, D., Hornuf, L., Karami, M., and Schweizer, D. (2023) 'Disentangling crowdfunding from fraudfunding', *Journal of Business Ethics*, 182, pp. 1103–1128.

Davis, E. and Stone, M.R. (2004) 'Corporate financial structure and financial stability', IMF Working paper WP/04/124.

Denis, D.J. (2004) 'Entrepreneurial finance: An overview of the issues and evidence', *Journal of Corporate Finance*, 10(2), pp. 301–326.

Drover, W., Busenitz, L., Matusik, S., Townsend, D., Anglin, A., and Dushnitsky, G. (2017) 'A review and road map of entrepreneurial equity financing research: Venture capital, corporate venture capital, angel investment, crowdfunding, and accelerators', *Journal of Management*, 43, pp. 1820–1853.

Ernst & Young (2016) 'UK FinTech on the cutting edge – An evaluation of the international FinTech sector'. Available at: http://www.ey.com/Publication/vwLUAssets/ EY-UK-FinTech-On-the-cutting-edge/%24FILE/EY-UK-FinTech-On-the-cutting -edge.pdf (accessed: 1 July 2023).

Fernando, C.S., May, A.D., and Megginson, W.M. (2012) 'The value of investment banking relationships: Evidence from the collapse of Lehman Brothers', *Journal of Finance*, 67, pp. 235–270.

Foley, S., Karlsen, J.R., and Putniņs, T.J. (2019) 'Sex, drugs, and Bitcoin: How much illegal activity is financed through cryptocurrencies?', *The Review of Financial Studies*, 32(5), pp. 1798–1853.

Gompers, P.A. and Lerner, J. (2000) 'The determinants of corporate venture capital success'. In Morck, R. (ed.), *Concentrated Corporate Ownership*, Chicago: University of Chicago Press, pp. 463–498.

Gompers, P.A. and Lerner, J. (2001) 'The venture capital revolution', *Journal of Economic Perspectives*, 15(2), pp. 145–168.

Haddad, C. and Hornuf, L. (2019) 'The emergence of the global fintech market: Economic and technological determinants', *Small Business Economics*, 53, pp. 81–105.

Hornuf, L., Klus, M.F., Lohwasser, T.S., and Schwienbacker, A. (2021) 'How do banks interact with fintech startups?' *Small Business Economics*, 57, pp. 1505–1526.

International Monetary Fund (2010) *World economic outlook: Rebalancing growth*, Washington, DC, April.

International Monetary Fund (2012) *New setbacks, further policy action needed*, Washington, DC, July.

International Monetary Fund (2013) *Global financial stability report: Old risks, new challenges*, Washington, DC, April.

Ivashina, V. and Scharfstein, D.S. (2010) 'Bank lending during the financial crisis of 2008', *Journal of Financial Economics*, 97, pp. 319–338.

Kamepalli, S.K., Rajan, R.G., and Zingales, L. (2021) 'Kill zone', SSRN. Available at: https://ssrn.com/abstract=3555915 (accessed: 1 July 2023).

Kaplan, S.N. and Lerner, J. (2017) 'Venture capital data: Opportunities and challenges'. In J. Haltiwanger, E. Hurst, J. Miranda, and A. Schoar (eds.), *Measuring Entrepreneurial Businesses: Current Knowledge and Challenges*. Chicago: University of Chicago Press, pp. 413–431.

Martin, F. (2013) *Money: The Unauthorised Biography*. New York: Alfred A. Knopf.

Nakamoto, S. (2008) 'Bitcoin: A peer-to-peer electronic cash system', White Paper. Available at: https://bitcoin.org/bitcoin.pdf (accessed: 1 July 2023).

Rossi, A. and Vismara, S. (2018) 'What do crowdfunding platforms do? A comparison between investment-based platforms in Europe', *Eurasian Business Review*, 8, pp. 93–118.

Small Business Administration (2022) Small Business Administration 7(a) Loan Guaranty Program. Available at: https://sgp.fas.org/crs/misc/R41146.pdf (accessed: 1 July 2023).

Sohl, J. (2015) 'The angel investor market in 2014: A market correction in deal size', Centre for Venture Research Report.

Sohl, J. (2022) 'The angel investor market in 2021: Metrics indicate strong market', Center for Venture Research.

Stiglitz, J.E. and Weiss, A. (1981) 'Credit rationing in markets with imperfect information', *The American Economic Review*, 71(3), pp. 393–410.

The World Bank (2013a) *Global Economic Prospects*, Volume 7, Washington, DC, June.

The World Bank (2013b) *Crowdfunding's Potential for the Developing World, Finance and Private Sector Development Department*. Washington, DC.

3.   The rise and evolution of Initial Coin Offerings: From genesis to now

INTRODUCTION

In this chapter, we will systematically explore the development and evolution of Initial Coin Offerings (ICOs) as a primary method for raising capital within the blockchain and cryptocurrency ecosystem. Our discussion will begin with an overview of the early ICO campaigns, highlighting the characteristics that made them appealing to both startups and investors. We will analyse the factors that contributed to the rapid growth of this unregulated market, resulting in a surge of projects and capital inflow.

As the ICO market grew, concerns about fraud, investor protection, and market manipulation became increasingly prevalent. The response of governments and financial authorities around the world, which led to the introduction of strict regulations and guidelines to govern ICOs, significantly impacted the ICO landscape, causing a decline in the popularity of ICOs as a fundraising method and the emergence of alternative fundraising models, such as Security Token Offerings (STOs) and Initial Exchange Offerings (IEOs). We will discuss the key differences between these new models and ICOs, as well as the benefits they offer to both projects and investors. Our analysis will delve into how these alternatives have shaped the industry, leading to a shift in focus from unregulated token sales to more compliant and secure fundraising methods.

Furthermore, we will explore the rise of Decentralized Finance (DeFi) and Non-Fungible Tokens (NFTs) as innovative developments within the blockchain and cryptocurrency space. We will discuss the underlying concepts, unique features, and the potential use cases of DeFi and NFTs that have captured the interest of both the public and the industry.

INTRODUCTION TO ICOs

Although Bitcoin, the first blockchain, was a revolutionary idea when it was introduced in 2009, by 2012, it became clear that it had some deficiencies that limited its potential for broader applications and use cases. As awareness of these shortcomings grew, the search for ways to address them and expand the capabilities of blockchain technology gained momentum. This led to the development of projects like coloured coins and, eventually, Mastercoin (now Omni Layer), and later Ethereum, which introduced new features and functionalities to overcome the limitations of the Bitcoin blockchain.

Funding through Blockchain

Mastercoin, now known as Omni Layer, was the first project to conduct an ICO as a fundraising method in 2013. The ICO allowed investors to purchase Mastercoin tokens in exchange for Bitcoin. While the concept of receiving funding for partial ownership of the company (equity financing), bonds, or loan contracts (debt financing) has been a traditional way of raising funds in the financial world, Mastercoin introduced a new approach to fundraising within the blockchain and cryptocurrency space. Investors in the Mastercoin ICO exchanged their bitcoins for newly issued tokens, which could be used within the Mastercoin ecosystem for various purposes, such as participating in decentralized exchanges, token creation, and other features provided by the platform. These tokens were not legally recognized as shares or debt instruments, or any other financial instrument that existed before in the conventional finance space.

Table 3.1 enumerates the significant advantages that the Omni Layer protocol introduced, compared to the original Bitcoin blockchain and coloured coins projects developed before 2013. It is evident that the Omni Layer protocol was considerably more advanced, boasting superior features compared to its predecessors.

Table 3.1   Characteristics of alternative early blockchain protocols

	Bitcoin	Coloured Coins	Omni Layer
Functionality	Primarily a digital currency with limited scripting language	Mostly asset representation with no standard to encode or manage tokens	Versatile financial assets and derivatives
Scalability	Limited due to its block size and block time	Limited due to operating on Bitcoin blockchain	Quicker, more cost-effective blockchain transactions via meta-protocol
Customization	Limited – implementation of layers (Lightning and Liquid networks)	Limited due to the lack of standardized protocol	Custom tokens with versatile functionality

	Bitcoin	Coloured Coins	Omni Layer
Smart contracts (SCs)	Bitcoin Script is not Turing-complete – no support	Limited – reliance on Bitcoin script language	Basic capabilities but no support for advanced SCs
Protocol extensibility	Limited	Limited by Bitcoin blockchain capabilities	High
Decentralized exchange	No	No	Possible to implement
Asset issuance and tokenization	No	Limited	High
Crowdfunding	No	Limited	Possible to implement
Financial engineering	No	No	High

Definition and Concept

In essence, an ICO is a fundraising mechanism where a project collects funds in exchange for newly created tokens or coins that represent an integral part of the developing project. This can be compared to a loan or a contract for a loan, as well as a money contribution in exchange for an equity stake, both of which allow investors to participate in future cash flows. Tokens issued in an ICO represent a digital asset that is built on blockchain technology. They can serve a variety of functions within the startup's ecosystem, such as providing access to products or services, enabling voting rights, or acting as a medium of exchange. The value of tokens is often tied to the success of the project, with their price expected to rise as the project develops and gains traction. However, tokens do not typically grant direct ownership rights or claims on a startup's assets or profits.

To gain a deeper understanding of tokens as a financial instrument, it can be insightful to draw comparisons with securitization, a significant financial innovation from the previous century. The securitization phenomenon shares some similarities with ICOs in that they both involve transforming an illiquid asset or investment opportunity into a more liquid, tradable, financial instrument. In securitization, assets such as mortgages and loans are pooled together and repackaged into tradable securities, which can then be sold to investors (Tavakoli 2008). This process allows investors to gain exposure to a diversified portfolio of assets and cash flows, while also providing the originators of those assets with access to new sources of funding.

Similarly, ICOs enable startups and projects to raise funds by issuing tokens or coins that represent a stake in the project's future development and success. These tokens can be bought, sold, and traded, providing investors with a liquid and accessible way to invest in the project. Like securitized assets, ICO tokens also give investors the opportunity to participate in the project's future cash flows and profits.

Shares, on the other hand, represent equity ownership in a company. By purchasing shares, investors become shareholders and acquire a proportional claim on the company's assets and future earnings. Shareholders may receive dividends as a portion of the company's profits, and they also possess voting rights, allowing them to influence the company's decisions and operations. Shares provide a more direct link between the investor and the startup's financial performance.

While both tokens and shares provide benefits to their holders, tokens are generally more versatile and flexible in their functions. However, they do not offer the same level of direct ownership, control, and claim on assets and profits that shares provide. Additionally, the regulatory environment surrounding tokens is often less established than for shares, which are subject to well-defined securities laws and regulations.

Nevertheless, tokens represent an innovative class of financial instruments that share certain similarities with traditional ones like shares, bonds, and options, but are built on digital principles, specifically blockchain technology. These digital assets leverage the decentralized, transparent, and secure nature of blockchain networks to offer new functionalities and investment opportunities. Like shares, tokens can represent a stake in a project or company, granting holders certain rights or benefits. However, they also possess unique features such as utility within a platform or ecosystem, serving as a medium of exchange or access to specific services. In this sense, tokens have expanded the scope of financial instruments by bridging traditional finance with the digital world, creating a new landscape for investment and innovation.

The First ICOs: Pioneers and Innovators

Mastercoin (Omni) had a successful token sale in 2013, becoming the first ICO in the cryptocurrency space. As a new protocol layer (also known as Bitcoin 2.0), it was designed to allow users to generate new smart contracts within the Bitcoin setup. The founding team created a Bitcoin address where participants sent their Bitcoins and received Mastercoin tokens in return. The dedicated thread on the Bitcointalk.org portal served as the only advertisement channel. The contributors included the project creator and numerous other individuals, as well as BitAngels (bitangels.network, 2013), the first investor network and incubator created to invest exclusively in cryptocurrency startups. The project managed to raise almost 4740 BTC, which generated more than 0.56 million Mastercoins distributed to users.

After the crowdsale, Mastercoin was initially traded on a dedicated website before being listed on various cryptocurrency exchanges, gaining traction within the market. The funds collected were primarily used for development, promotion, and expanding the project's ecosystem. However, some controversy surrounding the project's strategy, the weakening of the founders' efforts, and the creation of a competing network called Counterparty, dealt a blow to the project's popularity. Upon its emergence, Counterparty instantly captured the market, leaving Mastercoin behind. Even after rebranding as Omni, the project never managed to recapture its leading position.

Nevertheless, the legacy of the first ICO project should not be underestimated: the Omni platform hosted ambitious projects like the decentralized record-keeping network Factom, decentralized internet provider MaidSafe, and ultimately, the currency-backed token project Tether.[1] Tether (tether.to, 2014) is a blockchain-enabled platform designed to facilitate the use of fiat currencies in a digital manner. As its value was pegged to the US dollar, this token was called a stablecoin, and as of April 2023, it ranks as the third-largest cryptocurrency with a market cap in excess of $82 billion.

The first successful Mastercoin crowdsale was followed by the other projects that raised money in a similar fashion. These first ICOs (before Ethereum) shared some common characteristics. They were innovative projects aiming to expand the possibilities within the blockchain and cryptocurrency space, and they primarily used Bitcoin as a means of raising funds. These early ICOs were conducted in a more informal and decentralized manner compared to the later, more established offerings.

However, there were some differences among these initial ICOs as well. While Mastercoin aimed to create a platform for issuing custom tokens on top of the Bitcoin blockchain, other projects had their unique goals and use cases. For example, projects like Counterparty and MaidSafe focused on creating decentralized financial platforms and secure, decentralized internet services, respectively. Table 3.2 presents a chronological list of the first ICOs that took place prior to Ethereum, along with their respective statistics.

According to an extensive data search on the internet, there were 11 token sales done in the first year following the first ICO. Not one of these fundraisers was referred to as an ICO by its founder, instead, the majority of token sales were termed as either *donation* or *crowdsale*. These projects sought to raise funds to develop their blockchain-based platforms or introduce layers on existing Bitcoin ones, create new features and applications, and promote the adoption of their respective digital currencies and ecosystems. Indeed, projects like Omni, Counterparty, NEM, and Bitshares were all competing to create new ecosystems that would attract users to develop their ideas based on the toolkits provided. Counterparty protocol (counterparty.io), created in 2013, was especially successful in building a decentralized financial platform on top of the Bitcoin blockchain, allowing users to create and trade digital assets, execute smart contracts, and perform various other functions. Several ICOs prior to Ethereum issued their tokens on Counterparty platform and continued to do so for several years even post-Ethereum.

NXT (www.jelurida.com/nxt) and Bitshares (bitshares.github.io) projects, both originating in 2013, had their respective crowdsales shortly after that of Omni. These were the first ventures aimed to develop new blockchain platforms from scratch to address the limitations of the Bitcoin blockchain, such as transaction speed and scalability, while providing a more efficient and flexible infrastructure for its ecosystem. For example, NXT aimed to create a more scalable and versatile blockchain, introducing features like asset issuance, a decentralized marketplace, and a messaging system. Bitshares, in turn, developed a decentralized exchange (DEX) platform to trade cryptocurrencies and other digital assets without relying on centralized intermediaries. Bitshares first introduced the concept of the delegated proof-of-stake (DPoS) consensus mechanism, which has been adopted by several other blockchain projects since then.

Among the first ICOs was an interesting example of the American singer, Tatiana Moroz, who launched a campaign to raise funds by issuing in return the Tatiana Coin on Counterparty blockchain. Even though the project failed to raise the required sum (only $10 000 were raised, or 40 per cent of the sought funds), nor did it gain widespread adoption or create a significant impact on the broader cryptocurrency market, it remains the first example of how blockchain technology was leveraged to support artists and foster direct connections between creators and their fans.

Even though the initial ICO campaigns may seem trivial, amateurish, and low scale by later ICO standards, they showcased a variety of techniques and methods such as price determination, auction types, coin inflation, publishing of White papers, and more,[2] which laid the foundation for the evolution and refinement of the forthcoming ICO landscape. Moreover, in the absence of large marketing campaigns and involvement of financial intermediaries, the projects managed to attract enough investors (from 100–20 000) and raise non-trivial sums of money (up to several million US dollars in fiat equivalent).

ICO ACTIVITY

Looking back at the ICO activity from 2013, we see that it hit its peak in 2017 and 2018 when thousands of projects worldwide took this route to raise funds in the absence of unified regulatory response. The number of ICOs went down considerably from the second half of 2018, and the pure ICO model had virtually disappeared by 2021, giving way to regulatory-compliant models such as STOs, alongside DeFi projects and IEOs.

Table 3.2   *ICO campaigns run before Ethereum fundraising project*

Project name	Description	Date	Called itself as	Platform	Country	Identity of founders	No. of investors	Funds raised, $US	Success
Omni	Platform for creating and trading custom digital assets and currencies	Aug-13	donation	Bitcoin	USA	yes	551	616 342	yes
NXT	Platform supporting creation of other currencies, decentralized voting, and a marketplace	Nov-13	donation	own	unknown	no	99	14 720	yes
Counterparty	Open-source, decentralized platform that allows for peer-to-peer financial applications	Feb-14	burning	Bitcoin	USA	yes	3070	1 754 406	yes
NEM	Blockchain platform allowing the creation of assets, namespaces, and subdomains	Feb-14	fundraising	own	Japan	no	2740	38 245	max
MaidSafeCoin	Decentralized data storage and communications network that replaces data centres	Apr-14	crowdsale	Omni	UK	yes	2050	8 000 000	max
Siafunds	Decentralized cloud storage system	May-14	pre-IPO	NXT	unknown	no	134	147 593	yes
Crypti	Decentralized application (Dapp) platform	Jul-14	IPO	own	unknown	no	unknown	466 193	max
BitShares AGS	Decentralized exchange built on a blockchain	Jul-14	fundraising	own	USA	yes	20 000	3 734 870	yes
Tatiana Coin	Artist cryptocurrency	Jul-14	donation	Counterparty	USA	yes	unknown	10 000	no
Swarm	Decentralized storage and communication system	Jul-14	crowdsale	Counterparty	USA	yes	900	790 867	yes
Storj	Decentralized cloud storage platform	Aug-14	crowdsale	Counterparty	USA	yes	unknown	419 929	yes

Notes: Success column indicates if the campaign failed to raise the sought funds (no), raised the funds sought (yes), or reached the limit of funds set by the founder prior to the ICO (max). More details of various ICO characteristics are given in Chapter 4.
Source: Boreiko (2019).

Determining the exact number of ICOs that have occurred since 2013 is challenging for several reasons. Firstly, there was no reliable database that would track this activity, as is done in case of conventional financial deals such as venture capital investments (Crunchbase, Pitchbook), Initial Public Offerings (Refinitive, IPO Monitor), or mergers and acquisitions (FactSet Mergerstat, S&P Capital IQ). Secondly, the definition of what constitutes an ICO can vary. Some might consider only larger, public sales, while others might also count smaller, private token sales. Indeed, with Ethereum smart contract toolkit, the ease of creating, pitching, and running an ICO campaign for projects of any size is unparalleled. This toolkit allows even entrepreneurs with limited blockchain knowledge to create and distribute new tokens on its blockchain. Indeed, to deploy the smart contract for creating and selling new tokens takes very little time, and many services have promised to teach individuals how to run an ICO in as little as 5–20 minutes.[1]

As a result, at the height of ICO activity in 2017–2018, thousands of projects worldwide launched their own token sales. Sometimes, these were run by development teams consisting of a single person with only a vague idea of their project's viability. Often, they failed to raise any funds or managed to sell only a negligible number of tokens. In other instances, fraudsters deliberately published false information about the proposed project to collect funds in cryptocurrency and then disappear. Some projects sold their tokens and then abandoned development, leaving investors with worthless tokens of no value.

Lastly, over the years, dozens of ICO tracking portals were launched. These included both large, well-known platforms and smaller, niche websites (Boreiko and Vidusso 2019). However, as the ICO frenzy died down, many of these platforms ceased their tracking activities or went out of business. Moreover, the majority of them simply published the general information about ICOs, compiled from company announcements or from cross-sources, rarely validating the data. As a result, the ICO lists were mostly incomplete, reported erroneous information, or provided data that could not be confirmed by other sources. This was reported by many researchers who attempted to study the ICO phenomenon. Some studies preferred to focus only on large, publicly visible projects that raised funds in excess of some considerable threshold (Fahlenbrach and Frattaroli 2021), to rely on one source of data of higher quality (Fisch 2019), or leverage blockchain data to validate the actual ICO funds collection (Boreiko and Risteski 2021).

In order to look at the overall ICO activity across time, we have compiled several sources of data. First, we use the data from Boreiko and Risteski (2021) who studied ICOs from 2013 to 2017 and have constructed the most complete database of early ICOs. Second, we have obtained the database from Momtaz (2021), which contains a limited set of data for all potential ICOs announced between 2014 and 2021. Next, as of March 2023, we have found only two ICO portals (icodrops.com and Icomarks.com) that are still active and web-scraped the list of ICOs and funds collected. It must be stressed that after some screening of the deals listed on these two portals, we have some doubts about the numbers reported. First, the funds raised data that could not be confirmed or validated by other sources. Second, these two databases do not distinguish ICOs from STOs, IEOs, or Initial Dex Offerings (IDOs, discussed later in the chapter).

Table 3.3 reports basic statistics about the databases used in our study. As is obvious from the table, the reported figures differ wildly across the sources. Even though the total collected funds reported for the years 2014–2022 are similar (around $25 billion), the number of reported deals varies greatly across all sources. Whereas the Boreiko and Risteski (2021) database contains only the actual concluded fundraising campaigns, the other databases include all potential ICO announcements, and their data should be treated with caution. Indeed, exactly two-thirds of ICOs in Momtaz (2021) do not have information on the collected funds and for around 12 per cent of them, the database has no information on the campaign dates.

Table 3.3   *ICO databases statistics*

ICO databases	Boreiko & Risteski (2021)	Momtaz (2021)	Icodrops (2023)	Icomarks (2023)
Coverage	2013–2017	2014–2021	2014–2022	2015–2022
Funds collected, $m	6665	25 639	25 039	27 981
Total number of ICOs	948	6415	1567	1996
ICOs with missing dates	0	761	0	165
ICOs with missing funds	361	4276	52	0
Deals in 2017	852	813	189	422
Deals in 2018	-	3090	265	1048

Notes: The data includes all completed ICOs, STOs, and IEOs. *ICOs with missing dates* display the number of ICOs with no information about the campaigns' start and end dates. *ICOs with missing funds* reports the number of ICOs that do not have the information about collected funds.

Figures 3.1 and 3.2 illustrate the annual numbers of ICOs and total collected funds across time for all four databases. We can observe the peak of ICO activity in 2017 and in the first half of 2018, after which the numbers decline rapidly. Almost all deals reported for the subsequent years were either STOs or IEOs.

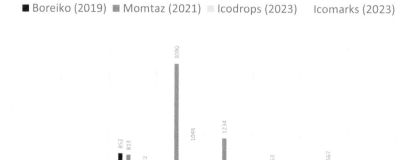

Figure 3.1   ICO activity by year, number of deals

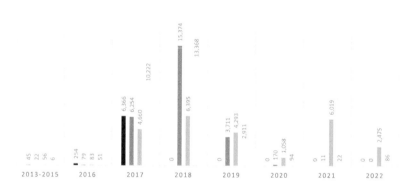

Figure 3.2   ICO activity by year, funds collected in $m

ICO STAGES

The entrepreneurial literature identifies the typical stages that startup development might go through (Churchill and Lewis 1983, Harper 2003). These stages represent common progressions that many businesses experience as they grow and evolve in time, and a similar framework might also be applied to blockchain funding (Boreiko 2019). Looking back at the panorama of ICO activity, we observe the full cycle of stages typical for any startup-like phenomenon and can identify several distinct periods of development of ICOs.

The first ICOs were conceptualized in 2013 (Idea Stage), with the first campaigns running in 2014 (Seed Stage), followed by ICOs growing bigger and featuring the involvement of institutional investors in 2015–2016 (Startup Stage), rapidly growing internationally and facing the first regulatory obstacles or opposition in 2017 (Growth Stage), culminating in the middle of 2018 (Established Stage), and quickly going into decline due to regulatory crackdown in 2019–2020 (Decline Stage). Since then, the industry has evolved, and other forms of fundraising such as STOs and IEOs have grown in popularity, along with DeFi projects, which we discuss briefly later in this chapter and provide an in-depth analysis later in the book.

Table 3.4 outlines the stages of ICO evolution while providing some common features and peculiarities of each. The Idea and Seed Stages were already discussed above. The Startup Stage was characterized by ICOs gaining traction within the cryptocurrency and blockchain communities. More projects started considering ICOs as a viable fundraising mechanism. There was growth in the development of token standards, like ERC-20 on the Ethereum blockchain, which facilitated the process of launching an ICO. During the Startup Stage, ICOs started to gain significant momentum. A larger number of projects launched, and the amount of funds raised through ICOs began to increase dramatically. Regulation was still unclear or non-existent in many jurisdictions, leading to a kind of *Wild West* atmosphere.

Table 3.4   ICO evolution stages

Stage	Period	No. of ICOs	Leading ICO	Prominent ICOs	Stage Features
1. Idea/ Concept	2013	2	Mastercoin	NXT	Bitcointalk.org forum announcements. Crypto-enthusiasts and projects' community as investors. No legal entity or compliance. First non-Bitcoin platform (NXT).
2. Seed	2014	10	Ethereum	Counterparty Maidsafecoin Bitshares	More frequent usage of social media and novel marketing campaigns. Experiments with various token sale types. Projects create independent blockchains platforms or use new ones developed. Limited investor base and lack of infrastructure to run the campaigns. First professionally organized ICO (Ethereum).

Stage	Period	No. of ICOs	Leading ICO	Prominent ICOs	Stage Features
3. Startup	2015–2016	84	The DAO	Waves Iconomi Lisk	Fast growth of number of ICOs, total and average funds raised. Higher investment in marketing campaigns. Selection of benevolent jurisdiction and attempts for self-compliance using legal advice. The term 'ICO' is used for the first time. Few VC-backed startups conducting crowdsales.
4. Growth	2017	800–850	Filecoin	Binance Tezos Bancor	Exclusion or limitations for investors from selected jurisdictions. Large investors (whales) participation. Many tokens sales raise unseen before funds in a very short time. Pioneering of SAFT sales. Chinese instigate complete ban on ICO activity. SEC guidance on ICOs as security offerings. Large-scale fraud activity.
5. Established	2018	1100–2970	EOS	Telegram TaTaTu Dragon	Legal debate about sold tokens' nature. Increased regulators' attention and comments. Increased participation of private and venture capital in private sales before / instead of public small pre-sale followed by several rounds of main token sales. Peak of ICO volumes in mid-2018. SEC enforcement actions on the rise.
6. Decline	2019–2023	~1700	Bitfinex	Avalance Algorand	Disappearance of ICOs as successful fundraising method. Mostly private sales to qualified investors. Subsequent smaller-scale fundraising activity through STOs and IEOs.

Note: The data for ICO volumes from 2018 to 2023 comes from various sources and is unconfirmed, thus only approximate.

Idea and Seed Stages

When Ethereum entered the scene with its ICO in 2014, it introduced several advancements that further differentiated it from the earlier ICOs discussed in previous sections. Ethereum aimed to create a blockchain platform that allowed developers to build and deploy decentralized applications (dApps) using smart contracts, a functionality not present in previous projects. It had a well-organized structure with the Ethereum Foundation, a Swiss non-profit organization, behind the project. Ethereum's ICO also attracted interest and investment from institutional investors, venture capitalists, and experienced players in the cryptocurrency and blockchain space. The ICO was supported by comprehensive documentation, including a White paper and detailed technical specifications, which set a new standard for ICO campaigns going forward.

Ethereum's ICO, which ended in August 2014, raised approximately 31 500 Bitcoins from over 9000 investors ($18 million). This was one of the largest ICOs in the early years, successfully reaching the maximum cap with all 60 million Ether (ETH) tokens sold to the public. Additionally, 12 million ETH were allocated to the Ethereum Foundation and early contributors to the project, bringing the total initial supply of ETH to 72 million. It was only The DAO ICO two years later that first collected more funds.

However, it was not the size of the offering, the well-organized structure, or the publicity that made ETH stand out from all other projects. Ethereum significantly contributed to the growth and popularity of ICOs by providing a powerful and flexible platform that made it easier for projects to create and distribute tokens. One of the key features of Ethereum is its smart contract capabilities, which allow developers to create versatile token sales and post-service using the Solidity programming language. This made it much more accessible for projects to create custom and secure ICOs with ease. Even though some of the later ICOs used other platforms to run their fundraising campaigns and issue tokens, by the middle of 2017, virtually every new ICO used its platform. Even those earlier alternative-platform-based tokens eventually migrated to the Ethereum platform, given its superior flexibility. Ethereum actually freed the founders of new blockchain startups from investing in the creation of their own platforms and provided a cost-effective toolkit to create new tokens.

Startup Stage

This period featured 84 ICOs that raised above $3 million on average. The first campaign that utilized the Ethereum blockchain after its ICO was the Augur token sale in September 2015, which raised $5 million both in Bitcoin and ETH, and by the end of 2016, only a dozen of ICOs followed suit. The majority of ICOs either developed their own platforms or issued tokens on earlier developed ones. Figure 3.3 illustrates that prior to becoming the number one token blockchain platform in 2017, Ethereum faced considerable competition from earlier platforms in this period, especially from concurrently developed alternative blockchains (own platform in Figure 3.3) and the Waves project blockchain (waves.tech, 2016) that was developed in 2016 and had a market share of 8 per cent and 7 per cent of the ICO market in 2016 and 2017, respectively.

In fact, Waves was developed as a blockchain platform that allowed for the easy creation of custom tokens, which could be used for a variety of purposes

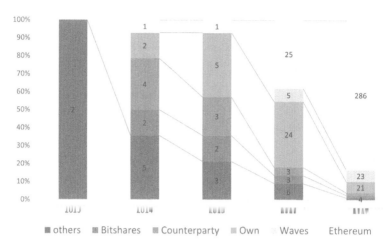

Notes: 'Own platform' stands for projects issuing tokens on their own, independently developed blockchain platforms. The numbers reported show the quantities of the projects issued on each platform.

Figure 3.3   *ICO tokens blockchain platform choice in 2013–2017, Q3*

including ICOs. Many projects used the Waves standard to issue tokens because the blockchain was easy to use, fast, scalable, had low fees, and, more importantly, had a built-in DEX. In fact, the DEX feature was a significant advantage of the Waves platform, as it allowed for immediate liquidity and trading of any token pairs without the need for a third-party intermediary. We will see in the forthcoming chapters how DEXs have become an important part of the fundraising landscape in the blockchain and cryptocurrency space, particularly with the advent of Initial DEX Offerings (IDOs).[4] Still, Ethereum blockchain's main feature of built-in smart contracts allowed for the creation of dApps and more complex token functionality. Coupled with a larger ecosystem with more developers, users, and dApps, and the developed ERC-20 Standard, which has become the industry standard for ICO tokens, the Ethereum blockchain has emerged as a winning blockchain platform.

Despite not being in the top 100 coins by market capitalization as shown in Table 3.5, and trailing behind the top ten crypto tokens in terms of LinkedIn followers, Waves has managed to sustain its relevance over the years, thanks to a robust and engaged community. Even in 2023, the project continues to command a significant following on X (formerly known as Twitter), comparable to many higher-ranked coins. This enduring popularity attests to Waves' ability to captivate public interest and underscores the project's resilience in a highly competitive market.

Table 3.5   *Waves platform and top ten crypto tokens*

Token	Ranking, Coinmarketcap	X followers ('000)	Rank, X	LinkedIn followers ('000)	Rank, LinkedIn
Bitcoin	1	5700	2	214	3
Ethereum	2	3000	4	16	8
Tether	3	367	8	7	9
BNB	4	10500	1	708	1
USD Coin	5	148	10	79	5
XRP	6	2600	5	320	2
Cardano	7	1300	7	33	7
Dogecoin	8	3700	3	1	10
Solana	9	2200	6	75	6
Polygon	10	70	11	142	4
Waves	153	244	9	1	11

Notes: Ranking data as of March 2023. *Coinmarketcap ranking* is by market capitalization of each token. *Rank, X* and *Rank, LinkedIn* stand for relative ranking by the number of followers among top ten tokens and Waves.

At the startup stage, the majority of ICO projects required some form of formal user registration before allowing investment. Approximately 40 per cent sought legal advice and drafted purchase agreements that outlined risks and emphasized the unique nature of tokens, distinguishing them from conventional securities. Not all fundraising campaigns warned or excluded US investors from participating, and around 25 per cent of all ICOs originated in the USA, where regulators were largely overlooking token sales at the time. Precisely 25 per cent of ICOs explicitly chose a governing jurisdiction for token sales, with 30 per cent opting for Swiss law, 30 per cent for US or Canadian law, and the remainder predominantly choosing the laws of their teams' countries of origin.

As early as August 2016, some ICOs either warned or outright prohibited the participation of all US residents. The Elastic ICO was the first token sale (referred to as a donation) that clearly stated in its sales terms and conditions document: 'By participating in our donation-based project support campaign, you attest that you are neither a corporation, an unincorporated association, nor a citizen/resident of, nor located in the USA (including any region under the sovereign jurisdiction of the federal government of the USA) or Canada, and neither a citizen/resident of, nor located in any jurisdiction where running this donation-based project support campaign as I do it, or participation in this donation-based project support campaign or the general use of Elastic's website or software or Bitcoin itself, might be illegal.' This was followed by the Flashcoin ICO in September 2016; however, neither of the founding teams conducted Know-Your-Customer (KYC) checks.

This stage also featured token sales that were structured with a pre-sale, followed by the main sale, and often involved venture capital (VC). In fact, it was the GetGems ICO in January 2015 that pre-sold approximately 15 per cent of its tokens in an invite-only round. This ICO also attracted VC funding from one of Israel's leading VC firms, Magma Venture Partners (magmavc.com, established in 1999), marking their first foray into the crypto space. Overall, only about 10 per cent of ICOs reported attracting VC investors, but 20 per cent of ICOs were conducted with pre-sales.

During this period, one-third of all ICOs successfully ran funding campaigns, raising the equivalent of millions of dollars, without publishing a formal White paper (which later became standard practice, much like issuing a prospectus in conventional IPOs). Most ICOs offered deep discounts (up to 50 per cent) to early buyers to create an impression of high investor interest and maximize the campaign's chances of success. Various distribution models were experimented with to allocate tokens to investors – including a Dutch auction in one instance – but the majority of these models set a cap on the accepted funds, either in terms of tokens or monetary value. This limit, later termed a *hard cap* in subsequent ICOs, was reached in seven ICOs (around 8 per cent of all sales). However, every eighth deal failed to collect funds above the declared minimum target (min cap).

Nine startups chose an uncapped model, where the firms were prepared to accept unlimited funding from investors, issuing an uncapped number of tokens, limited only by demand. One of these was 'The DAO', a well-known uncapped ICO that eventually met a tragic end and was the first to attract significant regulatory attention. The DAO's ICO was one of the largest in history, raising over $150 million in ETH at the time. However, The DAO is perhaps best known for its significant security vulnerability that was exploited in a hack shortly after the ICO, resulting in the theft of approximately a third of its funds. This event led to a hard fork in the Ethereum blockchain to recover the funds, creating what we now know as the Ethereum and Ethereum Classic (ETC) blockchains.

Apart from The DAO and Waves token sales, several other prominent projects conducted their ICOs during this period and are worth mentioning. Iconomi (iconomi.com, established in 2016), a digital asset management platform, allows users to easily invest in various digital assets or combinations of digital assets, known as Digital Asset Arrays (DAAs). The platform aims to provide the infrastructure for the decentralized economy, enabling users to manage and invest their digital assets. Iconomi's ICO took place in September 2016, and it was one of the more successful ICOs of that year, raising over $10 million. The project continues to be actively developed and attracted some VC funding in 2022.

Another successful ICO was conducted by Lisk (lisk.com, established in 2016), an open-source blockchain application platform written in JavaScript. Lisk bridges the gap between accessibility and web3 adoption. It allows developers to create, distribute, and manage decentralized blockchain applications, thereby making blockchain technology more accessible with a focus on user experience and developer support. Lisk's ICO took place in March 2016, and the project raised around 14 000 Bitcoin, which was worth approximately $6 million at the time, attracting around 4000 investors.

Growth Stage

The year 2017 was a time of intense excitement and activity in the ICO market, but it was also a period when the inherent risks and emerging regulatory challenges associated with ICOs became increasingly evident. Bitcoin's price reached an all-time high in December 2017, growing 20-fold from the start of the year, while Ethereum appreciated by 10 000 per cent. This had a ripple effect on the entire crypto market, including ICOs, leading to heightened media attention and increasing investment interest from outside the crypto community.

During this period, the ICO phenomenon began to evolve into the form we recognize today. Initial efforts often involved modest advertising and bounty campaigns via social media to garner crowd attention, followed by small-scale fundraising initiatives known as pre-sales. These pre-sales targeted large investors, business angels, or VCs, who could acquire tokens at substantial discounts. The funds raised from these pre-sales were then used to intensify advertising efforts ahead of the main public sale, which often offered significant discounts to early participants.

It became standard practice for startups to present their pitches in White papers, maintain active communication channels with the community through platforms like Slack, Discord, Telegram, or other blockchain forums, and release detailed information about fundraising and business development through blogs or specialized blockchain news websites. Tokens sold were often distributed automatically by smart contracts, either during the crowdsale or immediately after, with issuers arranging for the tokens to be listed on various online crypto exchanges. During this period, companies began to invest substantial funds in attracting potential investors. This was achieved through a variety of means, including PR articles and press releases, participation in hackathons or other blockchain events, and social media campaigns. Additionally, companies started to allocate tokens to active private promoters through what were known as *bounty campaigns*. Despite the increase in fraudulent activities during this time, the term 'ICO' did not carry a negative connotation.

Having sensed an opportunity to raise funds quickly and cheaply, many startups (deploying blockchain or not) rushed to announce and run their token sales. More than 800 ICOs raised in excess of $6 billion in total during the year. The median ICO size grew to above $10 million, with eight ICOs raising more than $100 million. Around a quarter of all ICOs reached their hard cap targets, and only one in ten failed to raise the minimum required funds. Every fifth ICO was backed by VC investors, and their involvement in pre-sales often served as a certification of projects' superior quality, attracting funds from retail investors in the main crowdsale.

In this period, technology company Block.one, specializing in high-performance blockchain software, conducted a year-long ICO for EOS, starting in June 2017. This record-breaking campaign raised $4 billion over a continuous one-year campaign. Other prominent projects developed during this time included the Binance (binance.com, established 2017) ICO in July 2017. Despite raising a modest $15 million, it later evolved into the world's largest crypto exchange. The Binance Coin (BNB), issued during the ICO, currently ranks third in terms of cryptocurrency market capitalization and serves multiple functions within the Binance platform, including offering reduced trading fees and facilitating participation in token sales, among other uses.

Tezos (Tezos.com, established 2014) ran its ICO in July 2017 and raised about $232 million, one of the largest amounts at the time. Tezos is a decentralized, open-source blockchain network that can execute peer-to-peer transactions and serve as a platform for deploying smart contracts. Its unique aspect is an on-chain governance model where all stakeholders can participate in network upgrades. However, the project faced several legal and internal challenges post-ICO, delaying the launch of its network.

Lastly, Bancor (bancor.network, established 2017) held its ICO in June 2017, raising approximately $153 million in ETH. Bancor was envisaged as an ecosystem of decentralized, open-source DeFi protocols to foster on-chain trading and liquidity. The Bancor Network Token (BNT) serves as a hub network connecting all tokens in the Bancor Network, allowing easy conversion between them.

Nothing seemed to be able to stop ICOs from taking the finance world by storm. However, regulators worldwide started to voice concerns and take a closer look at the activity. In response, many ICOs proactively allocated considerable funds to legal compliance, choosing Switzerland or Singapore as governing jurisdictions for token sales. Sixty per cent of sales prohibited US residents from participating, and founders began to take the identity of investors and the security of the fundraising process more seriously. The first significant regulatory signal came in July 2017 from the US Securities and Exchange Commission (SEC).

In the aftermath of the crypto attack on The DAO ICO, the SEC decided to investigate the case. In July 2017, the SEC released a report of its investigation, providing guidance on ICOs and marking a pivotal moment in the regulatory oversight of this new fundraising method.[5] The SEC determined that DAO tokens were securities and, therefore, subject to federal securities laws. Following the verdict, the ICO industry reacted in various ways. Many players argued that ICO tokens are predominantly utility tokens and thus not securities per se, so they are not subject to SEC regulation. An alternative approach was pioneered in August of 2017 when the US-based startup for a blockchain-based data storage network, called Filecoin, managed to raise $284 million from institutional and private investors. The company also aimed to comply with any future forthcoming regulation on ICOs. The campaign included running KYC checks on all investors, allowing only accredited investors from selected jurisdictions (such as the USA and the UK) to participate, warning investors from other jurisdictions (such as China and Canada), and selling a new product called a 'Simple Agreement for Future Tokens' (SAFT), which is not tradable on exchanges and will be converted into real tokens only after the network's launch.

SAFTs were modelled after Simple Agreements for Future Equity (SAFE), which were originally created by the startup accelerator Y Combinator in 2013. A SAFE is an agreement between a startup and investors that provides rights to the investor for future equity in the company without determining a specific price per share at the time of the initial investment. The SAFE investor receives the future shares when a priced round of investment or a liquidation event takes place. The SEC has not issued specific guidance on SAFEs but treats these instruments as securities, which means they are subject to federal securities laws.[6] A similar regulatory approach was taken regarding SAFT offerings. The third way was chosen by Blockchain Capital in its token sale in April 2017, as one of the first examples of a token that was explicitly marketed and sold as a security in compliance with existing securities offerings regulations. Such offerings were later termed as STOs (Security Token Offerings), and these will be discussed in detail later in the book.

Whatever the industry's response was to increased regulatory attention, it became clear that the uncontrolled growth of ICOs was coming to an end. First, China banned all ICO activity in August 2017, labelling it as fraudulent and detrimental to the development of the financial industry. Then, in September 2017, the SEC acted for the first time against two fraudulent ICO offerings run by the Recoin Group Foundation.[7] In December 2017 two more SEC interventions followed. First, its newly created Cyber Unit halted PlexCorps ICO fraud and, later that month, the SEC halted an ICO by a company called Munchee

Inc., which was the regulator's first action to halt an ICO for unregistered securities.[8] The age of explosive growth of token sales had come to an end.

Established Stage

Despite increased regulatory scrutiny, 2018 was a pivotal year for ICOs. Following the fundraising boom of 2017, the subsequent year kicked off with sustained momentum. As depicted in Figure 3.4, which illustrates the number of ICOs and total funds raised each month, ICO activity appeared relentless. Even when excluding the year-long EOS ICO that concluded in July and Telegram's $1.7 billion private placement in March, the momentum seemed unstoppable. However, as the year unfolded, the ICO market encountered a series of challenges.

First, the SEC intensified its efforts to monitor the crypto industry, and in that year, took 16 enforcement actions, with four of them being interventions in what the SEC deemed to be unregistered sales of securities in ICOs. Apart from that, the SEC quietly subpoenaed dozens of firms and their lawyers who conducted ICOs, asking for information on the sale's details and participating investors. This sent ripples through the market and indicated that the good old times of uncontrolled token issuance were gone. As it turned out later, the road

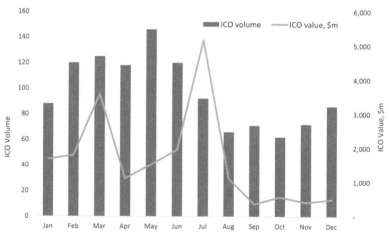

Source: The data is from Momtaz (2021). Number and funds raised are reported only for ICOs with funds raised data available (1166 out of 3091 ICOs reported for 2018).

Figure 3.4   ICO activity in 2018

of using SAFTs in token sales had not placated the SEC, and these were also treated as security offerings.

Second, the beginning of 2018 marked the end of the 2017 cryptocurrency bull market, with the prices of many cryptocurrencies, including Bitcoin and Ethereum, falling significantly from their all-time highs. This market downturn, often referred to as the *crypto winter*, had a negative impact on the ICO market, as both project founders and investors became more cautious.

Third, the ICO market was rapidly filled with low-quality projects that proposed blockchain implementation in virtually every business sector, with the sole purpose of obtaining funding through token sales. This trend was partially due to the market hype and crypto bull market in 2017, partially due to the low barriers to entry in this business, and largely due to the flexibility of the Ethereum toolkit that permitted the creation of proprietary tokens on its platform and the introduction of the ERC-20 standard, which eased listing and trading on various burgeoning crypto platforms.

Lastly, after the ICO boom of 2017, which saw many projects fail to deliver on their promises, investors became more sceptical and discerning. The quality of projects and their ability to deliver became more significant factors in the success of ICOs. Given the considerable fraud that permeated the ICO market, it was challenging for retail investors to identify genuinely promising projects. As a result, there was a drastic reduction in the value of the total funds raised by the ICOs, with many strong projects cancelling or postponing their token sales and urgently seeking alternative ways to attract financing.

Despite these challenges, several significant projects managed to sell tokens during this period, raising hundreds of millions of dollars. Among them was Dragon Coin, also known as DRG. This digital currency was introduced by Dragon Inc., a company aiming to revolutionize the casino gaming industry through the integration of blockchain technology. The DRG was one of the largest of the year, reportedly raising over $400 million. The saga surrounding this ICO could rival a Hollywood blockbuster, featuring a Finnish investor allegedly defrauded of $24 million, the arrest of a Thai film star's family for fraud, the backing of the project by a former triad leader known as Broken Tooth, and a staggering drop in the value of the DRG token by more than 80 per cent within the first week of trading.[9]

Another notable ICO from the 2018 period was conducted by TaTaTu, a social entertainment platform that leverages blockchain technology to incentivize user engagement and content consumption. Launched by Italian entrepreneur Andrea Lervolino, TaTaTu's ICO in June 2018 reportedly raised a staggering $575 million. This impressive amount came primarily from a select group of private investors, which included renowned investment firms such as BlockTower Capital and high-profile celebrities like Johnny Depp.

However, evaluating the project's subsequent progress proves to be a difficult task. The most concrete result seems to be the development of an app, available both on Google Play, where it has gathered around a thousand reviews, and on the App Store, where it has approximately 400 reviews. Critics of TaTaTu have labelled the token sale as opportunistic, a characterization that seems hard to refute. The TaTaTu token has not been listed on any cryptocurrency exchange, and there have been no transactions on its blockchain since 2021. Adding to the confusion, the legal entity behind the project later listed its shares on the Euronext stock exchange and seemingly shifted away from blockchain technology altogether.

This situation underscores the challenges and potential risks inherent in the rapidly evolving world of blockchain and cryptocurrency, particularly in the often-tumultuous landscape of ICOs. It serves as a cautionary tale and a reminder that due diligence is essential for both investors and regulators to navigate this complex and sometimes unpredictable sector.

Decline Stage

In 2019, the era of token sales via ICOs drew to a close. Regulatory bodies ramped up their efforts to prosecute the most blatant instances of ICOs that they considered illegal security offerings. Globally, investors grew increasingly wary of ICO campaigns, as fraudulent activities reached unprecedented levels. While Hornuf et al. (2022) identified one in five ICOs as fraudulent in their sample of 1393 ICOs from 2016 to 2018, Grobys et al. (2022) claimed that over half of their sample of 1014 ICOs conducted up until the end of 2019 were accused of scam activities. Two large SAFT offerings (Telegram and Kik) were halted and fined by the SEC, effectively banning this type of token sale in the US. Consequently, the SEC seemed to view the two-step SAFT issuance process as a mere artificial attempt to circumvent securities laws.

Fromberger and Haffke (2021) reported that of a thousand ICOs run in 2019 alone, only one-third had the data on collected funds. Even this self-reported and unreliable data of $3 billion of funds raised indicates a five-time fall in funds raised from the previous years. This seems to be a good indicator of the dramatically reduced ICO activity. Statista data (Statista Search Department 2023) shows an alternative view of virtually stopped ICO activity by the second quarter of 2019. The ongoing ICOs were attempting to circumvent the US regulation by running the offers privately, without sales to the general public, structuring sales as SAFTs, or implementing strict Know Your Customer (KYC) and Anti-Money Laundering (AML) procedures to identify the customers and exclude the US residents.

Despite the evident decline in the ICO market, several large ICOs still managed to secure funding. Bitfinex, one of the world's largest cryptocurrency exchanges, conducted a token sale for its native token, LEO, in 2019. This token sale reportedly raised $1 billion, primarily from private investors. However, US citizens were explicitly prohibited from participating in the offering. Avalanche, a decentralized, open-source platform designed to facilitate the launch of dApps, new financial primitives, and interoperable blockchains, conducted a public sale of its AVAX token in July 2020, raising approximately $42 million. The sale was open to retail investors, but citizens of the US and certain other countries were excluded.

SAFTs, STOs AND IEOs

In response to the above-mentioned challenges, many projects started to explore alternative fundraising methods. Many founders of ICOs, in an attempt to avoid falling under multiple jurisdictions, began to exclude investors from certain countries. This was particularly true for US investors, who were often excluded due to the complex regulatory environment in the United States. This approach mirrors the practices seen in traditional finance, such as Swiss banks' reluctance to open accounts for US citizens due to the extensive reporting requirements imposed by US tax laws. By excluding certain investors, these institutions aim to reduce their regulatory burden and potential legal risks.

Another strategy adopted by some projects was to limit participation to qualified or accredited investors. This is a concept borrowed from US securities regulation, where certain investments are only available to investors who meet specific income or net worth criteria. By limiting participation to these accredited investors, projects could further ensure compliance with securities laws and potentially avoid regulatory penalties.

SATFs

SAFTs emerged as a fundraising mechanism in the blockchain space as a response to the regulatory uncertainty surrounding ICOs. The framework was introduced in a White paper titled 'The SAFT Project: Toward a Compliant Token Sale Framework' (Batiz-Benet et al. 2017). Filecoin, a project by Protocol Labs, was among the first to use the SAFT framework during its ICO in August 2017.

SAFTs are investment contracts offered to accredited investors during a token pre-sale. These contracts entitle the investors to receive a certain number of tokens at a future date when the project's network or platform is functional. By focusing on accredited investors and tying token distribution to project development, SAFTs aimed to address regulatory concerns and reduce the risk of the token being classified as a security.

It is hard to identify exactly how many SAFTs were issued from the first one in 2017. However, the SAFT framework became increasingly popular following its introduction, with numerous projects adopting it for their token sales. Some well-known projects that used SAFTs include Telegram (2018) with $1.7 billion raised, Filecoin (2017) $257 million, Basis (2018) $133 million, Hedera Hashgraph (2018) $124 million, and Kik (2017) $98 million.

The SEC has not explicitly endorsed the SAFT framework as a compliant solution for token sales. However, it effectively quashed this innovation by bringing charges against two SAFT sales – those of Kik Interactive and Telegram – for conducting unregistered securities offerings through their respective ICOs. Both projects had used a SAFT-like structure to raise funds from accredited investors in the United States. The ensuing legal battles resulted in settlements, with Telegram returning $1.2 billion to investors and paying an $18.5 million penalty, and Kik paying a $5 million penalty. These cases underscored that the SAFT framework did not guarantee immunity from regulatory scrutiny.

STOs

Security Token Offerings (STOs) emerged as a response to the regulatory scrutiny that ICOs and SAFTs faced. They were seen as a way to offer tokens while complying with securities laws, providing a level of legal certainty that was often lacking with ICOs. Contrary to what the name suggests, the tokens sold in STOs do not represent the shares or other ownership claims on the project legal entity but refer to the representation of the token sales as offerings of the securities according to the regulation. There were some ICOs that were offering tokens that represented the conventional shares or bonds tokenized – these were not termed as STOs but classified as usual ICOs. One of the earlier examples is ICO of Lykke Corporation (Switzerland) in 2016, where it issued Lykke Coins (LKK). The LKK token is a cryptographic token that represents ownership in the Lykke Corporation. Each LKK token represents 1/100 of a share of Lykke Corp, a Swiss registered corporation, but without voting rights.

The vast majority of STOs in the United States have been limited to accredited investors due to regulatory requirements. Accredited investors are individuals or entities that meet certain income, net worth, asset size, governance status, or professional experience thresholds. In 2015, the SEC effected Regulation A+, a type of offering that allows companies to raise a limited amount of funds from the general public, not just accredited investors. However, the process to qualify for a Regulation A+ offering is rigorous and includes audited financial statements and filing an offering circular with the SEC. As a result, the first STO offering opened to retail investors was done in September 2019 only by Blockstack PBC (USA), followed by INX crypto exchange STO (Gibraltar) in 2000.

STOs emerged as a unique fundraising mechanism in the blockchain arena, blending features of traditional securities with the innovative potential of blockchain technology. While IPOs and private equity sales are time-honoured methods of raising capital, STOs present several unique advantages that have made them an appealing option for numerous firms. However, regulatory compliance proved to be complex and costly, and with the waning trend of token sales and a general decline in cryptocurrency market capitalization, STOs never reached the funding volumes seen with ICOs. Recently, South Korean regulators approved legislation permitting STOs in their country, indicating that STOs are not entirely obsolete. We delve into more detail about them in the forthcoming chapters.

IEOs

As previously discussed, by mid-2019, fundraising through ICOs had come to a standstill. The initial hype had waned, frauds and project failures had reached alarming levels, and regulators were actively investigating past issues for violations. The SEC was launching approximately 20 proceedings annually in the crypto industry, leading to a complete dry-up of the primary source of funds for blockchain startups. STOs were a rarity, occurring in very limited numbers. SAFTs had proven to be a weak shield against SEC scrutiny, and following the halt of Telegram's token sale, many firms ceased their SAFT offers. For instance, Basis, a notable project in the cryptocurrency space that aimed to create a stablecoin (a type of cryptocurrency designed to maintain a stable value relative to a specific asset or a pool of assets), returned money to its SAFT investors and cancelled the token sale in December 2018.[10]

Emerging crypto VC was still in its infancy and could only support a select few projects. However, at that time, another group of influential players were forming in crypto space – cryptocurrency exchanges. By that time, they had already established themselves as trusted platforms for trading digital assets, and they had the infrastructure and user base to facilitate large-scale token sales. By hosting projects' capital raising, exchanges could provide a more secure and regulated environment for token sales, which helped to restore investor confidence and opened up new funding opportunities for projects.

In an IEO, a cryptocurrency exchange conducts due diligence on a project and, if approved, lists the project's token for sale directly on its platform. This process adds an extra layer of trust, as the exchange stakes its reputation on the project's legitimacy. Additionally, the exchange handles many logistical aspects of the token sale, such as KYC/AML checks, as well as marketing, thereby reducing the burden on project developers. Furthermore, the exchanges provide immediate, much-sought-after listings of the tokens. Indeed, the earliest ICOs often had to secure their tokens' listing in order to attract a sufficient number of investors. In this case, it was offered as part of the service. Much like crowdfunding platforms, these new intermediaries were ideally positioned to offer their services in facilitating the flow of funds between interested investors and startups.

The first IEO on the Binance Launchpad was the sale of the Bread BRD token in December 2017, six months after Binance itself was created and raised funds through ICO. The first IEO ran relatively unnoticed as it was still the time of the full swing of the conventional ICO market. However, the launch of BTT token for the BitTorrent project in January 2019 was a great success. In times of dried ICO activity, it raised more than $7 million in a matter of minutes. This event marked the beginning of the IEO trend, with many other cryptocurrency exchanges launching their own ICO platforms shortly after.

Crypto exchanges play a crucial role in the IEO process. They not only provide the platform for the token sale but also handle KYC/AML checks, marketing, and sometimes even advisory roles for the project. This can significantly reduce the burden on project developers and increase the chances of a successful token sale. Furthermore, once the IEO is completed, the token can be immediately listed for trading on the exchange, providing instant liquidity. While most IEOs are conducted on crypto exchanges, there are also some platforms specifically designed for launching IEOs. These platforms provide a range of services to assist with the token sale process, including smart contract creation, token issuance, and marketing. We discuss in more detail, the cryptocurrency exchanges in forthcoming chapters.

IEOs have been hosted on a number of well-known exchanges, such as Binance, Huobi, and OKEx, among others. These platforms have launched numerous successful IEOs, contributing to the growing popularity of this fundraising method. In fact, IEOs have today replaced the ICOs completely. We discuss IEOs in greater details in the next chapters.

The Rise of Decentralized Finance

While IEOs provided a more secure and regulated platform for token sales, they were not without limitations. Firstly, the due diligence process for IEOs can be rigorous and time-consuming, and not all projects can meet the stringent criteria set by exchanges. Secondly, IEOs require a significant amount of resource, both in terms of time and money. Listing fees for major exchanges can be prohibitively expensive for many projects, particularly those in the early stages of development, which excluded many smaller or less-established projects from conducting an IEO. Thirdly, IEOs are typically limited to the user base of the hosting exchange. This means that a project's potential investor pool is restricted to users of that specific exchange, which can limit the reach and impact of the token sale.

Lastly, the whole idea of blockchain was decentralization and removal of inefficient intermediation in financial transactions. Here, the crypto industry found itself again dependent upon the will and benevolence of a particular exchange that was deciding on the fate of startups, not the investors and users themselves. Many have thought it was not right and against the spirit of the genesis blockchain idea. Indeed, as early as 2016, the Waves project created blockchain-powered custom tokens platform with built-in DEX. The Waves DEX is a key feature of the Waves platform, offering fast and secure trading with low fees. Even as recently as 2019 there were still projects that used Waves platform, rather than the Ethereum one, to create their tokens.

So, DeFi listings emerged as a response to the evolving needs of the block-chain and cryptocurrency industry. DeFi listings offer a more accessible and inclusive alternative. DeFi projects can list their tokens on a DEX or automated market maker (AMM) platform, such as Uniswap or SushiSwap, without the need for an extensive approval process or high listing fees. This opens up opportunities for a wider range of projects and allows for greater participation from the community. It is DeFi listings that align more with the ethos of decentralization that underpins much of the blockchain and cryptocurrency industry. They allow for permissionless innovation and open access, which can be appealing to many projects and investors in the space. We discuss DeFi in the last chapter of the book, where we focus more on its challenges and risks, including smart contract vulnerabilities, price volatility and liquidity issues, regulatory uncertainty, and scalability concerns.

THE DARK SIDE: SCAMS AND FAILED PROJECTS

The longer one studies ICOs and the blockchain and cryptocurrency industry, the more one can draw parallels to the era of stock market trading before the Great Depression. Both periods were marked by a surge in speculative investment, fuelled by the promise of high returns and the allure of a new, largely unregulated market. However, this lack of regulation and oversight also created an environment ripe for fraud, scams, and manipulation, leading to significant losses for many investors.

In the early 20th century, the stock market was a burgeoning field, attracting investors with the prospect of substantial profits. However, the absence of regulatory oversight allowed for widespread market manipulation and fraud-ulent practices. Pump-and-dump schemes, insider trading, and misleading or false information were common, creating an unstable market environment. This culminated in the stock market crash of 1929, which triggered the Great

Depression and led to the introduction of the Securities Act in 1933 to protect investors and ensure fair and transparent market practices.

Fast forward to the 21st century, and we see a similar narrative unfolding in the ICO market. The emergence of blockchain technology and cryptocurrencies has created a new frontier for investment. ICOs, in particular, have attracted significant attention due to their potential for high returns. However, the lack of regulation and oversight in this nascent market has also opened the door to fraudulent activities. ICO scams, such as exit scams where founders disappear after raising funds, and pump-and-dump schemes involving tokens, have become all too common.

Despite these similarities, the scale and nature of fraudulent activities have been greatly aided by technological advancements. ICO frauds are often global in nature, leveraging the borderless and pseudonymous characteristics of cryptocurrencies to evade detection. Additionally, the complexity of blockchain technology and the lack of understanding among many investors have made it easier for fraudsters to deceive investors.

An additional factor that has added greatly to widespread fraud is the anonymity and pseudonymity it affords to project developers. It is not uncommon for developers to be known only by aliases, particularly in the early stages of a project. This practice, while offering privacy protection, can also contribute to the opaqueness of the market, making it difficult for investors to verify the legitimacy of a project or the credibility of its team. This is reminiscent of the stock market in the early 20th century, where misleading or false information was often used to manipulate stock prices.

The use of aliases by developers is not always indicative of fraudulent intent. Some developers may choose to maintain their anonymity to avoid potential legal issues, protect their privacy, or simply because they prefer to let their work speak for itself. One of the most famous examples is Satoshi Nakamoto, the pseudonymous creator of Bitcoin, whose true identity remains unknown. However, this anonymity can also be exploited by malicious actors to perpetrate frauds and scams. In the ICO market, exit scams, where developers disappear after raising funds, have become a common occurrence. This has led to significant losses for investors and has tarnished the reputation of the ICO market.

Fraudsters were quick to recognize the opportunities presented by this new, largely unregulated market. The anonymity offered by cryptocurrencies, combined with the lack of cross-border enforcement, made it an ideal environment for scams and fraudulent schemes. This international investor base, coupled with the difficulty of enforcing regulations across borders, has made the cryptocurrency market particularly susceptible to fraud.

From the outset, scammers and opportunists have actively exploited these characteristics. The ICO market, in particular, has seen a surge in fraudulent activities, from exit scams where developers disappear after raising funds, to pump-and-dump schemes involving tokens. These activities have not only resulted in significant losses for investors but have also greatly tarnished the reputation of the cryptocurrency market. Some researchers went as far as identifying 80 per cent of all ICOs as frauds in 2018 (Dowlat 2018), even though, the actual reported total of funding stolen due to scams is only 11 per cent. Still, these numbers are by no means tiny. However, these numbers are only marginally higher than the losses due to credit card scams that account for below 7 per cent of the total transaction volume.[11] The ICO frauds are analysed in detail in the following chapters.

THE FUTURE OF ICOs AND TOKEN OFFERINGS

We have discussed that the traditional ICO era is gone, and the only surviving types of fundraising on blockchain that have remained are the IEOs and DEX offerings. It is unclear how long these will continue to dominate the scene, as the final word from the regulators is yet to be heard. At the same time, the crypto industry has continued to innovate and create new ways for startups to attract funds. As of the start of 2023, two main streams of innovation deserve to be mentioned here –NFTs and metaverse tokens.

Innovations in Tokenization and NFTs

As discussed in Chapter 2, the artistic industry was the driving force behind crowdfunding innovation as the first campaigns and platforms were in fact the artists trying to get funds to develop their projects. This was not the case for blockchain fundraising except for some non-representative cases at the early stage of ICOs development. ICOs democratized fundraising by allowing blockchain startups and projects to bypass traditional VC and directly access funds from the public. Similarly, NFTs have democratized the art world by allowing creators to sell their digital works directly to collectors and buyers on decentralized platforms. Unlike cryptocurrencies and tokens, which are fungible and can be exchanged on a one-for-one basis, NFTs are unique and cannot be replaced with something else. This uniqueness is what gives NFTs their value and sets them apart in the world of digital assets.

NFTs are digital assets that represent ownership or proof of authenticity of a unique item or piece of content, stored on a blockchain, which is a decentralized and distributed digital ledger. The blockchain technology ensures the security, transparency, and immutability of the NFTs, making it possible to prove ownership and trace the history of the asset. There are various types of NFTs, each with its own unique characteristics and uses. Digital art and collectibles are among the most popular types of NFTs. These include digital paintings, animations, music, and virtual collectibles. Virtual real estate and goods represent ownership of virtual land or items in virtual worlds or video games. Tokenized physical assets are NFTs that represent ownership of a physical item, such as a piece of real estate or a luxury good. Domain names and social media handles can also be tokenized as NFTs, providing a way to prove ownership and control over these digital properties. Sports, music, and event tickets can be issued as NFTs, providing a secure and transparent way to prove ownership and authenticity.

In reality, NFTs have opened up new avenues for the artistic industry to raise funds for various projects. Artists can create and sell NFTs of their work, providing them with a new source of income that can be used to fund future projects. This is a significant shift from traditional funding methods and has the potential to revolutionize the way artists finance their work by providing several distinct advantages.

1.   Removal of intermediaries. One of the key advantages of NFTs is that they allow artists to sell their work directly to collectors without the need for intermediaries such as galleries or auction houses. This direct-to-consumer model can result in higher profits for artists, as they are able to retain a larger portion of the sale price.
2.   Royalty automation. NFTs can be programmed to include 'smart con-tracts' that automatically pay the artist a royalty every time the NFT is resold on the secondary market. This means that artists can continue to earn from their work long after the initial sale, providing them with a sus-tainable source of income.
3.   Collaboration and community-driven projects. For example, artists can raise funds for a project by selling NFTs that represent a stake in the project or rights to future profits. This allows fans and collectors to directly support the artists they love and become stakeholders in their creative process.
4.   New collector experience. NFTs can be used to create unique experiences or rewards for collectors. For example, an NFT could include access to exclusive content, early access to new works, or even a personal experi-ence with the artist. This can add additional value to the NFT and create a deeper connection between the artist and the collector.

The first noticeable NFT project was started in June 2017 by Larva Labs, a two-person team of developers who wanted to conduct an experiment, an antipode to the malleable and centralized nature of mainstream collectibles like Pokémon cards. CryptoPunks, a set of 10 000 algorithmic 24 x 24 8-bit images, was randomly generated and unalterable once it went live on the Ethereum network. Nine thousand of them were freely distributed to those interested in possession of an Ethereum wallet. What started as a humorous experiment later turned into a billion-dollar industry of NFT trading, with the most expensive CryptoPunk NFT, No. 7523, sold at Sotheby's for $11.8 million.[12]

Later that year, a blockchain-based virtual game, CryptoKitties, was developed by Axiom Zen. The game allows players to adopt, raise, and trade virtual cats. These two projects and the launch of Decentraland (a decentralized virtual reality platform powered by the Ethereum blockchain, where users can create, experience, and monetize content and applications) in 2017, demonstrated the potential for unique digital assets and paved the way for the NFT boom that we see today. Currently, the value of the NFT market is projected to reach over $1.5 billion in 2023, with an expected annual growth rate of 18.6 per cent in the next five years.[13]

Various NFT marketplaces have emerged where users can create, buy, and sell NFTs. These include OpenSea, Rarible, SuperRare and many other places which cater to digital art and collectibles. These platforms provide a user-friendly interface for interacting with NFTs and facilitate transactions between buyers and sellers. As the NFT space continues to evolve, we are also seeing developments in cross-chain NFTs and interoperability. This allows for NFTs to be moved across different blockchain networks, expanding their potential use cases and increasing their accessibility.

The Role of ICOs in the Metaverse

The metaverse is the latest buzzword, ranking second in Oxford's Word of the Year 2022 list. The metaverse is a digital space that mirrors the physical world, evolving into a virtual reality with endless possibilities. It empowers a world where people can interact virtually, exchange digital assets for real-world value, own digital land, and much more. Several tech giants have recognized the viability and potential of the metaverse, among which is Facebook, now unsurprisingly renamed Meta. Today, we use this term to refer to many different types of enhanced online environments, from online video games to virtual workplaces. Given fierce competition and no barriers to entry, the current version of the metaverse is shaping up as a multiverse: a composition of metaverses with limited interoperability competing to gain the dominant position.

Metaverses are digital ecosystems built on various kinds of 3D technology, real-time collaboration software, and blockchain. Metaverse tokens are digital assets used to make digital transactions within the metaverse. Users holding the metaverse tokens can access multiple services inside the virtual space. While some tokens grant in-game abilities, others represent unique items for virtual avatars. The best part about metaverse tokens is their associated value both inside and outside the virtual world. Some examples of metaverse tokens are Decentraland (MANA), The Sandbox (SAND), Solana (SOL), Fantom (FTM), Render Token (RNDR), Harmony (ONE), and Axie Infinity (AXS). The Enjin metaverse has the ENJ token as the native token of its ecosystem, and is currently the world's largest game NFT networks.

The role of ICOs in the metaverse can be seen as a potential fundraising mechanism and as a catalyst for the development and growth of the virtual world. As the metaverse refers to a collective virtual space encompassing various interconnected digital environments, blockchain technology and cryptocurrencies are expected to play a significant role in its development in the following ways:

1. Fundraising for Metaverse Projects: ICOs can serve as a means to raise funds for various metaverse projects, enabling developers to create and expand virtual worlds, platforms, and applications. By offering tokens to investors, projects can gain the necessary capital to develop infrastructure, create content, and improve user experiences in the metaverse.
2. Tokenization of Virtual Assets: ICOs can facilitate the tokenization of virtual assets in the metaverse, enabling the creation of digital currencies and tokens representing virtual real estate, goods, and services. These tokens can then be traded, bought, and sold, fostering a thriving virtual economy.
3. Incentivizing Participation: ICOs can be used to incentivize participation in the metaverse by distributing tokens that serve as rewards for users who engage with the virtual world. These tokens can have utility within the metaverse, providing access to premium content, virtual goods, or services.

Even though the total market capitalization of metaverse tokens constitutes only around 1 per cent of the total cryptocurrency market capitalization, 11 tokens have made it into the Top 100 as reported by CoinMarketCap.[14] The metaverse token universe is expanding rapidly, with 206 metaverse tokens already listed and traded. This trend is expected to continue its growth trajectory in the coming years.

CONCLUSION: ICOs AND THE ONGOING DIGITAL ASSET EVOLUTION

ICOs marked a significant milestone in the evolution of digital assets. They demonstrated the potential of blockchain technology as a means of raising capital, paving the way for a new era of DeFi. The lessons learned from the ICO boom and its decline under subsequent regulatory scrutiny have shaped the development of the digital asset landscape and proved the viability of blockchain-based fundraising methods – they showed that it was possible to raise substantial amounts of capital quickly and from a global pool of investors. However, they also highlighted the need for greater transparency, accountability, and regulatory compliance in the crypto space.

The transition from ICOs to IEOs and IDOs was a response to these lessons. IEOs and IDOs provide an additional layer of trust and security for investors, as they are conducted by established cryptocurrency exchanges that perform due diligence on the projects they list. Later evolution in the form of NFTs opened up new possibilities for tokenization, allowing for the creation and exchange of unique digital assets. This has led to an explosion of creativity and innovation in the realms of digital art, virtual real estate, and beyond. The concept of the metaverse, a collective virtual shared space created by the convergence of virtually enhanced physical reality and physically persistent virtual reality, presents even more potential uses for digital assets. As we move towards increasingly virtual experiences, digital assets will likely play a crucial role in representing ownership and value in these spaces.

However, ten years after the first ICO, regulation remains a significant challenge. While regulators have made strides in recent years, the rapidly evolving nature of the digital asset space means that regulation is often playing catch-up. The legal status of various types of digital assets is still not settled in many jurisdictions, creating uncertainty for both projects and investors. Looking ahead, the future of digital assets is not entirely clear. However, one thing is certain: the evolution of digital assets continues and seems to be unstoppable. As technology advances and new use cases emerge, we can expect to see further innovation and growth in this exciting space.

NOTES

1   In total, our constructed ICO database have seven projects that created coins on Omni platform.
2   We discuss the ICO economics in more details in Chapter 4.
3   sudonull.com/post/14946-How-to-write-a-smart-contract-for-ICO-in-5-minutes.
4   An IDO is a type of ICO that is conducted on a DEX. This method of fundraising is more accessible and inclusive, as DEXs are typically permissionless, meaning that anyone can participate. It also provides immediate liquidity for the token, as it can be traded as soon as the IDO is complete. Furthermore, conducting an IDO on a DEX can be more cost-effective and efficient than traditional methods of fundraising. Lastly, it offers a level of transparency and security, as transactions are recorded on the blockchain and are not controlled by a centralized entity.
5   www.sec.gov/litigation/investreport/34-81207.pdf.
6   www.sec.gov/oiea/investor-alerts-and-bulletins/ib_safes.
7   www.sec.gov/news/press-release/2017-185-0.
8   www.sec.gov/litigation/admin/2017/33-10445.pdf.

9   fullycrypto.com/dragon-coin-the-floating-casino-ico-that-stole-24-million.
10   www.wsj.com/articles/stablecoin-project-basis-is-shutting-down-after-raising
     -135-million-11544730772?mod=article_inline.
11   moneytransfers.com/news/2022/09/21/credit-card-fraud-statistics.
12   www.sothebys.com/en/buy/auction/2021/natively-digital-cryptopunk-7523/
     cryptopunk-7523.
13   www.statista.com/outlook/dmo/fintech/digital-assets/nft/worldwide.
14   coinmarketcap.com/view/metaverse/.

REFERENCES

Batiz-Benet, J., Santori, M., and Clayburgh, J. (2017) 'The SAFT project: Toward a compliant token sale framework', White Paper. Available at: https://saftproject .com/static/SAFT-Project-Whitepaper.pdf (accessed: 1 July 2023).

Boreiko, D. (2019) *Blockchain-based Financing with Initial Coin Offerings (ICOs): Financial Industry Disruption or Evolution?* Mantova: Universitas Studiorum.

Boreiko, D. and Risteski, D. (2021) 'Serial and large investors in Initial Coin Offerings (ICOs)', *Small Business Economics*, 57, pp. 1053–1071.

Boreiko, D. and Vidusso, G. (2019) 'New blockchain intermediaries: Do ICO rating websites do their job well?', *The Journal of Alternative Investments*, 21(4), pp. 67–79.

Churchill, N.C. and Lewis, V.L. (1983) 'The five stages of small business growth', *Harvard Business Review*, 61(3), pp. 30–50.

Dowlat, S. (2018) 'Cryptoasset market coverage initiation: Network creation', Bloomberg Research. Available at: research.bloomberg.com/pub/res/d28giW28 tf6G7T_ Wr77aU0gDgFQ (accessed: 1 July 2023).

Fahlenbrach, R. and Frattaroli, M. (2021) 'ICO investors', *Financial Markets Portfolio Management*, 35(1), pp. 1–59.

Fisch, C. (2019) 'Initial coin offerings (ICOs) to finance new ventures', *Journal of Business Venturing*, 34(1), pp. 1–22.

Fromberger, M. and Haffke, L. (2021) 'ICO Market Report 2019/2020 – Performance Analysis of 2019's Initial Coin Offerings', SSRN. Available at: https://ssrn.com/ abstract=3770793 (accessed: 1 July 2023).

Grobys, K., King, T., and Sapkota, N. (2022) 'A fractal view on losses attributable to scams in the market for initial coin offerings', *Journal of Risk and Financial Management*, 15(12), pp. 1–18.

Harper, D.A. (2003) *Foundations of Entrepreneurship and Economic Development*, New York: Routledge.

Hornuf, L., Kück, T., and Schwienbacher, A. (2022) 'Initial coin offerings, information disclosure, and fraud', *Small Business Economics*, 58, pp. 1741–1759.

Momtaz, P.P. (2021) 'Token Offerings Research Database (TORD)'. Available at: https://www.paulmomtaz.com/data/tord (accessed: 1 July 2023).

Statista Search Department (2023) 'Total funding raised by blockchain initial coin offerings (ICO) worldwide in 2017 and 2019, by quarter (in million U.S. dollars) [Graph]', Statista. Available at: Statista.com/statistics/804748/worldwide-amount -crytocurrency-ico-projects/ (accessed: 1 July 2023).

Tavakoli, J.M. (2008) *Structured Finance and Collateralized Debt Obligations: New Developments in Cash and Synthetic Securitization*. New Jersey, US: Wiley.

4. Economics of Initial Coin Offerings

INTRODUCTION

In the early stages of their emergence, around 2013–2014, token sales were conducted in a relatively straightforward manner. There was little emphasis on roadshows, and the services of specialized investment banks to market the offerings and attract investors were rarely utilized, as is usual in the conventional financial industry. Instead, these early token sales borrowed tactics from the burgeoning crowdfunding industry and occasionally sought advice from angel investors, resulting in a rather ad hoc approach to fundraising. However, as the blockchain fundraising landscape matured, it began to attract professional advisors and investors. Initial Coin Offerings (ICOs) started raising substantial amounts, often in the tens of millions, and the campaigns themselves became more sophisticated. There was a greater emphasis on carefully planning the structure of the sale, the details of token distribution, marketing strategies, and security measures. Over time, a variety of methods and techniques were experimented with in the ICO space, providing a rich dataset for analysis. This evolution has allowed us to gain insights into which strategies have proven successful and which ones have not. In this chapter, therefore, we delve into the intricate world of ICOnomics, a term that encapsulates the economics of ICOs. ICOnomics is akin to tokenomics, but with a specific focus on the structure and functioning of ICOs. It encompasses the strategies, principles, and details that underpin the ICO process, from the initial setup of the startup to the final stages of token liquidity and smart contract deployment.

In the first section, we delve into the mechanics of ICOs across various stages of their development over the past decade. We begin with the initial setup of the startups, examining how the founders organized themselves before launching an ICO and the steps they took to secure funding. Next, we explore the importance of the White paper (WP), a crucial document that outlines the project's goals, technology, timeline, and token distribution plan. We then discuss the role of bounty programs, referral schemes, and incentive bonuses in promoting the ICO and incentivizing participation.

In the subsection on token sale design and timing, we examine the various factors that influenced the success of an ICO, including the structure of the token sale, the timing of the launch, and the pricing of the tokens. We also consider token distributions, founders' stakes, and vesting periods that served to demonstrate the project's quality to investors. The role of marketing and social media in promoting the ICO and engaging with potential investors is also scrutinized.

In the second section, we delve into the economics of tokens. We explore the different types of tokens, the concept of token inflation, and the importance of token liquidity. The final section focuses on smart contracts, self-executing contracts with the terms of the agreement directly written into code. We discuss the role of smart contracts in ICOs, with a particular focus on Ethereum and Solidity, the most commonly used platform and programming language for creating smart contracts. We also touch upon post-Ethereum chains and their role in the later ICO landscape.

ICO MECHANICS

The successful funding of a business idea is often predicated on a well-structured and thoughtfully planned startup with a robust operational structure in place. Investors often say that they invest in people, not just ideas. Therefore, it begins with a strong, experienced team supporting the founders. The team should have a mix of skills and experience relevant to the business idea and industry. A team with a strong track record and relevant experience can signal the quality of the project to potential investors. This is especially important in the context of an ICO, where the future of the project can be uncertain, and investors are essentially placing their trust in the team's ability to deliver on their promises.

The legal structure of the startup is another crucial factor. It can impact the startup's ability to raise funds, with different structures having different implications for liability, taxation, and the ability to issue shares or tokens. It is important to choose a structure that aligns with the startup's fundraising strategy and long-term goals.

At the heart of any successful startup is a compelling business idea. This idea should be innovative, scalable, and capable of solving a real problem or meeting a significant market need. It should also have a clear value proposition that sets it apart from competitors. In addition, investors also want to see that the startup has a clear path to profitability. This means providing detailed financial projections, including revenue, expenses, and cash flow. These projections should be based on realistic assumptions and supported by market research.

Various promotional strategies such as bounty, referral, and incentive bonuses are often used by ICOs to encourage participation, increase visibility, and attract more investors. These programs are designed to reward individuals who contribute to the project's success in various ways and attract more attention and a larger user base to the project's ecosystem. Moreover, clear and effective communication is key in a fundraising campaign. This includes the ability to articulate the business idea, value proposition, and growth strategy in a compelling way. It also involves maintaining open lines of communication with potential investors and keeping them informed about the startup's progress.

Next, the structure of the token sale and the distribution of tokens play a significant role as well. The structure of the sale needs to be designed in a way that it is attractive to investors, while the distribution of tokens needs to be fair and transparent. This can help build trust with investors and increase the chances of a successful ICO. However, even the most promising and well-structured ICOs can be severely impacted if the security of the process is not adequately addressed. The nature of ICOs, which involves the transfer and storage of digital assets, makes them a prime target for cybercriminals.

Finally, investors want to know how they will get a return on their investment. Unlike traditional forms of fundraising, where investors may need to wait for several years before they can exit and cash in on their investment, ICOs offer a much quicker path to liquidity. Once the tokens are issued and listed on a cryptocurrency exchange, they can be bought and sold freely, providing investors with the opportunity to realize gains (or losses) much sooner. This feature of ICOs is particularly attractive to investors who value the ability to quickly enter and exit positions. It also provides a level of flexibility that is often lacking in traditional investment scenarios, where exit opportunities may be limited and depend on specific events such as a sale of the company or an IPO.

Startup Setup

Traditional financiers like Venture Capital (VC) firms, angel investors, and banks typically prefer to deal with legally registered businesses. A formal legal structure offers a sense of security and accountability, making the investment less risky. It also lends credibility to the business, demonstrating that it is serious and committed to its long-term success. This formal structure is often a prerequisite for these traditional financiers to even consider investing or lending funds to a business. It was very much different in the crypto space a decade ago.

In the early days of ICOs, the setup of startups was often quite informal and lacked the traditional structure seen in other types of businesses. Many early ICOs were initiated by small teams of geographically dispersed developers with a shared vision, rather than established companies. The legal structure of these projects was often unclear, as the concept of raising funds through a token sale was new and largely unregulated.

In many cases, these early projects did not establish a formal legal entity before launching their fundraising. Instead, they operated as decentralized, open-source projects. The teams behind these projects often remained anonymous or used pseudonyms, further distancing themselves from traditional business structures. This practice was partly inspired by the pseudonymous creator of Bitcoin, Satoshi Nakamoto, whose true identity remains unknown. The use of aliases in the crypto space can serve several purposes.

Firstly, anonymity can provide a layer of protection for developers, especially in the nascent stages of a project. Given the experimental nature of many blockchain projects and the regulatory uncertainty surrounding ICOs, developers may choose to use aliases to avoid potential legal issues. Secondly, anonymity can also be a way to maintain privacy. The crypto space values decentralization and individual freedom, and some developers may prefer to let their work speak for itself without drawing attention to their personal identities. Lastly, in the unique context of the crypto space, reputation can indeed be built around an alias. In a community that values the technology and ideas over personal identity, the consistent delivery of valuable contributions can earn respect and trust, regardless of the identity behind the alias.

However, it is important to note that while anonymity can have its advantages, it can also raise concerns among investors and regulators. Anonymity can make it easier for fraudulent projects to evade accountability, which is why transparency about team members has become a standard best practice in more recent ICOs. Anonymous developers, little details about the team, or outright fake identities have become one of the clearest ICO red flags, signalling potential fraud.[1]

Figure 4.1 illustrates the frequency of anonymous founders in ICOs up until the end of 2017, represented as percentages of the total number and of funds raised. It is evident that anonymity was more common in the early stages of ICO activity but steadily declined as investors grew wary of potential scams involving teams with unclear identities. It is worth noting that larger ICOs were predominantly conducted by identifiable teams, as indicated by the significantly lower percentage when considering the value of funds raised. Furthermore, the primary business sectors featuring anonymous teams were betting, online casinos, and gaming, where anonymity also served as a protective measure against potential regulatory prosecution for illicit activity within certain jurisdictions.

As the ICO market matured and attracted more attention from regulators and institutional investors, the approach to setting up an ICO startup began to change. Recognizing the need for greater transparency and accountability, many projects not only provided full details on teams' composition, but also started to establish formal legal entities before launching their ICOs. Throughout the years, ICO founders have opted for a variety of legal structures

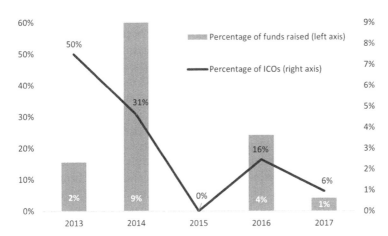

Source: Author's calculations.

Figure 4.1   Percentage of ICOs with anonymous founders

for their organizations, each tailored to their specific needs, objectives, and the regulatory landscape of the jurisdictions they operate in.

Foundations have been a popular choice, particularly for those focusing on non-profit activities. As independent legal entities, foundations are governed by a board and are obligated to utilize their funds for a designated purpose. Foundations are typically exempt from certain taxes, which can be a significant advantage for a startup looking to maximize its available funds. Additionally, a foundation structure can provide a level of transparency and trust, as it is required to act in the best interests of its beneficiaries – in this case, the community of token holders. Many large and successful projects have chosen this legal form, among them, Ethereum (Switzerland), IOTA (Germany), Tron (Singapore), and many others.

Corporations have also been a common choice, particularly for startups that aim to generate profit. This structure offers limited liability, which can be attractive for founders and investors alike. Corporations are also subject to specific governance rules, which can provide additional transparency and trust. Several notable ICOs have chosen the corporation structure for their organizations, such as Ripple Labs Inc. (USA), Filecoin (USA), and Block.one (Cayman Islands), to name a few.

In some cases, ICOs have been launched by existing businesses, which may already be structured as limited liability companies (LLCs), partnerships, or other forms of business entities. These businesses may choose to launch an ICO as a way to raise funds for a specific project or to pivot into the blockchain space. Overstock.com, a well-known online US-based retailer, launched an ICO through its subsidiary, tZERO, which was structured as a corporation. Bitfinex (China) was founded in 2012 and had been operating as a crypto-currency exchange for several years before it launched the UNUS SED LEO token in 2019. Kodak (USA) planned to launch a photographer-oriented block-chain cryptocurrency – KodakCoin – with an ICO in 2017, then with a SAFT in 2018, but finally abandoned the idea, removing all mention of the project from its website.

The choice of jurisdiction also gained more importance as the ICO market grew. These include the regulatory environment, tax implications, the legal system, and the overall business-friendly nature of the jurisdiction. This often involved incorporating a company in a jurisdiction perceived to be crypto-friendly, such as Switzerland or Singapore. These jurisdictions are known for their progressive regulatory environments, which can provide a level of certainty and security for blockchain startups. We will discuss the geography of ICOs in the subsequent chapters of the book.

Unlike earlier ICOs, it was quite common for ICO startups in 2017–2018 to have a well-defined legal structure, a transparent team, and a detailed roadmap for their project. While this represented a significant shift from the early days of ICOs, it was a necessary evolution that reflected the growing maturity of the blockchain industry.

Team Composition

The success of an ICO is often closely tied to the strength and credibility of its founding team. Investors, in their assessment of a project's potential, will scrutinize the founders, who are typically the leaders of the blockchain project. However, it is important to note that being a visionary in the blockchain space does not necessarily equate to being a competent manager or planner. The ICO history is full of cases where the promising genuine projects were stalled or failed partially due to the founders' incompetence.

For example, The DAO, was a complex smart contract built on the Ethereum blockchain with the aim of serving as a VC fund for the cryptocurrency and decentralized space. It gained significant attention and became one of the most prominent ICOs of its time in 2016. However, the DAO suffered a major setback when a vulnerability in its smart contract code was exploited by a hacker. This resulted in the theft of a significant portion of the funds raised. The flaw in the code was attributed to a lack of understanding and expertise in Ethereum smart contract security on the part of the DAO's creators. At the time, the blockchain industry was still relatively new, and security practices and standards were not as well-established as they are today. The DAO incident served as a wake-up call to the industry, highlighting the need for experienced security specialists or advisors to the teams.

Another promising ICO, Tezos, faced significant issues due to internal conflict. A dispute between the project's founders and the president of the Swiss foundation they established to manage the funds raised in the ICO led to delays and legal trouble. The initial mismanagement and conflict significantly hampered its early progress and probably contributed to its lagging behind more successful peers. Similarly, Envion, a German startup promising to create mobile mining units powered by renewable energy, raised $100 million in its ICO back in 2017. However, internal conflicts between the founders and hired managers led to legal battles, and the project was eventually liquidated by a Swiss court.

In the early stages of a startup, founders often seek the guidance of business angels to consult on various tasks. Venture capital, while a significant source of funding for many startups, has traditionally been somewhat hesitant to invest in ICOs. This has led ICO founders to assemble a robust team and advisory board, as well as to form partnerships and alliances, to avoid falling short of their fundraising goals.

An advisory board can also be a valuable asset to an ICO. By recruiting industry experts and advisors, ICOs can gain guidance, credibility, and connections. These advisors can provide strategic insights, help navigate regulatory complexities, and open doors to potential partnerships. In the early days of ICOs, the advisory space was relatively unstructured. Many of the first advisors to ICOs were individuals with deep experience in the crypto-currency space or in traditional finance. They helped companies navigate the uncertainties and complexities of launching an ICO, including how to structure the offering, manage the process, and communicate with potential investors. Mostly, individuals, either early investors in crypto, such as Roger Ver, or founders of successful blockchain startups, such as Vitalik Buterin, were advising the new projects on various aspects of running a successful ICO. An online database of ICO advisors demonstrates that these are very important players in the industry, with top advisors having consulted on 50–100 projects each.[2]

As the ICO market heated up, and more companies sought to raise funds via ICOs, the advisory market also grew and became more professionalized. People from traditional finance backgrounds, who understood the dynamics of fundraising and could bring that knowledge to bear on the ICO process, started to move into the ICO advisory space. In more recent years, specialized firms dedicated to providing ICO advisory services have emerged. These firms usually offer a broad range of services, from strategic and operational advice, through to legal and regulatory guidance. They often have teams with a mix of backgrounds, combining expertise in traditional finance, blockchain technology, and law, to provide a comprehensive service.

As an alternative to employing an advisor or blockchain consulting firm, building strategic partnerships and alliances can significantly enhance a project's standing. By aligning with established businesses, industry leaders, and other ICO projects, startups can expand their network, gain access to additional resources, and enhance their project's credibility. These partnerships can also provide a level of validation, signalling to potential investors that the project is recognized and supported by other players in the field.

Examples of such alliances include, for example, Chainlink, a project that had previously undergone a successful ICO, and Google Cloud, which in 2019 formed a partnership aimed to allow Google Cloud's big data analytics platform, BigQuery, to interact with Chainlink's blockchain interoperability platform. This partnership was a significant endorsement for Chainlink. Similarly, in 2017, Ripple announced a partnership with American Express to improve cross-border transactions using Ripple's blockchain technology. In addition, the Basic Attention Token project, which had a successful ICO, has been deeply integrated with the Brave browser as part of a partnership.

White Paper

In the world of ICOs, the WP stands as the cornerstone of communication between a company and its potential investors. Similar to how prospectuses function in Initial Public Offerings (IPOs), business plans serve in VC pitches, and how presentations play a crucial role in crowdfunding campaigns, WP has a pivotal role in an ICO process. It is a comprehensive document that outlines the details of the company's technology, the architecture of its business model, and the tokenomics – the economic underpinnings of the proposed token. Essentially, it forms a bridge of understanding, linking complex technical ideas to potential investors by presenting an understandable and clear vision of the product.

Even though the WP lacks the depth and complexity of the standard business plan produced to get VC funding, the role of the WP in an ICO cannot be overstated. One of its primary purposes is to deliver a detailed explanation of the technology driving the token or coin. Often, it delves into intricate details about the underlying blockchain protocol, consensus algorithm, and other vital technical facets. This component is especially critical to potential investors with a technical inclination, who seek to understand the underlying mechanics of the ICO.

The WP also exposes the business model of the ICO, reminiscent of the function a business plan serves in traditional startup contexts. It delineates the company's milestones to be reached post-funding, its plans to generate revenue or attract the users to the project, the proposed use of funds raised through the ICO, and other pertinent details about the business strategy. This component of the WP provides potential investors with an understanding of how the company plans to navigate the business landscape, and thus, forms an essential part of their decision-making process.

Lastly, the WP examines the tokenomics (or the economics of the token) being offered. It provides a clear understanding of the token's utility within the ecosystem, its distribution plan, pricing, and other important details. This analysis offers investors insights into the potential growth and value of the token, helping them gauge the potential returns on their investment.

Lastly, the WP should present a detailed roadmap that outlines the project's future development plans. It gives investors an understanding of the project's direction and the team's ability to deliver on their promises. Carefully structured ICOs also feature a Legal Disclaimer and Terms, which details the legal considerations and risks associated with the ICO. While this document does not guarantee absolute legal safety, it does demonstrate transparency and responsibility on the part of the project's team. Occasionally, such disclaimers may be included as a separate section within the WP.

Table 4.1   *WP, Legal Terms, and ICO success*

	WP			Legal Terms			
	Yes	Missing	No	Disclaimer	Yes	Missing	No
N, % of all documents	87.1	2.1	10.8	8.4	53.3	3.0	35.3
Listed tokens, %	66.5	30.0	60.7	65.0	69.4	64.3	58.7
Average funds raised, $m	9.9	8.7	1.6	4.0	14.3	9.1	1.9
Average number of investors, 000s	3.4	0.05	3.3	1.4	4.4	2.1	1.9

Note: WP / Legal Terms is either available (Yes), could not be located (Missing), or not published (No).
Source: Authors' calculation on the sample of 473 ICOs in 2013–2017, Q3.

Table 4.1 presents data on the availability of WP and Legal Terms documents, and the corresponding performance of ICOs in the sample under consideration. Interestingly, around a tenth of all ICOs did not publish a standard WP, while a third did not draft a Legal Terms document. The table reveals that ICOs that had a WP tend to raise more funds, attract a greater number of investors, and their tokens are listed more frequently on cryptocurrency exchanges. Similar trends are apparent when a Legal Terms document is present.

Unsurprisingly, the existence of a comprehensive WP, particularly one featuring a detailed technical description of the project, has been proven to have a significantly positive effect on multiple aspects of ICO success, including fundraising outcomes and token price performance. This is supported by academic research such as the papers by Momtaz (2020) and Belitski and Boreiko (2022) where it was observed that well-drafted WPs positively influence both the amount of funds raised during an ICO and subsequent token market performance. Similarly, Fisch (2019) found a robust correlation between the quality of WPs and the overall success of ICOs. These findings emphasize the importance of high-quality WPs, as they significantly contribute to an ICO's successful fundraising and the strong performance of its tokens.

Promotional Strategies

When ICOs were still a young concept, the founders usually possessed very limited or no budget to market their campaigns through the conventional channels, and promotional strategies provided low-cost alternatives. While these strategies can certainly be more cost-effective compared to traditional advertising or marketing methods, their primary goal was to build community engagement, create viral growth, and increase the project's visibility in a crowded market.

As the ICO market matured and grew rapidly, it led to a highly competitive environment with each ICO battling to capture investors' attention and capital. In such a setting, these promotional strategies serve as critical differentiators, helping specific ICOs stand out from the crowd. Moreover, the technology underlying blockchain projects, tends to be technical and, often, overwhelming for the average investor. Therefore, ICOs' promotional strategies served as a way to present the project's details in a more palatable manner. This helps foster understanding and interest among potential investors.

In the blockchain space, community involvement plays a critical role. These promotional strategies help ICOs to establish a strong, engaged community which is beneficial for the project's long-term success. They encourage early adopters and enthusiasts to contribute to the project by rewarding them with tokens. This can stimulate network effects, whereby the project becomes more valuable as more people participate. Moreover, these strategies help to decentralize token ownership, a key aspect in many blockchain projects. When tokens are more widely distributed, the risk of manipulation or concentrated control over the project decreases and this might send a positive signal to other potential investors.

However, like any marketing strategy, the success of these promotional campaigns relies on the underlying value and credibility of the ICO itself. An effective promotional campaign cannot compensate for a poorly conceived project or a lack of transparency. In fact, over-reliance on promotional strategies at the expense of product development and transparency could send a negative signal to potential investors.

Among the most popular promotional techniques used by ICOs were bounty, referral, and incentive bonus programs. Bounty programs are designed to incentivize and reward individuals who contribute to the ICO project in various ways, often through non-monetary tasks. These tasks can range from software development and bug reporting to creative activities such as article writing, graphic design, or social media promotion.

In a typical early-stage ICO bounty program, the project allocated a certain portion of their tokens (usually expressed as a percentage of the total supply) to be distributed as rewards or *bounties* to participants. These tokens were then distributed among the participants upon the successful completion of the ICO. Participants in a bounty program, known as *bounty hunters*, usually had to register and agree to terms and conditions before they could start working on tasks. Each task or action had a specific reward associated with it, usually based on the difficulty of the task, the skill required, or the potential impact it could have on the ICO's success.

Bounty programs in ICOs are often divided into categories. For instance, the 'Social Media Bounty' involves promoting the ICO on platforms such as X (formerly known as Twitter), Facebook, and Reddit. Another category, the 'Content Creation Bounty', rewards bloggers, video creators, and graphic designers for creating high-quality content about the ICO. The 'Translation Bounty' caters to those who can help translate ICO documents into different languages. As the interest from the multilingual community grew, virtually all smaller-budget ICOs employed bounty hunters to translate their WPs into different languages. Interestingly, in the early days of ICOs, between 2013 and 2015, when most were marketed with a thread on Bitcointalk.org forum, there were no bounty programs. Later, however, the first pages of the ICO threads often came from potential bounty hunters who advertised their skills, or from people aggressively asking for bounties to be distributed.

An important thing to note is that bounty programs were not without their risks and controversies. Some argue that they can be exploited by individuals who are more interested in quick profits rather than the long-term success of the project. Moreover, there were plenty of cases where the founders did not pay, or paid very little to the bounty hunters, undermining the project's image.

Other promotional techniques, for example, referral programs, use the power of networking and word-of-mouth marketing to increase the reach of the ICO, often leveraging the social networks of current investors or participants. This has the potential to generate a much larger pool of interested investors than traditional marketing methods. However, the success and integrity of a referral program are highly dependent on the overall quality and legitimacy of the ICO itself. If the ICO is of high quality and is run by a trustworthy team, a referral program can further enhance its reputation and reach. Investors are generally more inclined to trust and participate in an ICO that has been recommended by a friend or peer, making the referral program an effective strategy.

On the other hand, if the ICO is of low quality or has dubious credibility, a referral program might be perceived as a desperate attempt to attract funds. In this scenario, the referral program could inadvertently signal a red flag to potential investors. It is worth noting that, due to the unregulated nature of the ICO market, there have been instances of projects using referral programs primarily to generate quick funds without having a solid project or even a legitimate operation behind them.

Sometimes, excessive use of aggressive promotional campaigns, such as large referral bonuses, is a sign of an outright Ponzi scheme. Examples abound in the crypto space. One of the largest ICO frauds, OneCoin, was a well-known cryptocurrency that was later exposed as a Ponzi scheme. The ICO was launched in Bulgaria, and it promised high returns with minimal risk. OneCoin was heavily promoted through referral marketing, rewarding its investors for bringing more people into the fold. Despite having no blockchain nor any technological backing, OneCoin was able to raise $4.4 billion before it was shut down and the founder disappeared.

Another startup, BitConnect, ran a highly publicized ICO and operated a high-yield cryptocurrency investment platform, promising extraordinary returns for investors through a 'lending program'. The company's aggressive promotional strategies included referral bonuses, encouraging existing investors to bring in new ones. However, it turned out to be a Ponzi scheme, and BitConnect shut down its exchange platform in 2018 following warnings from regulators. Many investors lost their money, demonstrating the risks of promotional strategies that promise exorbitant returns without clear business justification.

Incentive bonuses, on the other hand, are employed to stimulate early investment or large-scale participation in the ICO. These bonuses often take the form of extra tokens and are designed to reward early adopters or those who invest a certain amount into the ICO. The principle here is simple: the earlier you invest, or the more you invest, the greater the bonus you receive. This strategy not only accelerates fundraising but also encourages larger investments.

From a scientific perspective, the effectiveness and implications of incentive bonuses in ICOs are subjects of ongoing research and debate. On the one hand, incentive bonuses can be viewed as an effective tool for attracting investors and raising funds quickly. They create a sense of urgency and exclusivity which can spur potential investors into action. Moreover, inducing investors to contribute funds earlier in a campaign may create informational cascades, i.e., an observational learning process that is based on the actions of other individuals. Such a behaviour was observed in conventional crowdfunding (Vismara 2018) and in ICO campaigns (Boreiko and Risteski 2021).

However, on the other hand, there are also concerns. Incentive bonuses might contribute to the volatility and speculative nature of token prices. This is particularly the case if a large number of investors, motivated by the bonus, sell their tokens once they are listed on an exchange. Furthermore, offering high bonuses might signal desperation or lack of confidence in the underlying value of the project, which could raise red flags for savvy investors.

The effectiveness of incentive bonuses in any fundraising tool ultimately hinges on their utilization within the broader context of the project's comprehensive strategy. When managed appropriately, they can provide valuable initial momentum. However, when misused, they can lead to damaging consequences. In a similar vein to generous referral bonuses, substantial incentive bonuses could potentially serve as indicators of potential fraud. This is because the founders may aim to secure contributed funds as early as possible in order to abscond before the community identifies other red flags about the scam project. PlexCoin ICO in 2017, Prodeum in 2018, Pincoin in 2018, and many other fraudulent projects offered aggressive bonus structures aimed at incentivizing early investment.

Table 4.2 illustrates this point and highlights some other intriguing statistics about promotional strategies. ICOs with a hard cap reached, denoting very successful campaigns, typically demonstrate a lower frequency of using referral and early-investor bonuses than ordinary ones, as indicated by the 'Funded ICO' label in the table. This might be due to the superior quality of the project, which negates the need for aggressive marketing. Unsuccessful campaigns exhibit similar, though less pronounced, statistics. However, in these cases, the generous bonuses might signify an attempt to create artificial buzz for projects that would otherwise fail to attract investors.

Table 4.2   Incentive bonuses statistics

	All ICOs	Hard cap reached	Funded ICO	Min cap not reached
Number	473	118	300	55
With any incentive bonus, %	66.8	52.5	73.7	60.0
Average size of investment bonus, %	26.5	14.7	43.3	39.4
With referral bonus, %	**10.3**	**4.4**	**13.3**	**7.4**
With early-bird-time bonus, %	**45.5**	**37.7**	**50.3**	**35.2**
Average size, %	38.1	30.3	40.1	40.3

	All ICOs	Hard cap reached	Funded ICO	Min cap not reached
Min, %	3.0	7.4	3.0	5.3
Max, %	350	67.0	350	167
With early-bird-tier bonus, %	**15.2**	**7.9**	**17.4**	**18.5**
Average size, %	62.8	41.6	66.7	61.5
Min, %	8.1	9.0	8.1	10.0
Max, %	710	150	710	125
With larger-contribution bonus, %	**6.9**	**4.4**	**7.8**	**7.4**
Average size, %	20.5	35.0	20.0	7.6
Min, %	0.0	0.0	0.0	0.0
Max, %	150	150	75	30.4

Notes: The table depicts the frequency of various promotional strategies, as well as the average, minimum, and maximum bonuses awarded to investors across different ICO groups within a sample of 473 ICOs spanning from 2013 to the third-quarter of 2017. The 'Hard cap reached' and 'Min cap not reached' categories correspond to ICOs where the collected funds have either reached the targeted maximum or have failed to reach the targeted minimum, respectively. An 'Early-bird-time bonus' is granted to investors who contribute early in the ICO, while an 'Early-bird-tier bonus' is awarded to those who invest before a pre-specified level of funds has been attained. The 'Larger-contribution bonus' is allocated to larger investors.

On the whole, approximately only 10 per cent of the ICOs in our sample used referral bonuses, but around two-thirds of them awarded bonus tokens to early investors. On average, around 25 per cent of tokens were given to early investors as a reward for their timely participation. However, only about half of the very successful ICOs used bonus schemes, and these granted less than 15 per cent as bonus tokens.

Token Sale Design and Timing

Apart from incentivizing investors with bonus token schemes, many campaigns were run with different sale designs. Even the earlier ICOs in 2013–2014 didn't follow the same strategy but experimented with various mechanisms of fixing the price, defining fundraising goals, and structuring the sale. Over time, with larger and more complicated campaigns, various types of token sales have emerged, each with its mechanics and characteristics. Below, we briefly discuss various token sales designs that were used in classical ICOs.

One of the first questions that stands before the token sales organizer is how to determine the price of the token to be offered to investors. The conventional financial methods were not very suitable to employ in this setting. For example, the price determination of shares in an IPO is often conducted through the book-building method where underwriters and the issuing company solicit expressions of interest in the shares from institutional investors, indicating the number of shares they'd like and at what price (Boreiko and Lombardo 2011). Based on the demand, underwriters determine the final price. In VC funding, the price of a share is usually determined during a funding round when the company and investors negotiate the company's valuation. The per-share price is then derived from this negotiated valuation and the number of existing and newly issued shares. These traditional methods are often impractical or unsuitable for ICOs for various reasons, such as reliance on valuation, well-defined concept of a financial instrument sold, and so on.

Due to these challenges, ICOs have often adopted innovative sale designs that are more appropriate for their unique needs and characteristics. There are two most frequently used mechanisms of token price determination – fixed-price token sales and proportional sales with price determination occurring at a later stage. Each method has its unique advantages and disadvantages, and the choice between the two largely depends on the specifics of the project and the expectations of the team and investors. Table 4.3 illustrates each method's pros and cons.

Table 4.3   Fixed-price auction vs. proportional sale of tokens

	Fixed-price auction	Proportional sale
Simplicity	High	Low
Transparency	High	Low
Flexibility	Low	High
Market-driven	No	Yes
Uncertainty	Low	High

In a fixed-price token sale, the price of the token is set before the ICO begins. This price does not change during the course of the sale, and potential investors know exactly how much they have to pay for a specific number of tokens. (Earlier-bird bonuses may alter this amount as discussed in the previous section.) The straightforward nature of this design makes it easier for investors to understand since they know exactly what they are getting for their money. Moreover, there is very little ambiguity or unpredictability about the token price, which can instil additional confidence in investors.

However, establishing the fair price of the token is not an easy task, especially for blockchain-based risky and uncertain projects. If the fixed price is too high or too low relative to market demand, it can lead to an unsuccessful ICO or a subsequent drop in token price post-ICO. In addition, the token price is not adjustable based on market conditions or demand trends, which can result in potential losses for both the project team and investors.

In a proportional sale, tokens are distributed proportionally based on the amount of funds contributed by each participant, and the final token price is determined once the ICO ends. So, if founders are selling one million tokens and total raised funds are equivalent to $5 million, then the token price is set at $5 and each investor gets the number of tokens equal to their contribution divided by five. This model allows for a fair distribution of tokens based on market demand, and the token price is automatically adjusted based on market conditions and total funds raised, allowing the potential for a more successful ICO. However, this model can be more difficult for potential investors to understand due to its inherent complexity. In addition, investors may not know the exact price of the token until the end of the sale, which can lead to uncertainty and potential hesitancy to participate.

Some projects have attempted to mix these two methods in order to overcome the deficiencies of each. Filecoin conducted a token sale in 2017 that used a combination of the two mechanisms. It incorporated elements of a fixed-price sale for advisors and large investors and a proportional model for the broader public. The structure of this token sale was a bit complex, with the Filecoin token price floor fixed at $1 and increasing progressively with each subsequent investment.

Some other ICOs have experimented with hybrid structures or running more conventional auction designs. The EOS token sale was a sequence of proportional token sales divided into two main phases: a short initial distribution of 200 million tokens (20 per cent of the total) followed by a year-long distribution period of 700 million tokens (70 per cent of the total) where the total Ether (ETH) contributed during each period determined the EOS/ETH exchange rate.

Some other ICOs employed auctions or other methods to sell tokens. For instance, the Gnosis ICO in 2017 utilized a Dutch auction mechanism. The price started high and then gradually decreased until all tokens were sold, or the sale period concluded. This approach aimed to find a fair price for the tokens but resulted in a concentration of tokens within a few wallets, as participants held off until the last moment to buy in at a lower price. It is important to note, however, that there were very few ICOs that used this method. Figure 4.2 shows that four-fifths of all ICOs used a fixed-price mechanism, and only 1 per cent experimented with hybrid or auction methods.

Since the first ICO campaigns in 2013, the founders always wanted to signal to the potential investors that they are not merely speculative ventures. Proving the viability and soundness of their projects was not easy for non-specialists, and they had to find other ways to demonstrate their worth. One of the ways to do that was to introduce various caps on sales proceeds as a strategic move

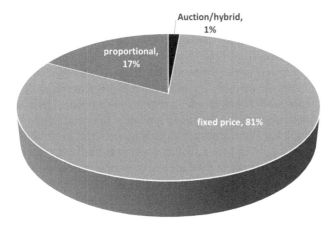

Source: Author's calculations.

Figure 4.2   *Price determination mechanisms in ICOs from 2013 to 2017, Q3*

designed to manage the fundraising. The industry practice quickly adopted different milestones that a project aimed to reach during its token sale. These goals became a de facto standard and provided investors with a better understanding of the project's financial requirements. The list of the funding goals is as follows:

1. A *minimum cap*, often referred to as a minimum goal or min cap, is the least amount of funds that an ICO aims to raise. If the ICO does not reach this threshold, it is typically considered unsuccessful, and the funds are often returned to the investors, providing a degree of protection. The minimum cap is usually set to cover the basic costs of initiating the project. The first ICO that used min cap was Swarm in July 2014, which set its min cap at 1000 bitcoins (BTC) and later successfully raised 1270 BTC. Our ICO data for the period 2013–2017, Q3, shows that slightly above 40 per cent of all ICOs have set some sort of min cap on their token sales.

2. A *soft cap* is an intermediate fundraising goal in an ICO. Once a project reaches its soft cap, it typically signifies that sufficient capital has been raised to become fully operational and deliver on its promises. However, there might be additional objectives that require further funding. Originally, meeting the soft cap either triggered a set closing period or activated a hard cap, which would close the sale when met. This

allowed last-minute buyers a chance to participate while preventing excessive fundraising beyond the announced goal. Interestingly, over time, since 2018, the term soft cap has been adopted as the minimum cap,[3] and nowadays, the terms are used interchangeably, with no distinction made between the two.[4]

3. The *hard cap* represents the maximum amount of funds that an ICO aims to raise. Once the hard cap is reached, the project will not accept any additional funds, and the token sale is considered complete. Hard caps are set to avoid overfunding, as well as to provide a clear end point for the ICO. By setting a hard cap, a project signals its financial needs and limits the risk of oversupply of tokens, which could potentially devalue the tokens. It also ensures the project does not overcapitalize and potentially mismanage investor funds due to having more money than they can realistically use efficiently. During the early stage of ICO development, the hard cap was set not in monetary terms but as a number of tokens for sale under the fixed-price token sale model. So, the first ICO that ever used a hard cap in its fundraising was MaidSafeCoin that, in April 2014, offered 400 million-plus tokens for sale at a fixed price with early-bird bonus and reached the hard cap, collecting 12 200 BTC or $8 million in equivalent. The first ICO to set up a hard cap in monetary terms was Crypti CO in July 2014. They capped their token sale at 750 BTC and stopped it once the funding goal was reached. Our ICO data for the period 2013–2017, Q3, shows that the vast majority of ICOs (almost 95 per cent) have set the hard cap on their token sales.

4. A *hidden cap* is a variant of the hard cap where the maximum funding limit is not disclosed to the investors until it is reached. The purpose of a hidden cap is to prevent late investors from rushing in to close the sale and to provide everyone who is interested with a chance to participate. Once the hidden cap is reached, there is typically a final period for last-minute investments. Hidden hard caps were occasionally used during the peak of the ICO boom, around 2017–2018. For example, the Status Network held an ICO for its Status Network Token (SNT) in June 2017. The team has implemented a smart contract algorithm that they called *dynamic ceilings*, a series of mini 'Hidden Hard Caps' at specific block intervals. However, this practice was met with controversy and criticism due to the lack of transparency and was not pursued by many ICOs.

Some teams went even further and conducted *uncapped sales*, or ICOs that didn't set a maximum limit on the funds that they could raise. While this approach allowed the project to raise a substantial amount of capital, it occasionally led to concerns about project valuation and fund allocation. Uncapped sales are relatively rare and can potentially lead to issues of token oversupply.

In our sample of 473 ICOs up to the end of the third-quarter of 2017, we identified only 29 ICOs with uncapped sales. Among these uncapped ICOs are seminal blockchain projects such as Ethereum, The DAO, Bancor, Tezos, Polkadot, and EOS, among others, which collectively raised over $5 billion. This represents around 60 per cent of the total funds raised by ICOs in our sample.

Apart from setting caps on total funds raised, some ICOs also defined minimum and maximum contribution caps, that referred to the limits on the amount that a single investor could contribute during the token sale.

A *minimum contribution cap* is usually set to prevent the blockchain network from becoming flooded with numerous micro-transactions that could clog the system. This is often used in ICOs to ensure that each individual's investment is meaningful enough to the project's fundraising goals. A small minimum investment requirement can also help manage administrative work by reducing the total number of contributors. Our ICO data for the period 2013–2017, Q3, shows that slightly above 20 per cent of all ICOs have set some sort of min contribution cap on their token sales.

The *maximum contribution cap*, on the other hand, is intended to prevent a single investor or a small group of investors from gaining too much control over the token supply. This can be critical for projects that want to ensure a wide distribution of tokens to create a diverse and decentralized network of token holders. The maximum contribution cap is a way to promote fairness, allowing more individuals the opportunity to participate in the token sale. In our sample, only 10 per cent of all ICOs specified the max cap on individual contribution.

The final point worth mentioning in this chapter is the structuring of token sales in stages. These stages offer a methodical process for fundraising and enable projects to engage with different types of investors at various stages of their development. The initial ICOs were conducted in a single stage, however, later developments introduced a more complex sale structure. The established industry practice identifies the following stages that may be present in an ICO:

1. A *private sale* represents the initial stage of the ICO process and is typically targeted at institutional investors, venture capitalists, and high-net-worth individuals. Private sales offer substantial discounts on token prices and may stipulate a minimum investment threshold. Given the limited audience and the significant investment requirements, private sales often take place before the public announcement of the ICO. Acquiring reliable information about such private sales is typically challenging, even for experienced researchers in the field.
2. A *pre-sale* is a stage that follows the private sale, targeting early investors who are interested in the project but may not meet the requirements for

the private sale. Pre-sales usually offer tokens at a discount compared to the main sale, and there may be a minimum investment amount. Pre-sales help generate early interest and raise initial funding for the project. Many ICOs that were run from 2016 structured their sales with an advertised pre-sale. Some ICOs even stopped fundraising after running a pre-sale. Whereas during earlier years of ICOs this was not a frequent activity pursued (slightly above 30 per cent of ICOs in our sample before 2017 Q3 had a pre-sale), the data from Momtaz (2021) indicates that over 45 per cent of all ICOs that had data on raised funds were run with one.

3. The *public sale*, or *crowdsale*, is the main event of an ICO, where the majority of tokens are offered to the general public. Token prices are usually higher than in private sales or pre-sales, but still discounted compared to the expected market price after the ICO. In earlier years that was the only major fundraising event, but later, the majority of tokens were usually distributed in private sales or pre-sales to strategic buyers or professional investors.

Marketing and Social Media

Marketing and promotion are key to attracting a sufficient number of investors both by promoting the project and building a strong community around it. This can be achieved through various channels, including social media, forums, and blockchain events. Social media platforms provide a powerful tool for promotion and communication. Campaigns use social media to announce the launch of their projects, keep investors updated on progress, and engage with their community. They provide a direct line of communication between projects and potential investors, facilitating a sense of transparency and trust. Moreover, social media platforms have facilitated virality, a crucial component for the success of many crowdfunding campaigns. The ease of sharing information across social networks allows campaigns to reach a much wider audience than they would through traditional methods.

Social media has played a vital role in crowdfunding campaigns prior to ICOs. Long before ICOs came onto the scene, social media had already become an integral part of the crowdfunding landscape, enabling creators to connect with potential backers in a way that is direct, personal, and engaging. The impact of proficient social media utilization on the success of a campaign has received attention in both industry reports and academic research. Studies such as Vismara (2016) underscore that ventures with broader social networks have higher chances of successful funding. Similarly, Nitani and Riding (2017) emphasized the significance of an extensive social network on campaign success, among other factors. Further research by Nitani et al. (2019) demonstrated that social media offers investors an opportunity to validate information that may otherwise lack credibility. Thus, the influence of social media on crowdfunding extends beyond promotion to also include aspects of trust-building and information validation.

While social media has been integral to crowdfunding efforts prior to ICOs, the decentralized and global nature of ICOs have made social media even more important in these types of fundraising efforts. Social media has been instrumental in their evolution and success. Not surprisingly, its role in token sales has been a significant focus of academic and industry research. This vast body of literature covers a range of topics, exploring how social media influences the success of ICOs, the dynamics of investor interactions, and the impact of various marketing strategies.

Many researchers have investigated the correlation between social media activity and the financial success of ICOs (Ackermann et al. 2020, Albrecht et al. 2020, Campino et al. 2021). Several studies suggest that a robust social media presence can positively impact ICOs' fundraising efforts. Factors such as the number of followers, frequency of posts, and the overall engagement on platforms like X, Facebook, or Telegram, are often associated with higher levels of funding (Perez et al. 2020).

Another key topic addressed in the literature is the role of social media in fostering communication and trust between project founders and potential investors. Given the decentralized and often anonymous nature of ICOs, social media platforms can serve as essential tools for projects to demonstrate transparency, relay updates, and respond to investor inquiries.

In the early days, the first ICOs, like Bitcoin, used platforms like BitcoinTalk as the only channel to engage potential investors, particularly those with blockchain knowledge. These forums provided a platform for in-depth discussions, enabling a core community of crypto enthusiasts to explore and understand the intricacies of the project. As the ICO landscape evolved, projects began to utilize a broader array of channels to connect with potential investors and supporters. Professional discussion forums and code-sharing repositories, such as GitHub and Discord, became popular. These platforms allowed developers to share code, discuss technical details, and provide transparency into the development process, thereby building credibility and trust among the technically inclined investor community (Amsden and Schweizer 2019, Fisch 2019).

In addition, ICOs began to leverage mainstream social media platforms like X, Facebook, and LinkedIn to raise awareness and disseminate information to the interested public. These channels were primarily used for announcements and news updates, broadening the reach beyond the tech-savvy communities to include less technical, but still interested, audiences. Within the ICO industry, X emerged as one of the primary communication channels for ICO teams, with regular updates and posts from the founders serving as clear signals that the projects were active and progressing. In subsequent years, Telegram has grown to become a significant platform for communication between investors and project teams, facilitating real-time interaction and discussion.

Lastly, ICOs started to employ marketing campaigns involving celebrities to further boost their visibility and appeal. The role of celebrity endorsements in ICOs has sparked much discussion, presenting both potential advantages and significant risks. While such endorsements can bring visibility to ICOs and potentially enhance their success, they also entail notable risks for both investors and the endorsing celebrities.

One primary concern is the lack of expertise that celebrities often bring to the projects they endorse. They may not possess a comprehensive understanding of the projects or the underlying technology, with their endorsements possibly being driven more by the financial gains they stand to receive rather than a thoughtful assessment of the project's potential or viability. Another risk is tied to the potential for misleading marketing. Celebrity endorsements can generate hype and draw investors who may not fully grasp the risks associated with investing in ICOs. This can culminate in marketing campaigns that mislead potential investors, relying on their trust in the celebrity's judgement rather than a robust understanding of the investment.

Legal and regulatory implications also present considerable challenges. In some jurisdictions, celebrity endorsements of ICOs may be viewed as the promotion of unregistered securities, which could lead to legal complications. For instance, in the United States, the Securities and Exchange Commission (SEC) has issued warnings and even taken actions against celebrities who have endorsed ICOs without providing proper disclosures[5]. Moreover, many ICO scam schemes hired celebrities to promote their ICOs. Celebrity endorsements could inadvertently lend credibility to these scams, making it more challenging for potential investors to discern legitimate projects from fraudulent ones.

An interesting recent research paper by White and Wilkoff (2023) studied the impact of celebrity endorsements on the outcomes of ICOs. The researchers found that while celebrity endorsements did not replace ICO pre-sales, they increased the anticipated success of the ICOs, resulting in more funds raised and more exchange listings. However, there was no evidence that these celebrity-endorsed ICOs had more success post-launch, and they were even associated with potential red flags such as a higher likelihood of scams.

TOKEN ECONOMICS

In ICOs, the token that is issued serves a variety of purposes. Primarily, it is an integral part of the project's economy and network, its blood, representing a unit of value and the primary building block within the project's ecosystem. The token's utility could range from granting access to certain services within the platform, serving as a form of payment, providing voting rights, or simply representing an investment in the project.

The token was needed because it provides a way to pre-fund blockchain infrastructure. Before ICOs, fundraising for decentralized projects was challenging. These projects are designed to be decentralized from the start, which often means there's no business model or revenue stream for the founding team. Tokens serve as a way to incentivize early participants and also raise upfront funds for development. By purchasing tokens, investors essentially fund the infrastructure needed for these decentralized networks to operate.

Simply promising future participation would be less attractive to investors. Tokens not only provide a tangible representation of their stake in the project, but they also offer a form of liquidity as these tokens can be traded on various exchanges. Furthermore, as the project gains users and popularity, the demand for these tokens can increase, leading to potential price appreciation. These potential benefits and risks are elements of what is known as tokenomics, the study of the supply and demand characteristics of cryptocurrency tokens, as well as the incentives systems built into their structure. Tokenomics is vital to a successful ICO because it influences everything from the project's long-term viability to the potential return on investment for the early adopters.

Several factors go into the tokenomics of a cryptocurrency project. The choice of blockchain is one such factor. Some tokens are based on existing blockchains like Ethereum, while others opt for independent blockchains. This choice influences the token's security, scalability, and interoperability with other projects. The type of token also matters. There are different token standards, each with its unique properties and capabilities. For instance, ERC-20 tokens are widely used in Ethereum-based projects, while ERC-721 tokens are used for Non-Fungible Tokens (NFTs).

In addition, the token's consensus mechanism (such as proof-of-work or proof-of-stake) can influence the tokenomics. These mechanisms determine how new tokens are minted and how transactions are validated. For instance, proof-of-work requires miners to solve complex mathematical problems and consume a lot of energy, while proof-of-stake allows users to validate transactions and create new blocks based on the number of tokens they hold and are willing to 'stake' for the purpose.

The monetary policy of a token, an integral aspect of tokenomics, plays a pivotal role in determining its long-term viability and value. Key components of this policy include aspects such as inflation rate and total supply. These elements can have a profound effect on the token's price dynamics and market perception. For instance, a high inflation rate, which signifies a higher rate of token creation, might cause the token's price to decrease over time due to the increased supply. This depreciation could discourage investors and devalue the token's utility within its associated ecosystem. On the other hand, an adequately managed inflationary model can also incentivize network participation and healthy token circulation, contributing to the overall growth of the platform.

On the contrary, a low total supply could potentially enhance each token's value, provided there is a consistent demand. A finite or scarce supply often creates a perception of exclusivity and value, akin to assets like gold. However, it is essential to ensure that this limited supply does not hinder the network's growth or lead to excessive price volatility, which could discourage usage or lead to speculative bubbles.

Token distribution and allocation are also critical components of good governance practices in ICOs, drawing on experiences from traditional financial transactions. This involves determining when and how the tokens will be distributed, and who will receive them. The details of this allocation can significantly influence investor confidence and the project's long term success. For instance, retaining a large portion of tokens may indicate the founders' confidence in the project, while giving away a significant percentage to the community can foster engagement and decentralization. Furthermore, distribution policies often include vesting periods or lock-ups for team tokens, which can reassure investors that the team is incentivized to stick around and deliver on their promises. Transparent and fair token distribution practices can enhance the legitimacy of the project, attract more investors, and ultimately contribute to the sustainability and success of the project.

Token liquidity is another important factor to consider in tokenomics. A token needs to be widely available and easy to trade on the market to maintain its value. If a token is difficult to buy or sell, it might deter potential investors and users, affecting its overall market value.

Lastly, due to unique legal and regulatory contexts, the classification of tokens into utility and security tokens is not arbitrary; rather, it plays a crucial role. The reason why this classification is important is that securities are subject to strict regulatory oversight, including disclosure requirements and investor protections. If a token is classified as a security but has not complied with relevant securities laws, the project founders could face severe legal consequences, including fines and enforcement actions from regulators.

Blockchain Choice and Token Standards

Blockchain choice and token standards are among the key considerations for an ICO. Initially, many early blockchain projects sought to build their own blockchains to improve upon Bitcoin. These were predominantly infrastructure projects, competing to create new, improved standards that would allow for the issuance of new types of tokens. Projects such as Omni, NXT, Lisk,

NEM, NEO, Bitshares, and, later, Waves, are examples of early blockchains that hosted ICOs.

However, the advent of Ethereum and its smart contract capabilities proved to be a game changer. Ethereum's smart contracts allowed non-infrastructure projects to focus on developing their ecosystem without having to worry about the technicalities of the underlying blockchain. This is comparable to startups receiving funding from venture capitalists in the form of cash, deposited in a bank, without having to worry about the internal workings of bank transfers and payment systems.

However, this ease of token creation has a double-edged sword. While it democratized access to capital and fostered innovation, it also opened the door for scams and fraudulent projects. The ease of token creation and the lack of regulatory oversight made ICOs an attractive option for individuals or groups looking to raise funds quickly, without necessarily having a viable or legitimate project.

The standardization provided by Ethereum, particularly its ERC-20 token standard, greatly simplified the process of token creation. This lowered the barriers to entry and made it possible for a wider range of projects to raise funds through ICOs. Ethereum's introduction of smart contracts was also a significant development in the blockchain technology landscape. Smart contracts are self-executing contracts with the terms of the agreement directly written into code that automatically execute transactions once the predetermined conditions are met, eliminating the need for an intermediary and ensuring the trustworthiness of the transaction. As was shown in Figure 3.1 (Chapter 3), by 2017, Ethereum quickly became a de facto standard to be used for new token issues.

The Ethereum network, since its inception, has been grappling with several challenges. Among these, the issues of scalability and high transaction costs have been quite prominent. As Ethereum grew in popularity, the network started facing scalability issues. The network was limited in terms of the number of transactions it could process per second. This was largely due to the proof-of-work consensus mechanism used by Ethereum, which was relatively slow and inefficient in handling large volumes of transactions. Consequently, this led to network congestion, slower transaction speeds, and an increase in transaction costs.

In response to these scalability issues, Ethereum's transaction fees, otherwise known as gas fees, rose significantly. The price of these fees was determined by supply and demand dynamics within the network, which meant that during periods of high demand, these fees could become quite exorbitant. This rendered Ethereum less affordable for some users and, back in 2017, raised questions about its long-term sustainability.

These challenges faced by the Ethereum network spurred the development of several alternative solutions. Ethereum itself continued to upgrade and in September 2022 switched to the proof-of-stake consensus mechanism.[6] There has also been a rise in alternative blockchains to Ethereum, offering improved scalability, lower fees, or other distinctive features. Some of these include Binance Smart Chain, Polkadot, Cardano, Avalanche, Solana, and Fantom. Each of these blockchains brings unique attributes to the table, but also potential trade-offs.

As a result, we observe a large variety of blockchain platforms that enable startups to issue tokens under their respective standards. At present, tokens have been issued on 140 such platforms, each having a total token value exceeding $1 million. Table 4.4 showcases information about the top five largest blockchain platforms as of April 2023, ranked by the number of tokens issued on them.

Table 4.4   *Top five largest blockchain platforms by number of tokens issued, as of April 2023*

Name	Launched in	No. of tokens	Market cap
Ethereum	2014	830	$227.8b
Binance Smart Chain	2020	618	$48.6b
Polygon	2017	434	$8.4b
Arbitrum	2021	350	$1.6b
Avalanche	2020	319	$5.0b

Source: Coinmarketcap.com.

As can be seen in Table 4.4, the Ethereum platform still dominates the market, however, the competing platforms are getting closer. Binance Smart Chain (BSC) is a blockchain developed by Binance in 2020, one of the world's largest cryptocurrency exchanges. BSC was designed to run parallel to Binance Chain, Binance's original chain, to enable smart contracts and to be compatible with Ethereum. The main appeal of BSC is its low transaction fees and fast block times, making it an attractive option for developers and users who find Ethereum's costs and speed prohibitive.

An alternative solution, Polygon (previously known as Matic Network), developed a framework for building and connecting Ethereum-compatible blockchain networks back in 2017. Polygon combined the best of Ethereum and sovereign blockchains into a fully fledged multi-chain system. This made Polygon a highly suitable platform for issuing tokens, particularly for projects that need scalability while still wanting to leverage the Ethereum network's security and capabilities. Additionally, Polygon provides a much faster and cheaper transaction environment than Ethereum, which can be highly beneficial for projects that need to manage a high volume of token transactions. Therefore, despite being a newer player compared to Ethereum, Polygon is increasingly becoming a preferred choice for projects looking to issue tokens, especially in the Decentralized Finance (DeFi) and NFT spaces.

Token Monetary Policy

While traditional fiat currencies are issued by central banks and regulated through mechanisms like interest rates and reserve requirements, the issuance and regulation of tokens are often conducted by the project teams behind the ICOs. Despite the potential for missteps due to the lack of formal monetary policy training, many projects have managed to establish thriving token economies. They have done so by adapting principles from traditional economics and finance, learning from the successes and failures of past projects, and experimenting with innovative new approaches to monetary policy.

At its core, a token economy works much like a traditional economy. Tokens, like money, are used as a medium of exchange within a certain ecosystem. The value of the tokens is derived from the supply and demand dynamics within that ecosystem. However, unlike traditional economies, where monetary policy is used to control inflation and stabilize the currency, token economies lack a centralized authority with the ability to adjust monetary policy on-the-fly in response to economic changes.

Take, for example, Bitcoin, which is sometimes called *digital gold*. Much like gold, Bitcoin has a limited supply, with a total of 21 million Bitcoins ever to be created. This supply limit is coded into the Bitcoin protocol and cannot be changed. New Bitcoins are introduced into the market through a process called mining, similar to how gold is extracted from the earth. This mining process slows down as we approach the maximum supply limit, adding a scarcity factor to the asset.

This fixed, limited supply makes both Bitcoin and gold deflationary assets, meaning they aren't subject to arbitrary inflation. Unlike fiat currencies, where a central bank can increase the money supply leading to inflation, both Bitcoin and gold have a cap on their total quantity. However, the fixed supply also leads to some challenges. It can contribute to price volatility as demand for the asset increases or decreases. Additionally, if the demand for Bitcoin or gold suddenly surges, the limited supply can lead to significant price spikes.

Thus, Bitcoin's fixed supply was intentionally designed as part of its foundational code in order to prevent inflation, ensure predictable monetary policy, and incentivize early adoption in the absence of a central monetary authority. The early ICO tokens followed suit and were predominantly launched with fixed supply. In fact, this model remained the predominant one – in our sample of 473 ICOs up to 2017 Q3, exactly three-quarters of ICOs issued a fixed number of tokens. A handful of projects opted for an inflationary model where new tokens are continually issued, similar to how a central bank might print money. For example, Ethereum does not have a maximum supply limit like Bitcoin. This means that Ethereum technically could be considered inflationary, as new ETH coins are created with each new block added to the Ethereum blockchain. In total, around one-fifth of ICOs in our sample chose this model of token issuance.

Some projects chose to implement a deflationary model where a certain percentage of tokens are permanently removed from circulation after each transaction, effectively reducing the supply over time. The purpose of such a model is to create scarcity, and thus potentially increase the value of each individual token as the supply decreases. This can incentivize early adoption and investment in the token, as tokens might become more valuable in the future if the project becomes successful. This is the rarest token issue model, and only 22 ICOs (less than 5 per cent) implemented it for their tokens.

For example, Binance Coin (BNB) was initially created with a fixed supply of 200 million coins. As part of their WP and commitment to the community, Binance stated that they would use a portion of their profits each quarter to buy back and burn BNB tokens, until 50 per cent of the total BNB supply (100 million BNB) is burned. This effectively reduces the supply of BNB over time. Binance has so far kept its word, and in each quarter to date, around two million BNB tokens have been burned.[7]

Token Distribution and Allocation

A well-structured token distribution policy is critical for the success of an ICO campaign. This policy determines who gets the tokens and when, which can significantly impact the future of the project. The ICO's distribution policy typically mirrors some of the established practices in traditional finance, such as IPOs, where equity distribution involves considerations around owner retention, lock-ups, and vesting periods.

Like in an IPO, it is common for a portion of tokens to be retained by the project's founders and team in an ICO. This can demonstrate that the team has skin in the game, aligning their interests with those of the token holders. However, the percentage retained should be balanced and not too excessive so as to prevent centralization of token ownership (Boreiko and Lombardo 2011, Giudici and Adhami 2019).

Lock-up periods, which restrict the ability of certain token holders (usually the team and early investors) to sell their tokens for a set period after the ICO, are often used to promote price stability. This approach prevents large quantities of tokens from being dumped onto the market immediately after the ICO, which could depress the token price (Boreiko and Lombardo 2012). Vesting schedules, similar to those used in employee stock option plans, can also be implemented in ICOs. These schedules gradually release tokens to team members over time, incentivising them to remain with the project and contribute to its long-term success.

Figure 4.3 presents the token distribution statistics for the sampled ICOs. Notably, the proportion of tokens offered to investors is quite substantial but seems to decline in later years. The average stake sold is around 60 per cent, a figure considerably higher than the stakes typically sold in IPOs. The stake attributed to founders ranges between 15 and 20 per cent of all tokens. However, considering the reserve tokens, which remain under their control, the figure goes up to around a third of all tokens.

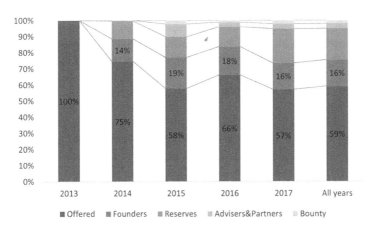

Note: The data illustrates the proportions of all tokens allocated for sale (Offered), given to founders (Founders), reserved for future distribution or maintained at the startup's discretion (Reserves), dispensed to advisors, partners, and early adopters (Advisors & Partners), and planned for bounty awards (Bounty).
Source: Author's calculations.

Figure 4.3   *Distribution of allocated tokens in ICOs between 2013 and 2017 Q3*

Concerning the lock-up of tokens and vesting periods, data for approximately 90 per cent of ICOs in our database was found. Interestingly, exactly one-third of these ICOs provide for the lock-up of the founders' shares to assure investors that these will not be immediately sold on the market post-token sale. On average, tokens are locked up for a period of one year and four months. This commitment demonstrates the founders' faith in the project's long-term prospects and aligns their interests with those of the investors, thus encouraging trust and stability in the ICO.

Token Liquidity

Token liquidity is the ease with which a token can be bought, sold, or exchanged for other assets in the market. High liquidity is desirable because it allows token holders to convert their tokens quickly and easily into other assets, such as fiat currency or other cryptocurrencies. Factors affecting token liquidity include the number of exchanges listing the token, trading volume, market depth, and the token's overall market demand. Ensuring adequate token liquidity is vital for the success of an ICO, as it can impact investor confidence and the token's value.

Token liquidity is indeed a significant factor in the success of an ICO. It stands as a vital consideration for investors who need the assurance that they can easily exit their investment if needed. Given the high-risk nature of investing in ICOs, the availability of an easy exit strategy often becomes the determining factor for participation. It is important to note that the motives for investing in ICOs are varied. While some investors are driven by speculative reasons, others are passionate about the technology or are motivated by different factors. Using a survey of ICO investors, Fisch et al. (2021) found that for the majority, technology motives are considered more important than financial and ideological ones. Regardless of the reasons, liquidity remains a key concern for most. Indeed, during the early days of ICOs, their dedicated threads on platforms like Bitcointalk.org were commonly filled with questions about which exchanges would list the tokens from ICOs.

Quite a few academic studies have focused on the listing of ICO tokens as a factor of success. Boreiko (2019), Amsden and Schweizer (2019), Belitski and Boreiko (2021), Momtaz (2020), and other researchers provided statistical evidence that the tokens that are more likely to get listed on exchanges tend to be associated with higher fundraising success, greater liquidity, higher market capitalization, lower volatility, and they attract a higher investor base.

During the ICO boom in 2017–2018, exchanges understood the critical role token listing held for these projects and began to levy substantial sums for this service. This evolution highlighted the vital function that exchanges fulfilled within the ICO ecosystem. They served as gatekeepers, determining which tokens received a listing and thereby gaining access to the liquidity they offered. Unsurprisingly, this dynamic greatly propelled the introduction and rapid expansion of decentralized exchanges (DEXs), where the intermediary role is performed by smart contracts or automated market makers. On these decentralized platforms, tokens can be listed and traded without the need for a centralized authority, thereby democratizing access to liquidity and reducing dependence on traditional exchanges.

However, the requirement for high liquidity and the corresponding desire for exchange listing also come with their own set of challenges. For one, the high listing fees could pose a significant barrier for many ICOs, especially for those with limited funding. Furthermore, the listing process can often be opaque and influenced by various factors beyond the control of the ICO team.

Utility vs. Security Tokens

The distinction between utility and security tokens in the ICO landscape emerged primarily as a response to regulatory scrutiny, rather than the organic evolution of ICOs. Each type of token carries specific implications and presents unique advantages and challenges. Utility tokens function as a sort of 'digital coupon' for a future product or service. The purpose of these tokens is to provide the holder with access to a particular functionality within the network or platform. For example, tokens can grant voting rights, facilitate the use of certain features, or act as a payment mechanism within a decentralized application. The value of utility tokens stems from their usability and the demand for the service or product they provide access to. They are not designed as investments per se and, therefore, they typically fall outside the jurisdiction of securities regulations.

Security tokens, on the other hand, denote an investment in a project and typically give holders the right to dividends, profit-sharing, or other forms of financial returns. They are akin to traditional securities, such as stocks or bonds. Because of this, security tokens are subject to the regulations and laws that govern securities, which can vary significantly from one jurisdiction to another.

However, it is worth noting that this dichotomy isn't always clear-cut. The classification of a token as a utility or security can be ambiguous and often requires detailed analysis. This classification can also vary depending on the jurisdiction and the specific regulatory framework in place. A prominent example of this ambiguity is the Ripple token (XRP), which was classified as a security by the SEC, but was never sold in an ICO or regarded by users as a security.[8] The case is still ongoing and has sparked significant debate in the crypto community. Adding to this complexity, in 2023, SEC Chairman Gary Gensler stated that, from the SEC's perspective, most tokens (excluding Bitcoin) could be classified as securities.[9]

The academic discourse surrounding ICOs was dominated by the legal theme of classification of the tokens issued in these offerings. Many papers in the academic literature address the legal classification of ICO tokens (Boreiko et al. 2020, Zetzsche et al. 2019, and many others). The question here is whether a given token should be classified as a utility or a security? This classification is crucial as it determines the regulatory framework that applies to the token. This is a complex issue, as the classification can depend on various factors including the token's characteristics, the rights it provides to its holders, and the jurisdiction in which it is issued. Much of this legal scholarship has emerged in response to the regulatory ambiguity surrounding ICOs and the high-profile enforcement actions taken by regulators.

SMART CONTRACTS

The concept of smart contracts predates blockchain technology and was first proposed by computer scientist and cryptographer Nick Szabo (Szabo 1994). Szabo aimed to use computer protocols to facilitate, verify, and enforce contract negotiations and performance digitally. He believed that digital contracts could make transactions more secure, efficient, and cost-effective by removing the need for intermediaries like lawyers or notaries. However, at that time, there was no suitable underlying technology to implement and widely adopt smart contracts.

Before Ethereum introduced smart contracts, there were a few projects that attempted to implement similar concepts using blockchain technology. Even Bitcoin's scripting language itself allowed users to create basic programmable logic within transactions, enabling multi-signature wallets and other simplest use cases. Mastercoin (now Omni Layer), introduced in 2013 with the first ICO, aimed to create a protocol layer on top of Bitcoin's blockchain that enabled the creation of new digital assets and smart contracts. It was a pioneer in tokenizing assets on a blockchain and introducing digitalization of contracts. It was followed by Counterparty (2014) that enabled smart contracts on the Bitcoin blockchain.

Ethereum's introduction of smart contracts into the blockchain landscape brought about a significant shift in the ways in which distributed ledger technology could be applied. The novelty of Ethereum lies in its programmability. While Bitcoin was created as a digital currency system, Ethereum was designed to be a flexible platform upon which decentralized applications (dApps) could be built.

In the context of ICOs, Ethereum's smart contracts were pivotal. They provided a framework to automatically process transactions between project founders and investors. Upon receiving funds from an investor, the smart contract would instantly issue the corresponding amount of tokens, greatly simplifying the fundraising process. However, the application of Ethereum's smart contracts extends far beyond ICOs, touching areas such as DeFi, supply chain management, digital identity verification, and more.

Following Ethereum, a number of other blockchain platforms have sought to improve and expand upon the concept of smart contracts. Blockchain protocols such as Cardano, Polkadot, and Tezos, among others, have introduced innovations to address limitations associated with Ethereum, such as scalability issues, high gas fees, and the complexity of the Solidity programming language. They have implemented new consensus algorithms, on-chain governance models, and interoperability solutions to enhance the versatility and efficiency of smart contracts.

The Role of Smart Contracts

A smart contract, in essence, is a self-executing contract with the terms of the agreement directly written into lines of code. These contracts automatically execute transactions when pre-set conditions are met, without the need for a third-party intermediary. This level of automation has the potential to significantly reduce frictions and increase the efficiency of a wide array of processes across many industries. The smart contracts were introduced in blockchain to facilitate secure, transparent, and automated transactions and agreements. As the next step in the evolution of the blockchain, they help in achieving the following objectives:

1. Trustless execution. Smart contracts allow parties to engage in agreements without the need for trust or intermediation, as the code enforces the contract terms. The decentralized nature of blockchain ensures that there is no way to hamper with the contract, and no single party can manipulate or control the contract's outcome.
2. Automation. Smart contracts automatically execute actions when predefined conditions are met, reducing manual intervention and speeding up processes.
3. Cost reduction. By automating processes and removing intermediaries, smart contracts can significantly reduce the costs associated with contract negotiation, execution, and enforcement.
4. Transparency. Blockchain-based smart contracts enable all parties to have a transparent view of the contract's terms, conditions, and execution status, at the same time providing a high degree of privacy for negotiating parties.
5. Immutability and security. Once a smart contract is deployed on a blockchain, it cannot be altered or tampered with, providing a high level of security and integrity.

Navigating the adoption of smart contracts comes with a unique set of challenges that need to be addressed to ensure their mainstream implementation:

1. Ensuring accuracy. As smart contracts are essentially computer programs, the explicit terms and conditions of the contract have to be translated into code. This process could potentially introduce errors, misinterpretations, or omissions by the coder, leading to exploitable loopholes.
2. Addressing unreliable inputs. Erroneous or false inputs can lead to invalid contracts or contract non-execution. In traditional contracts, parties can resort to judicial intervention for dispute resolution, whereas currently the smart contracts are not necessarily legally binding. Currently, most countries are still in the process of determining how they will enforce smart contracts, although these might eventually fit into one or another category of electronic signatures, which are recognized already in many jurisdictions.
3. Contending with bugs and coding errors. Bugs or coding mistakes could lead to disputes and procedural challenges. The responsibility of identifying the parties accountable for these errors, and addressing the subsequent issues, can be quite difficult. Indeed, there were already numerous instances where errors in code have led to substantial funds being stolen, lost, or frozen.
4. Preserving confidentiality. While transparency is a core feature of blockchains, many enterprises hesitate to place their sensitive contractual data on this public ledger due to the potential exposure of strategic information. The Ethereum platform lacks private smart contracts, requiring enterprises to choose their blockchain platforms judiciously.
5. Addressing complexity. Creating complex smart contracts requires advanced programming skills, which can be a barrier to adoption for non-technical users.

Smart contracts are transformative and versatile tools with applications spanning several industries, reshaping the way business and transactions are conducted. Supply chain management is one area where smart contracts are making a profound impact. They can be programmed to track goods from manufacturing to delivery, ensuring transparency at every step. Payments can be automated upon meeting specific conditions, reducing the need for paperwork and manual processing.

The real estate industry is also embracing smart contracts. From managing property sales and rental agreements to dealing with title management and fractional property ownership, smart contracts are streamlining complex processes and making transactions more transparent and efficient. Smart contracts are revolutionizing the field of intellectual property as well. They are facilitating licensing and the distribution of royalties for digital content, ensuring that creators get fair compensation for their work. In the sphere of voting systems, smart contracts enable the creation of decentralized voting and governance models. These can be implemented in organizations and communities, making voting processes more secure, transparent, and resistant to manipulation.

In the financial sector, smart contracts serve as the backbone of DeFi. They power innovative platforms for lending, insurance, and asset tokenization, circumventing traditional intermediaries and offering more efficient and inclusive financial services. The automation and irrevocability of smart contracts bring a level of transparency and trust that is reshaping the landscape of finance. ICOs have utilized smart contracts to streamline fundraising processes, allowing projects to raise capital directly from investors worldwide.

Smart Contracts in ICOs

Smart contracts played a crucial role in the post-Ethereum ICOs by automating the process of token distribution and fundraising. The earlier ICOs required a significant amount of manual work, were prone to human error, and lacked transparency and trustless execution. Between 2013 and 2016, many ICOs were run in similar fashion to Omni, the very first ICO in 2013.

Instead of using smart contracts, the Omni ICO used a simple process on the Bitcoin blockchain. Investors would send Bitcoin to a specific Bitcoin address controlled by the project's founders, and in return, they would receive the newly minted Mastercoin tokens. The process of distributing tokens to the investors was handled manually. The team running the ICO would take note of the Bitcoin addresses from where the investments came and the amount of Bitcoin each address sent. They would then manually send the appropriate number of tokens to each contributing address.

Apart from tedious work on correctly distributing tokens, another issue was with mistrust and risks associated with investing in a new, unproven venture. The ICOs teams frequently used escrow services to mitigate these risks. The concept of escrow is common in traditional finance and involves a third party holding assets (in this case, the funds raised in the ICO) on behalf of the transacting parties.

The use of an escrow in ICOs worked as follows. Instead of funds raised during the ICO going directly to the project's founders, they would be held by a trusted third-party escrow agent. The escrow agent was typically a respected individual or organization within the cryptocurrency community, and their role was to hold and protect the funds raised during the ICO. The funds held in escrow would only be released to the project's founders once certain predetermined conditions were met, such as the achievement of project milestones. This helped to protect investors and to hold the project founders accountable.

It ensured that the funds would be used for their intended purpose, and that the project founders could not simply disappear with the funds without delivering on their promises.

This method of conducting an ICO was quite primitive compared to later ICOs that utilized Ethereum's smart contracts. The advent of smart contracts on Ethereum and other platforms significantly improved this process, automating the token distribution, enhancing transparency, and reducing the potential for errors or fraud.

It was Augur, a decentralized prediction market platform, that first conducted its ICO on the Ethereum blockchain in August 2015. Moreover, the startup employed Vitalik Buterin, the creator of Ethereum, as its principal advisor, and used Ethereum's smart contract functionality to create their platform, a decentralized forecasting tool that rewards users for correctly predicting future events. The Augur ICO was innovative in many ways and showed how Ethereum's smart contracts could be utilized to create a dApp with its own set of rules and incentives. The successful launch and operation of Augur helped establish Ethereum as a platform for deploying complex dApp, setting a precedent for future projects.

With time, smart contracts have proven to be an effective mechanism to be used in ICOs of various size and origin. The main tasks that smart contracts took care of in ICOs were the following:

1. Token creation. Projects created their custom tokens using Ethereum's smart contract standards, such as ERC-20 or ERC-721. These standards define a set of rules and functions that the token must implement, allowing them to be compatible with various wallets, exchanges, and other dApp.
2. Crowdsale contracts. Projects set up smart contracts to handle the ICO process, often called crowdsale contracts. These contracts define rules such as the token price, the total supply, the start and end dates of the ICO, minimum and maximum investment caps, and any bonuses or discounts for early investors.
3. Automated distribution. When an investor participated in an ICO by sending ETH to the crowdsale contract, the smart contract automatically calculated the number of tokens the investor had to receive based on the predefined rules and sent the tokens to the investor's Ethereum address. This automation ensured a transparent, efficient, and secure token distribution process.
4. Fund management. Funds raised during the ICO were typically held in the smart contract until the end of the crowdfunding period. Some projects implemented additional security features, such as multi-signature wallets, to protect the funds. Once the ICO ended, the collected funds could be released to the project team according to the terms specified in the smart

contract, such as releasing funds in phases or based on the completion of project milestones.

5. Vesting and lock-up periods. Smart contracts were used to enforce vesting schedules and lock-up periods for team members, advisors, and early investors. This helped to prevent sudden token dumps and ensured that the involved parties had a vested interest in the project's long-term success.

6. Refund mechanisms. In case the ICO did not reach its minimum funding goal or was cancelled for any reason, some smart contracts implemented a refund mechanism that allowed investors to claim back their invested ETH.

Overall, smart contracts have made ICOs more efficient, secure, and transparent, allowing projects to raise funds and distribute tokens in a decentralized manner, without the need for intermediaries, such as investment banks or escrow agents.

Despite the high-profile misstep of the DAO, it was the third ICO that utilized Ethereum blockchain, raising a staggering $150 million but ending in a major loss due to a coding loophole[10] – however, the underlying technology's potential was far from being undermined. Ethereum's smart contracts capabilities had been demonstrated to the world, and the unfortunate event served as a wake-up call to the industry, highlighting the importance of rigorous security and auditing measures.

Instead of deterring future projects, the DAO's failure was instrumental in catalysing an industry-wide push for more robust security practices and led to the proliferation of a new era of ICOs leveraging the capabilities of Ethereum's smart contracts. In the years that followed, many projects (such as Golem, Bancor, and EOS), each with their unique visions and solutions, successfully conducted their ICOs on the Ethereum blockchain.

All of these ambitious projects were facilitated by Ethereum's smart contracts, reinforcing its position as the leading blockchain platform for token issuance. From 2016 through to 2018, Ethereum became synonymous with ICOs and token creation, underpinning a new wave of blockchain innovation and solidifying its role as a fundamental piece of the blockchain ecosystem.

Post-Ethereum Chains

Since the advent of Ethereum and its innovative smart contracts, a number of other blockchain platforms have emerged, each offering their own unique features, strengths, and approaches. These platforms emerged largely due to the evolving needs of different blockchain applications and to address certain limitations inherent in the Ethereum platform. For instance, scalability issues, high transaction costs, and complexity in programming have been persistent challenges within the Ethereum ecosystem throughout the years.

Platforms such as Binance Smart Chain, Polkadot, Cardano, and Solana have been built to offer alternative solutions. Binance Smart Chain, for example, provides a lower-cost, high-performance platform with a strong focus on facilitating decentralized trading. Polkadot aims to solve the scalability issue with a multi-chain architecture that enables different blockchains to interoperate, whereas Cardano has placed a strong emphasis on rigorous academic research to ensure high standards of security and scalability.

These newer platforms have gained significant popularity, driven by unique selling points and backed by vibrant communities of developers and users. Despite Ethereum's early mover advantage and massive developer base, these platforms have shown that they can attract significant interest and activity.

However, it is important to note that these platforms aren't necessarily in direct competition with Ethereum but often provide complementary offerings. They represent diversity in the blockchain ecosystem, offering a variety of tools, capabilities, and environments that can serve different types of applications and user needs.

Whether any of these platforms will ever surpass Ethereum in popularity or usage remains to be seen. Ethereum has a substantial lead and is also evolving, with the implemented Ethereum 2.0 upgrade addressing many of its earlier limitations. However, the growth and success of these alternative platforms underline the dynamism and diversity of the blockchain technology landscape. They collectively push the boundaries of what is possible, contributing to the ongoing evolution of the blockchain space.

CONCLUSION

In this chapter we have shown that the fundamental structures of an ICO, particularly the tokenomics and sale structure, play a crucial role in shaping its potential success. Tokenomics involves understanding the supply, demand, and utility of the token within the project ecosystem. It requires a careful balancing act to ensure that tokens are valued properly and serve a meaningful purpose, whether that's governance, access to services, or some other utility.

The sale structure of the ICO is another key component. This includes aspects like the token distribution plan, pricing strategy, and the sale timeline. An ICO needs to decide how many tokens to distribute, at what price, and over what period. Additionally, it might offer bonuses or incentives for early participation.

However, while these aspects are vital, they are just the beginning of the ICO process. The ecosystem surrounding an ICO, involving various stakeholders such as founders, investors, intermediaries, and regulators, has an equally significant impact on the overall success of the ICO. As we delve into the next chapter, we'll explore this ecosystem, examining the roles and interactions of the key players in an ICO.

NOTES

1   www.wsj.com/articles/buyer-beware-hundreds-of-bitcoin-wannabes-show
     -hallmarks-of-fraud-1526573115.
2   icoholder.com/en/ico-advisors.
3   bitcointalk.org/index.php?topic=2261103.0.
4   coinmarketcap.com/alexandria/glossary/soft-cap.
5   www.sec.gov/news/press-release/2018-268.
6   ethereum.org/en/roadmap.
7   www.binance.com/en/blog/ecosystem/23rd-bnb-burn-2841286413235339089.
8   www.sec.gov/litigation/complaints/2020/comp-pr2020-338.pdf.
9   cryptoslate.com/sec-chair-gensler-confirms-everything-other-than-bitcoin-is-a
     -security-implications-and-analysis.
10   Augur, based in the USA, and DigixDAO, from Singapore, were indeed the first
     and second ICOs respectively to be conducted on the Ethereum blockchain.

REFERENCES

Ackermann, E., Bock, C., and Buerger, R. (2020) 'Democratising entrepreneurial finance: The impact of crowdfunding and Initial Coin Offerings (ICOs)'. In A. Moritz, J.H. Block, S. Golla, and A. Werner (eds.), *Contemporary Developments in Entrepreneurial Finance*. Cham, Switzerland: Springer, pp. 277–308.

Albrecht, S., Lutz, B., and Neumann, D. (2020) 'The behaviour of blockchain ventures on Twitter as a determinant for funding success', *Electronic Markets*, 30(2), pp. 241–257.

Amsden, R. and Schweizer, D. (2019) 'Are blockchain crowdsales the new "Gold Rush"? Success determinants of Initial Coin Offerings', SSRN. Available at: https://ssrn.com/abstract=3163849 (accessed: 1 July 2023).

Belitski, M. and Boreiko, D. (2022) 'Success factors of Initial Coin Offerings', *Journal of Technological Transfer*, 47, pp. 1690–1706.

Boreiko, D. (2019) *Blockchain-based Financing with Initial Coin Offerings (ICOs): Financial Industry Disruption or Evolution?* Mantova: Universitas Studiorum.

Boreiko, D. and Lombardo, S. (2011) 'Shares' allocation and claw back clauses in Italian IPOs', *Journal of International Financial Markets, Institutions & Money*, 21, pp. 127–143.

Boreiko, D. and Lombardo, S. (2012) 'Lockup clauses in Italian IPOs', *Applied Financial Economics*, 23, pp. 221–232.

Boreiko, D., Ferrarini, G., and Giudici, P. (2020) 'Blockchain startups and prospectus regulation', *European Business Organization Law Review*, 20(4), pp. 665–694.

Boreiko, D. and Risteski, D. (2021) 'Serial and large investors in Initial Coin Offerings (ICOs)', *Small Business Economics*, 57, pp. 1053–1071.

Campino, J., Brochado, A., and Rosa, A. (2021) 'Initial Coin Offerings (ICOs): The importance of human capital', *Journal of Business Economics*, 91(8), pp. 1225–1262.

Fisch, C. (2019) 'Initial Coin Offerings (ICOs) to finance new ventures', *Journal of Business Venturing*, 34(1), pp. 1–22.

Fisch, C., Masiak, C., Vismara, S., and Block, J. (2021) 'Motives and profiles of ICO investors', *Journal of Business Research*, 125, pp. 564–576.

Giudici, G. and Adhami, S. (2019) 'The impact of governance signals on ICO fundraising success', *Journal of Industrial Business Economics*, 46, pp. 283–312.

Momtaz, P.P. (2020) 'Initial Coin Offerings', *PLOS ONE*, 15(5): e0233018.

Momtaz, P.P. (2021) 'Token offerings research database (TORD)'. Available at: https://www.paulmomtaz.com/data/tord (accessed: 1 July 2023).

Nitani, M. and Riding, A. (2017) 'On crowdfunding success: Firm and owner attributes and social networking', SSRN. Available at: https://ssrn.com/abstract=2945081 (accessed: 1 July 2023).

Nitani, N., Riding, A., and He, B. (2019) 'On equity crowdfunding: Investor rationality and success factors', *Venture Capital*, 21(2–3), pp. 243–272.

Perez, C., Sokolova, K., and Konate, M. (2020) 'Digital social capital and performance of Initial Coin Offerings, *Technological Forecasting and Social Change*, 152, pp. 1–14.

Szabo, N. (1994) 'Smart contracts'. Available at: http://www.fon.hum.uva.nl/rob/Courses/InformationInSpeech/CDROM/Literature/LOTwinterschool2006/szabo.best.vwh.net/smart.contracts.html (accessed: 1 July 2023)

Vismara, S. (2016) 'Equity retention and social network theory in equity crowdfunding', *Small Business Economics*, 46(4), pp. 579–590.

Vismara, S. (2018) 'Information cascades among investors in equity crowdfunding', *Entrepreneurship Theory and Practice*, 42(3), pp. 467–497.

White, J.T. and Wilkoff, S. (2023) 'The effect of celebrity endorsements on crypto', SSRN. Available at: https://ssrn.com/abstract=4380845 (accessed: 1 July 2023).

Zetzsche, D.A, Buckley, R.P., and Arner, D.W. (2019) 'The ICO gold rush – A challenge for regulators', *Harvard International Law Journal*, 63(2), 267–315.

5. Key players in Initial Coin Offerings

INTRODUCTION

In the Initial Coin Offerings (ICOs) ecosystem, each player indeed has a crucial role in a token sale's success and in the project's long-term viability. Founders or developers come up with the vision and implement it, creating the groundwork for the ICO project. Investors, both retail and institutional, provide the necessary financial support for the ICO project, purchasing tokens and essentially bringing the project to life. These key stakeholders are at the heart of the token sale process, with tokens being traded for financial investments.

From 2013–2015, the earliest ICOs, such as Mastercoin, NXT, Counterparty, NEM, and MaidsafeCoin, took a streamlined, fully decentralized approach to fundraising. Using only Bitcointalk threads, these projects were able to describe their vision, call for funding, communicate with potential investors, and update on token sale results and project development. The simplicity of these initial ICOs showcased the potential of this new fundraising mechanism, demonstrating that a project could be successfully launched without a plethora of intermediaries.

However, as the scale and complexity of projects grew, the need for intermediaries became more apparent. The reasons for this shift included the need for more sophisticated marketing to reach a broader audience, ensuring regulatory compliance in a rapidly evolving legal landscape, and providing more robust security measures to protect investor interests. Intermediaries such as advisors and industry experts, ICO listing and rating portals, exchanges, wallet providers, auditors/security firms, legal advisors, regulatory authorities, and the community, have since proved indispensable in the ICO landscape.

Advisors and industry experts lend their expertise and reputation to the project, providing guidance and instilling confidence in potential investors. ICO rating portals provide valuable assessments and rankings of ICO projects, aiding potential investors in decision-making. ICO listing portals, on the other hand, serve as directories for ongoing and upcoming token sales, increasing visibility and credibility for these projects among potential investors.

Exchanges play a multifaceted role, providing a platform for token trading, enabling liquidity and price discovery, and later acting as token sales platforms themselves, lending their reputation to convince investors of a project's quality and viability. Wallet providers offer secure storage solutions for tokens, an essential element in a landscape where security breaches could lead to significant losses. Auditors/security firms ensure the project's security, examining smart contracts and other technical elements to prevent potential attacks.

Legal advisors have turned out to be crucial in navigating the complex regulatory environment around ICOs, ensuring compliance with relevant laws and regulations to avoid potential legal repercussions. Regulatory authorities, in turn, attempt to enforce compliance with relevant regulations, maintaining investor protection and market integrity. Their role became increasingly important as the ICO market matured and became more regulated. Lastly, the community of developers, users, and supporters contributes valuable feedback, provides support, and engages with the project, contributing to the project's overall success and long-term sustainability. Their participation often extends beyond the ICO stage, contributing to the ongoing development and success of the project.

In this chapter, we will closely examine each participant in the ICO ecosystem. We will look into who they are, what they do, and the roles they play in token sales. In addition, we will look at the challenges they face and the solutions they employ to overcome them, providing a comprehensive view of the inner workings of the ICO ecosystem. By doing so, we aim to give you a better understanding of how these different pieces fit together to make an ICO successful. This is a crucial part of understanding the ICO process as a whole, and how innovative ideas in the world of cryptocurrencies are brought to life.

STARTUPS

In this section we focus on the key role of founders in ICOs. These individuals and their background, experience, and expertise often serve as the driving force behind a startup's success or failure. Initially, the ICO landscape was dominated by blockchain enthusiasts, but over time, entrepreneurs from various sectors recognized the potential of blockchain technology and entered the fray.

The geographic location of a startup, along with its proximity to technological resources and favourable regulation, can undeniably play a significant role in its success. However, the advent of the internet has made the world a smaller place, reducing the importance of physical location and enabling teams spread across the globe to collaborate effectively.

In the beginning, ICOs were exclusively a realm of blockchain infrastructure projects. However, as the ICO wave grew, this trend saw a shift. At the height of ICO activity, startups from a myriad of industries were using ICOs as a fundraising mechanism. Interestingly, even businesses with tenuous links to blockchain technology began to launch token sales, lured by the surge of investor enthusiasm reminiscent of the internet boom in the 1990s. This block-chain hype fuelled financing for a wide range of ventures, including plenty of fraudulent ones, so long as they could claim some association with blockchain technology.

Schueckes and Gutmann (2021) delved into the various economic and behavioural aspects that guided entrepreneurs towards funding their startups through ICOs. Through comprehensive interviews with executives and found-ers of startups that have benefited from ICO funding, this study revealed four key factors that influence the decision to initiate an ICO. These include the necessity of funding, the aim of building a community, the strategic impli-cations of tokenomics, and a range of personal and ideological motivators. A noteworthy finding from the study is the role of the entrepreneur's identity, exhibited through behavioural and ideological drivers, in deciding to opt for an ICO. This is a unique factor that may not typically be considered in other forms of fundraising.

Teams

The success of a startup and an ICO project is significantly influenced by the entrepreneur and the team of developers involved. The entrepreneur plays a critical role in the early stages, as their vision and leadership drive the startup's direction, growth, and eventual success. The entrepreneur's ability to inspire and motivate the team is also vital, as it can have a direct impact on the morale and productivity of the entire organization. A strong leader can encourage the team to work towards a common goal, which is essential for overcoming the various challenges that startups typically face. Moreover, the entrepreneur's networking skills and connections can help attract the right talent, funding, and other resources necessary for the startup to flourish.

In the case of crowdfunding, an accumulated body of research repeatedly underscores the importance of the team and founders in the success of fund-raising campaigns. For example, Mollick (2014) looked into the determinants of success and failure in crowdfunding campaigns and discovered that the background and reputation of the project creator are crucial. Campaigns led by individuals with proven track records or with clear expertise in a relevant field were more likely to succeed.

Building upon this, Ahlers et al. (2015) expanded the understanding of this phenomenon by examining how venture quality signals, such as the back-ground of the founding team, can influence investor decisions in crowdfunding platforms. They found that well-educated and experienced teams were often seen as more credible and, therefore, attracted more funding.

Furthermore, research by Kuppuswamy and Bayus (2017) points out the critical role of the founders' commitment and passion. Their findings suggested that teams demonstrating high levels of dedication and enthusiasm are often more successful in their crowdfunding efforts. Lastly, the influence of the founders' network has been validated by several studies, including the work of Agrawal et al. (2014), which found that the size and activity level of the founders' network significantly contribute to crowdfunding success.

In the case of ICO projects, the team of developers holds significant importance for the success of the project. The technical expertise, experience, and skills of the developers play a crucial role in ensuring that the underlying technology, such as blockchain, smart contracts, or decentralized applications, is designed and implemented effectively. A capable development team can deliver a robust and secure platform that meets the needs and expectations of the project's stakeholders. The founders of a successful ICO project should ideally have valuable industry connections that can help attract talent, additional funding, and other resources necessary for the project's success.

Furthermore, the credibility and reputation of the development team can significantly influence investor confidence in the ICO. A skilled team with a strong track record is more likely to attract investors and gain their trust, ultimately leading to a successful fundraising campaign. In addition, a well-coordinated development team can effectively handle project management, ensuring that milestones and deadlines are met, and the project progresses as planned.

Similar to crowdfunding literature, the body of research examining ICOs strongly emphasizes the role of human and social capital in success. For instance, studies have found that entrepreneur traits such as self-efficacy and media presence significantly influence ICO outcomes (Campino et al. 2021). Characteristics of the project team, including their location and network strength, are also considered vital (Roosenboom et al. 2020). Another aspect that is stressed is the diversity of knowledge within the team and the management team's confidence. This confidence, even when conveyed non-verbally (for example, through facial expressions), is seen as a positive signal impacting the funds raised (Huang et al. 2021).

Digital social capital, which includes factors such as positive language tweets, active community building, appointment of well-networked advisors, and overall social network activity, is found to be crucial in influencing the success of ICOs and their post-valuation (Giudici et al. 2020, Perez et al. 2020). Finally, CEO loyalty is highlighted as an important aspect. As a representation of entrepreneurial quality, loyalty has been found to reduce the cost of interactions between entrepreneurs and investors, improving the ICO's success (Momtaz 2021).

In summary, academic studies robustly support the idea that human and social capital, demonstrated through various traits and actions, play a pivotal role in the success of ICOs, influencing both the amount of funds raised and the post-ICO valuation of the project. This fact was tacitly acknowledged by fraudsters, who quickly realized the importance of presenting a credible team for their projects and, consequently, frequently posted fake identities of the founders to add credibility to their scam ICOs. Figure 5.1 illustrates that fake identity was found to be present in exactly one-quarter of all potentially fraudulent ICOs that tried to collect funds from investors between 2019 and 2021, through advertising their fundraising campaigns on Bitcointalk.org.

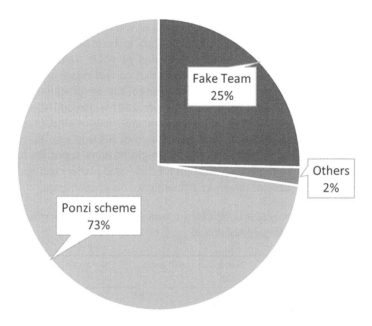

Note: Fake Team stands for fake identity of the founders or replicated data from the original genuine ICO project.
Source: Bitcointalk Scam Accusation thread by tvplus006 that identifies potential scam ICOs between 2019 and 2021, and the reasons for the accusation.[1]

Figure 5.1   Scam ICOs red flags

Nevertheless, a substantial number of ICO campaigns were launched and successfully concluded by the developer teams that stayed anonymous, even though it was most often regarded as a clear red flag of a potential fraud (see Figure 4.1, Chapter 4, for more details). The teams of various projects such as NXT, NEM, and also projects from the gambling industry, run their fundraising campaigns without disclosing their identities. Anonymity helped teams avoid legal and regulatory scrutiny, particularly if the ICO involves untested or controversial technology or concepts. It also made it more difficult for hackers and other cybercriminals to target team members individually, reducing the risk of personal information theft or extortion. Moreover, anonymity in some way shifted the focus of the ICO from individual team members to the project itself, which was supposed to be beneficial if the team believed that the project's merits should have spoken for themselves.

Geography of ICOs

Were ICOs a truly international phenomena or were these confined to a particular set of countries? Indeed, there appears to be a distinct geographical distribution when it comes to the origination of ICOs. Data derived from multiple sources (see Table 5.1) indicates that certain countries seem to be particularly favoured as locations for launching ICOs. Specifically, the United States, Russia, the United Kingdom, Singapore, and Switzerland have emerged as leading hubs, collectively hosting approximately half of all ICOs launched up to 2020. This disproportionate concentration of ICOs in specific countries prompts us to question why these regions might be more appealing to blockchain startups when choosing a location for their headquarters and operations. It seems there are several factors contributing to this phenomenon.

Table 5.1   *Geography of ICOs by country of incorporation (founder's country of residence)*

Boreiko (2019)		Huang, Meoli, and Vismara (2020)		Momtaz (2021)	
USA	23%	USA	20%	Singapore	14%
Russia	11%	Russia	12%	USA	10%
UK	8%	UK	9%	UK	9%
Unknown	7%	Singapore	8%	Estonia	6%
Singapore	6%	Switzerland	5%	Switzerland	6%
Canada	4%	Canada	3%	Russia	4%
Switzerland	4%	Estonia	3%	Hong Kong	4%
China	4%	Hong Kong	2%	Cayman Islands	3%
Israel	2%	Slovenia	2%	British Virgin Islands	2%
Slovenia	2%	Australia	2%	Gibraltar	2%

Notes: The data shows the top ten countries of ICO origin and is sourced from Boreiko (2019): time period 2013–2017, Q3; Huang et al. (2020): time period 2017–2018, Q1; Momtaz (2021): time period 2014–2020.

The regulatory environment of a country is a pivotal consideration for blockchain startups planning to launch an ICO. For instance, countries such as Singapore and Switzerland have crafted clear and comprehensive regulatory frameworks for ICOs. These guidelines offer a degree of certainty and safety, which can be particularly enticing to startups. Given the legal intricacies surrounding token sales, this can significantly mitigate the risk of regulatory hurdles. Additionally, these countries are known for having strong technological infrastructures and rich ecosystems of technological talent, making them attractive locations for tech startups more generally. These locations often also have a reputation for being innovative and forward-thinking, values which align well with the ethos of many blockchain startups.

However, not all countries have such welcoming regulatory landscapes for ICOs. A notable example is the United States, where, since 2018, the regulatory environment for ICOs has been viewed as less friendly. This reality is evident in the data presented by Momtaz (2021) in Table 5.1, which covers a later period and reveals a noticeable decrease in ICOs originating from the United States. The implications of the regulatory climate on the geographical distribution of ICOs clearly demonstrate how crucial these considerations are for startups in their decision-making processes.

Lastly, financial factors may also play a role. Countries like the United States and the United Kingdom have large, well-developed financial sectors. This not only makes it easier for startups to access capital, but it can also increase the visibility and perceived legitimacy of an ICO. This, combined with a broader and deeper pool of potential investors, can make these countries particularly attractive locations for launching an ICO.

In a comprehensive study examining 915 ICOs spanning 187 countries between January 2017 and March 2018, a set of compelling insights emerged (Huang et al. 2020). It was observed that ICOs are more prevalent in nations with well-structured financial systems and equity markets, significant investments in Information and Communication Technology (ICT) infrastructure and human capital skills, and comprehensive regulations regarding ICOs. Interestingly, the presence of ICOs in a country showed a positive correlation with the advancement of its crowdfunding markets. This finding emphasizes the increasing preference of innovative ventures for digital fundraising technologies, which also cater well to the investment needs of small investors. The study suggests that the more direct and disintermediated the fundraising mechanism is, the more prevalent ICOs are likely to be in a given country.

In contrast to the relationship between ICOs and crowdfunding, there were no observed associations between ICOs and traditional alternative finance methods, such as debt financing, venture capital (VC), and private equity funds. This suggests a divergence in the factors influencing the prevalence of ICOs and more conventional financing routes. Lastly, preliminary findings from the study indicate that tax considerations do not play a significant role in the decision-making process of where to launch an ICO. This may reflect the global nature of ICOs and the relative ease of operating across borders in the digital domain.

Industry Classification

When ICOs first emerged as a means of raising capital, they were utilized by startups primarily in the blockchain and cryptocurrency sector. This is perhaps unsurprising given the inherent synergies between these industry sectors and the ICO fundraising mechanism, which itself is based on blockchain technology. Early projects in 2013–2014 were the pioneers, setting the stage for other cryptocurrency projects to follow suit. The success of these initial ventures illustrated the potential of ICOs to facilitate capital raising for projects that were otherwise underserved by traditional financing mechanisms, particularly in the context of the blockchain industry where ideas were often unconventional, and the technology was not fully understood or appreciated by mainstream investors and financial institutions.

As ICOs gained popularity and acceptance, their appeal began to expand beyond the blockchain and cryptocurrency sector. By 2017–2018, startups from a wide array of industries had started exploring and adopting ICOs as a method of fundraising. Industries such as software development, finance, real estate, entertainment, and even healthcare, saw a surge in ICO activity. Several factors made these sectors particularly amenable to the ICO model. For one, many of these sectors are characterized by rapid innovation and a high degree of technological involvement, much like the blockchain sector itself. Startups in these sectors often require significant upfront capital to fund their innovative projects, and the traditional funding sources may not be willing to take the perceived risk.

Furthermore, the tokenization potential offered by ICOs has a unique appeal in certain sectors. For instance, in the entertainment industry, tokens could potentially be used to give investors a stake in a film's profits or enable access to exclusive content. In the software industry, tokens could be used to access certain services or features within a platform. Distributed ledger technology, with its inherent attributes of anonymity and immutability, has demonstrated considerable potential for various business sectors. Sectors such as trade, healthcare, and sustainable agriculture, which heavily rely on transparent, secure, and efficient data management and transaction systems, are particularly well-poised to benefit.

In the trade sector, the blockchain technology underlying distributed ledgers can streamline complex supply chains, enhance traceability, and improve overall efficiency by eliminating intermediaries. In healthcare, it can enable secure sharing of patient data among different providers while maintaining patient privacy, potentially leading to better coordination of care and improved health outcomes. Sustainable agriculture, too, can leverage this technology to verify the origin of produce and ensure adherence to sustainable farming practices, thereby building consumer trust.

Furthermore, the immutability of distributed ledger technology, which prevents any post-transaction manipulation, serves as a guarantee of data integrity. This is invaluable in fields where tampering with information can have severe consequences, such as in legal contracts, financial services, or quality assurance systems. The anonymity that distributed ledger technology provides can also enhance privacy in data-sensitive sectors. In a world where data breaches are increasingly common, this feature is particularly attractive to both businesses and their customers.

Analysing the statistics on the primary sectors that had startups conducting ICOs reveals some interesting trends. As per a report by Ernst & Young (2018), blockchain infrastructure; finance; social networks, content and ads; data storage; and gaming and VR were the top five business sectors for ICO activity in 2017. However, it is important to note that this report was based on a limited sample of only 87 ICOs, and so might not fully represent the overall market trend.

Contrastingly, the data from Icomarks, which includes a much larger sample of 1898 ICOs from 2015–2022, presents a slightly different picture. The top industry sectors by total ICO activity in this sample were cryptocurrencies, banking, business services, blockchain platforms, and AI. Figures 5.2 and 5.3 provide the relevant statistics by number of ICOs and total funds raised, respectively.

Cryptocurrencies were the leading sector in terms of ICO activity, reflecting the growing interest, and investment, in this domain. This trend suggests an increasing recognition of cryptocurrencies as a legitimate and lucrative investment vehicle. The prominence of banking and business services in ICO activity underscores the potential of blockchain technology to transform these traditional sectors. With its promise of enhancing efficiency, reducing costs, and providing transparency, blockchain technology has immense potential for these industries. Blockchain platforms, the backbone of all these applications, also showed significant ICO activity, unsurprisingly. These platforms provide the necessary infrastructure for developing blockchain applications, indicating a growing demand for such services. Lastly, the AI sector also featured significantly in ICO activity. This perhaps reflects the synergistic potential of combining blockchain and AI technologies, two of the most transformative technologies of our time.

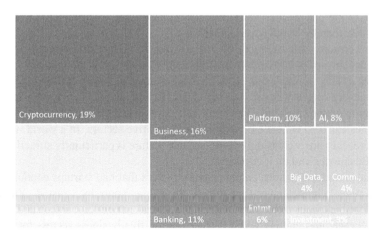

Notes: Entmt. stands for entertainment segment; *Comm.* stands for communication segment.
Sources: ICOmarks.com, ICO portal, and author's calculations.

Figure 5.2   Top business segments with highest ICO activity by number of fundraising campaigns between 2015 and 2022

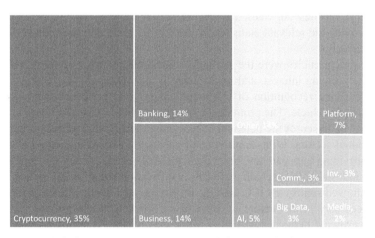

Notes: Inv. stands for investment segment; *Comm.* stands for communication segment.
Sources: ICOmarks.com, ICO portal, and author's calculations.

Figure 5.3   Top business segments with highest ICO activity by total funds raised between 2015 and 2022

ICO INVESTORS

The investor base in ICOs has witnessed a dynamic evolution since their inception. It began primarily with cryptocurrency enthusiasts who were quick to grasp the potential of this novel fundraising method. As ICOs gained popularity, they began to attract a broader range of investors, from ordinary retail investors drawn by the hype to professional serial investors scouting for early-stage investment opportunities.

This shift was further amplified by the emergence of crypto funds and venture capitalists specializing in cryptocurrency investments, who brought an increased level of sophistication and selectivity to the process. These entities brought traditional investment analysis techniques to the crypto world, critically evaluating projects based on their business models, teams, and market potential. Their involvement also helped to lend legitimacy to the ICO market, drawing in even more investors.

One distinctive feature of ICOs was their ability to attract a truly global investor base. Unlike traditional crowdfunding, which is often limited by regional restrictions, and considered by many to be mostly a national phenomenon, ICOs could be participated in from anywhere in the world, thanks to the borderless nature of cryptocurrencies. This international appeal not only broadened the potential investor base but also contributed to the dynamism and volatility of the ICO market.

Types of Investors

In the early days of ICOs, the investment landscape was significantly different from what we see today. The pioneering phase of this fundraising mechanism was dominated by retail investors – individuals who invest personal capital rather than investing on behalf of institutions. The primary audience for ICOs at this stage were blockchain enthusiasts. ICOs were a novel concept around 2013–2015, and awareness of them was limited primarily to those who were active within the blockchain and cryptocurrency communities. Even the Ethereum ICO in 2014 was run as a purely democratic campaign, where anybody could contribute Bitcoins in return for Ether. There is no information that this campaign had some pre-sale or private sale to a large investor, nor was there an announcement of a large commitment from some professional investor. The motivation of these early investors often extended beyond the mere expectation of financial returns; they were supporters and believers in the transformative potential of blockchain technology.

As ICOs started to mature and the sums of capital being raised grew, the investor base began to evolve. ICOs started to gain attention beyond the core blockchain community, attracting a more diverse group of retail investors. With their potential for high returns, ICOs began to catch the eye of institutional investors as well. This new wave of investors included VC firms, hedge funds, and family offices, all of whom brought substantial resources and experience to the table. They were able to conduct more thorough due diligence, mitigating some of the risk associated with investing in an emerging, unregulated space.

The advent of these professional investors marked a shift in the ICO landscape. As ICOs began to be more regulated and scrutinized, institutional investors found themselves better equipped to navigate this changing landscape. Their entry into the space signalled a new stage in the evolution of ICOs, as their participation introduced a higher level of professionalism, scrutiny, and regulatory compliance. This shift was reflective of the overall maturation of the ICO market, transforming it from a niche fundraising mechanism into a mainstream investment strategy.

In general, crowdfunding investors tend to be less sophisticated than ICO investors, especially when comparing them to institutional investors who participate in ICOs. Crowdfunding investors usually invest smaller amounts of money, and their primary motivation is often to support projects they are passionate about or to receive perks and rewards. ICO investors, on the other hand, may be more focused on the potential financial returns, especially as the ICO market matured and attracted more experienced investors.

The role of serial investors (also known as experienced, informed, or sophisticated investors) in ICOs is an intriguing area for exploration. In the context of ICOs, these investors have been involved in previous token sales and can use their accumulated knowledge to make informed decisions. This is in stark contrast to uninformed or novice investors, who may lack such knowledge and experience. The theoretical models of sequential decision-making, or of sequential information acquisition, suggest that informed investors are often the first movers. They are equipped to act earlier because of their ability to identify valuable information or detect subtleties that uninformed investors might miss.

In ICOs, this could translate into serial investors being more adept at identifying successful token sales amidst the multitude of offerings. They could leverage their experience to predict the success potential of an ICO, based on various factors like the team's expertise, the project's viability, and the utility of the token. As a result, they might be better positioned to invest in successful ICOs and avoid less-promising ones or pure frauds.

On the other hand, uninformed investors, without prior experience or comprehensive understanding, might find it challenging to navigate through the complex and unregulated ICO landscape. They may struggle to identify promising token sales, making them more susceptible to scams and unsuccessful investments. The extreme information uncertainty and lack of regulations surrounding ICOs exacerbate this issue.

Moreover, the role of serial investors could also influence the actions of other investors. Their involvement and backing could serve as a signal to other potential investors about the viability of a particular ICO. This could lead to a cascade effect, with later investors following the initial informed investment decisions, thus impacting the overall fundraising success of the ICO.

Who Invests in ICOs and Why?

The anonymity of blockchain transactions complicates the analysis of the investor base. Even though it is possible to identify some pattern in investor behaviour by analysing blockchain transactions (like was done in Boreiko and Risteski 2021), it is impossible to identify the origin and exact type of each investor who contributed to ICO campaigns. Here, ICO teams might come to help. Frequently, many ICOs have published the results of the token sales, and in case they were conducting the Know Your Customer (KYC) checks, they knew exactly the origins of the investors. For example, as announced by Airswap (USA), their token sale that raised more than $12 million in October 2017 attracted more than 12 000 participants from 135 countries. Similarly, German startup Request Network has raised more than $32 million from more than 11 000 contributors from 135 countries. As claimed by Howell et al. (2019), the public sale of Filecoin (USA) raised $154 million from more than 2100 investors in over 50 countries.

Anecdotal evidence suggests that ICO investing has truly become an international phenomenon. Sending money to another party in a distant land has never been so easy. Therefore, unlike crowdfunding, token sales have attracted a genuinely international base. This widespread interest can be attributed to several factors. Firstly, cryptocurrencies, by their nature, are decentralized digital assets that transcend borders. This characteristic has made it possible for people from any country to invest in ICOs with ease, bypassing the restrictions that typically accompany traditional investments. Next, ICO investments often require minimal capital and documentation, enabling individuals from diverse economic backgrounds to participate. This ease of access has encouraged participation from investors across the globe.

Additionally, the lure of high returns on investment and the easy exit possibilities have attracted considerable attention from potential contributors. Stories of successful ICOs that have yielded significant returns have drawn investors from various countries, all hoping to capitalize on the next big opportunity. Finally, the increasing penetration of the internet worldwide has allowed more people to learn about ICOs, cryptocurrencies, and blockchain technology, thereby creating a global community of investors keen to invest in new projects.

While the international nature of ICO investors brings advantages, such as increased diversity and a broader range of ideas and opinions, it also carries potential downsides. For instance, regulatory frameworks can vary significantly between countries, leading to confusion and difficulties for both investors and projects. Moreover, the ease of investing in ICOs has attracted scammers who have taken advantage of inexperienced or uninformed investors, leading to calls for increased regulation and oversight in the sector.

Some studies have attempted to infer basic information on investors' behaviour at large, without the possibility to identify them. The study by Fahlenbrach and Frattaroli (2021) aimed to analyse the composition and trading behaviour of ICO investors. They examined whether investors primarily purchase utility tokens out of interest in the product or for speculative purposes. The research utilized primary sources including ICO White papers, social media pages, and Ethereum blockchain data, to construct a hand-collected sample of successful ICOs.

The study found that the median investor in their sample invests only $1200 in an ICO and each ICO has approximately 4700 investors, suggesting that ICOs have managed to attract a new type of investor to finance innovation. However, the typical investor often sells a significant fraction of tokens shortly after the ICO, indicating an interest in financial gain rather than the underlying product. Additionally, the investors in their sample did not hold a diversified portfolio of ICOs in the same wallet.

Boreiko and Risteski (2021) also provide comprehensive evidence about investor behaviours in ICOs, focusing on their investment patterns and their influence on the success of campaigns. The data was gathered from 472 public token sales during the period 2013–2017. The study identifies that some contributors, referred to as *serial investors*, often invest in more than one campaign and usually contribute earlier. However, these serial investors do not necessarily demonstrate better judgement in identifying high-quality ICOs. In contrast, it is only the larger serial investors who are more likely to invest in campaigns that successfully raise more funds, attract more contributors, achieve their hard caps, and distribute tokens that eventually get listed on crypto exchanges. These findings highlight the potential need for regulatory or self-regulation measures within the industry to protect smaller retail ICO investors who tend to display naïve reinforcement learning behaviour.

The paper by Fisch et al. (2021) is probably the only study so far that has attempted to directly survey the ICO investors. The goal of this study was to explore and profile ICO investors based on their motives. Three key research questions were addressed: the motives of ICO investors, their relative importance, and profiling ICO investors based on these motives. To answer these questions, a survey of 517 ICO investors was conducted, and an exploratory factor analysis was carried out to identify the underlying investment motives. Using the self-determination theory as a foundation, it was found that ICO investors are driven by ideological, technological, and financial motives. Technological motives were found to be more important to ICO investors than financial or ideological motives.

Through regression analysis, the study was able to profile investors according to their motives, which revealed significant differences among them. A risk-prone attitude was found to have a positive correlation with technological motives. Conversely, a professional background in technology had a negative correlation with financial motives. Investors who made earlier ICO investments were found to have stronger ideological motives. Interestingly, a careful reading of a White paper was found to be positively correlated with both ideological and technological motives, but not with financial ones.

Institutional Investors and Crypto funds

Institutional investors, including VC firms, hedge funds, family offices, and asset management firms, have increasingly been attracted to ICOs. While the earliest ICOs were predominantly financed by retail investors and, to some extent, business angels, the landscape began to shift around 2016–2017. This shift coincided with a surge in media attention towards ICOs and the maturation of the market.

Institutional investors brought substantial capital infusion to ICOs, often helping projects meet funding goals and expedite development. Unlike retail investors, they possessed more extensive resources and experience for assessing investment opportunities, leading to a more rigorous vetting process and more robust projects. The participation of these reputable investors also added credibility to ICOs. It signalled confidence in the project, attracting other investors and generating positive market sentiment. These investors often advocated for better governance, transparency, and financial management in the projects they invested in, which led to the overall improvement of the ICO market.

As the ICO market matured, so did the regulations around it. Jurisdictions like the United States distinguished between accredited investors (typically high-net-worth individuals or institutions meeting specific financial criteria) and retail investors. This regulatory distinction paved the way for accredited investors to participate in more complex, higher-risk offerings like ICOs.

When comparing institutional investors to retail investors, several differences are apparent. Institutional investors typically invest larger sums, conduct thorough due diligence, and can exert more influence on the projects they invest in. They often participate in ICOs during the pre-sale or private sale stages, before the public token sale, drawn in by early-stage investment incentives. Finally, the involvement of prominent institutional investors in an ICO can serve a certification role. This participation signals to the market that the project is legitimate and has potential, thereby attracting additional investors and generating positive momentum for the ICO. This evolution and the rising institutional interest in ICOs underscore the increasing maturation and acceptance of the ICO financing mechanism in the broader investment ecosystem.

The first recorded participation of VC in an ICO happened in the GetGems ICO of January 2015 that pre-sold approximately 15 per cent of its tokens in an invite-only round and attracted funding from one of Israel's leading VC firms, Magma Venture Partners (magmavc.com 1999), for whom it was the first crypto investment ever. Prior to this ICO, some business angels and VCs did invest in blockchain projects (for example, Li Xiaolai, a Chinese billionaire and Bitcoin investor, who supported the Bitshares AGS project in 2014), however, this was done through direct cash investment and acquisition of the projects' stakes, not through tokens in an ICO.[2]

As the ICO industry evolved and matured, venture capitalists indeed started seeing opportunities rather than threats. The traditionally high-risk appetite of VCs aligned well with the ICO landscape. While the legal ambiguity surrounding tokens and the heightened risk of fraud presented significant challenges, VCs leveraged their competitive advantage – their experience and expertise in identifying and nurturing high-potential startups. This expertise extended to the realm of ICOs, enabling them to separate promising token sales from potential frauds or doomed projects.

Furthermore, VCs recognized an unusual feature in ICO investments compared to traditional VC funding – a readily available exit option. In a standard VC investment, the exit options, such as an IPO or acquisition, often take years to materialize and can be uncertain. On the contrary, ICOs offer a more immediate and liquid exit route as tokens can be traded on various cryptocurrency exchanges once the token sale is completed.

A key indicator of this trend was the emergence of specialized crypto venture funds solely focusing on investing in token sales. These funds carved out a unique niche for themselves, leveraging their expert understanding of blockchain technology, crypto assets, and tokenomics. Some of the early and notable crypto-focused funds include Andreessen Horowitz's 'a16z crypto', Pantera Capital, and Polychain Capital. Each of these funds has distinguished themselves through successful investments in the ICO and broader crypto space.

In fact, currently, there are plenty of crypto funds involved in ICO investment. For example, the Cryptofundresearch database lists more than 800 such funds and the Cryptofundresearch portal provides information about 430+ funds. By actively participating in the ICO space, these VC firms and funds have validated the potential of ICOs as a mechanism for financing innovation. They have paved the way for more institutional investors to enter the sector, contributing to its ongoing evolution and maturity.

Several academic papers have looked into the behaviour of VCs and professional investors in ICOs. For example, Hackober and Bock (2021) employed the resource-based view and signalling theory to highlight the crucial role of professional investors, particularly reputable and specialized ones like Corporate Venture Capitals (CVCs), in providing essential complementary assets and resources to blockchain ventures in the later stage of ICO activity. Notably, the specialized technical and market knowledge that these investors bring to the table emerges as a crucial success factor. Additionally, a longer investment period positively correlates with the success of these firms, reinforcing the importance of sustained resource provision.

In terms of signalling theory, the involvement of VCs in an ICO is interpreted as a positive signal of the venture's quality, thereby attracting further investors. This signal also proves beneficial in drawing in other stakeholders such as skilled employees and potential customers. This certification via VC investment becomes particularly significant in the ICO context, which often lacks the conventional signals found in other funding scenarios, like audited accounts.

Another study by Fisch and Momtaz (2020) also investigated the influence of institutional investors on the performance of ICOs. Analysing a sample of 550+ ICO projects, the researchers aimed to understand how these professional investors affect the post-ICO performance of the issued tokens. The researchers suggested that the expertise of institutional investors in identifying promising ventures (selection effect) and their ability to guide the development of these ventures (treatment effect) could help mitigate the inherent information asymmetries in the ICO environment. The results indicated that ICOs backed by institutional investors generally performed better post-ICO. Therefore, the study underscores the significant role institutional investors play in the ICO space.

Dombrowski et al.'s recent study (2023) examines the strategic behaviour of crypto venture funds that exploit available exit strategies, investing in ventures only to quickly sell tokens at peak valuations. The research found that ICO ventures backed by institutional investors often demonstrate weaker operating performance and are more prone to early failure than those funded solely through crowdsourcing. However, if these institutionally backed ventures survive, they financially outperform their counterparts. This divergence between operational and financial performance is consistent with the notion of certification arbitrage. This concept suggests that institutional investors use their reputation to inflate valuations, subsequently making a swift exit post-ICO.

ICO INTERMEDIARIES

While the initial concept of cryptocurrencies and ICOs aimed to eliminate intermediaries, the reality is that several types of intermediaries have emerged in the space over time. This development is primarily due to the necessity for structure, security, and regulatory compliance in a burgeoning and complex market. It became clear that without various types of intermediaries, the ICO mechanism, which functioned fairly well during its early stages, became increasingly problematic with the rise in volume and number of participants.

Issues of asymmetrical information and moral hazard reached unparalleled proportions in ICO financing. The market was inundated with fraudulent campaigns, perpetrated by scammers who saw an easy opportunity to make a quick buck off inexperienced investors hungry for double-digit returns. Moreover, many founders, having received funding in the form of rapidly appreciating cryptocurrencies during the bull crypto market of 2017, felt no obligation to use the collected resources for their intended purposes, leading to minimal progress on their project development.

This situation highlighted the crucial need for intermediaries to establish a sense of order, fairness, and trust in the cryptocurrency market. As the ICO market expanded and matured, attracting increased scrutiny from regulators, the need for compliance with various regulatory frameworks grew in importance. Intermediaries such as ICO portals, legal advisors, and compliance service providers emerged to help projects navigate these complex regulatory landscapes. Moreover, with a growing number of ICOs competing for investors' attention, projects needed to differentiate themselves and effectively communicate their value proposition. This led to the rise of marketing agencies, public relations firms, and social media influencers specializing in promoting ICOs.

As scams and failed projects tarnished the reputation of the ICO market, intermediaries emerged to help protect investors by conducting due diligence and vetting projects. These intermediaries include platforms that rate and review ICOs, as well as advisors who offer guidance on the quality of the projects. At the same time, platforms like ICO portals and crypto exchanges have become crucial intermediaries, streamlining the process of participating in token sales, managing funds, and distributing tokens to investors. These platforms also offer additional services such as KYC and Anti-Money Laundering (AML) checks, further legitimizing the process, and signalling the best token sales to investors.

Advisers and Industry Experts

Advisers and industry experts hold significant influence over the fate of an ICO due to their provision of crucial services, invaluable insights, and expansive connections. Their involvement in an ICO often serves to enhance its credibility, boost its visibility, and instil a greater sense of trustworthiness in potential investors. Not surprisingly, ICO teams attempt to attract top professional advice and promptly display their support in all the media advertising token sales.

One notable area where advisers offer their expertise is in the technical evaluation of a project. They meticulously assess the feasibility of an ICO's technical aspects, pre-empt potential challenges, and recommend enhancements when necessary. Regulatory guidance is another essential area that advisers address. Given the complexity of laws governing ICOs and cryptocurrencies, their insights on legal and regulatory compliance greatly assist in navigating this intricate terrain.

Furthermore, advisers often provide a significant contribution to an ICO's marketing strategies. They possess the ability to connect ICOs with influential figures in the industry and potential investors, which can immensely boost the project's visibility. In the realm of business development, advisers provide guidance to refine the business model, identify target markets, and establish strategic partnerships. They also aid in the identification and mitigation of potential risks that could affect an ICO's success.

There are numerous renowned advisers in the world of ICOs. Among them are Ian Scarfe, a serial entrepreneur, investor, and consultant with business experience from around the world who has consulted for around 126 ICO projects. Another noteworthy figure is Tim Draper, a legendary venture capitalist who has backed, and invested in, an array of blockchain projects such as Bancor, Tezos, and Factom. The likes of Simon Cocking, a co-founder of Irish Tech News and CryptoCoinNews, and Nikolay Shkilev, a serial entrepreneur and blockchain expert, have also advised numerous blockchain startups. Jason Hung and Michael Terpin have demonstrated a strong track record in advising successful ICOs, making them notable figures in the industry as well.

However, it is essential to recognize that the involvement of experienced advisers and industry experts doesn't guarantee the success of an ICO. Other factors such as market conditions, investor sentiment, and the overall quality of the project significantly influence its outcome. For instance, Unikrn, an eSports betting platform advised by renowned entrepreneur and investor Mark Cuban, managed to raise only $31 million out of its targeted $100 million and was later fined by the Securities and Exchange Commission (SEC) in 2020 for an unregistered sale of securities. Similarly, Kik's Kin ICO, despite being backed by Fred Wilson, a renowned venture capitalist known for his early investments in X (formerly known as Twitter), Etsy, and Kickstarter, fell short of its hard cap, raising $98 million out of a targeted $125 million and was later prosecuted by the SEC on similar grounds.[3] These instances underscore that the success of an ICO is contingent on a combination of factors, not just the calibre of advisers and experts involved.

Legal Advisors and Compliance Service Providers

In the early days of ICOs, a somewhat casual approach towards legal and regulatory considerations was evident. Simple disclaimers were often considered adequate, with little attention given to detailed term sheets or legal documentation. The focus tended to be more on the technological and business aspects of the projects rather than legal compliance. However, as ICOs gained prominence and began attracting significant capital, they also drew increased scrutiny from regulators worldwide. The once laissez-faire approach became untenable, and the role of legal advisors and compliance service providers became indispensable. They helped these projects navigate the complex and ever-evolving regulatory landscape, advising on legal aspects that the projects initially overlooked.

Figure 5.4 presents the frequency of legal documents produced for token sales from 2013 to 2017. In the earlier years, 50–60 per cent of all ICOs were conducted without any legal documents, indicating a lack of assistance from legal advisors. By 2017, however, this percentage dropped to below 30 per cent, primarily for smaller-scale ICOs. Terms of Sale and Purchase Agreements became integral components of many ICOs' documentation, alongside the White paper. The frequency of these documents increased steadily throughout the years.

One key development was the introduction of Simple Agreement for Future Tokens (SAFT) and security tokens. These were innovative legal structures designed to meet the requirements of securities regulations while still allowing for the innovation and flexibility inherent in blockchain-based fundraising. Legal advisors, such as Cooley LLP (cooley.com), a law firm known for its technology and financial expertise, played a significant role in developing these concepts. Perkins Coie (perkinscoie.com), another prominent law firm in the crypto space, was often sought after for its expertise in blockchain and crypto-related regulations. Many additional legal firms, such as Selachii, Gordon Law, and Davis Polk, have also advised ICO startups around the globe. This has resulted in the emergence of a quite profitable industry segment.

Despite professional legal advice, many high-profile projects were still prosecuted for various regulatory violations. These incidents underscored the challenge that legal advisors faced in navigating uncharted legal territory. The complexity of the regulatory environment, the novelty of the ICO mechanism,

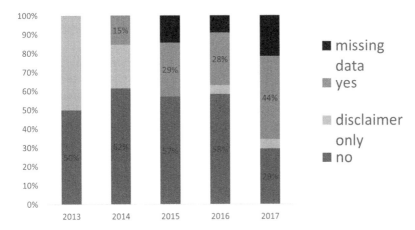

Source: Author's calculations.

Figure 5.4   Frequency of legal documents in ICOs across years

and the pace at which these projects evolved meant that even the best legal advisors could not guarantee complete insulation from regulatory actions. Thus, while their role was crucial in aiding ICOs to comply with regulations, their effectiveness was also reflective of the broader uncertainty surrounding the legal status and treatment of ICOs during the period.

ICO Promoters

Promoters, community managers, social media influencers, and even celebrities have also played notable roles in the ICO ecosystem. Their primary function was to create awareness, build hype, and attract potential investors for ICO projects. Community managers, usually well-versed in blockchain technology and cryptocurrencies, managed online communities on platforms like Reddit, Telegram, and Bitcointalk. Their role was crucial in fostering community engagement, answering questions, and promoting the ICO's vision and potential.

Social media influencers and celebrities acted as endorsers for ICO projects, leveraging their follower base to generate buzz. High-profile endorsements came from celebrities such as, for example, boxer Floyd Mayweather and musician DJ Khaled, both of whom promoted the Centra Tech ICO. However, the practice of endorsing ICOs came under scrutiny when it was revealed that many influencers, promoters, and rating platforms were compensated for their promotions without adequately disclosing these arrangements to the public.

This lack of transparency raised ethical and legal questions, leading to the SEC acting. The SEC notably prosecuted both Mayweather and DJ Khaled for their failure to disclose payments received for promoting the Centra Tech ICO, which was later found to be fraudulent.[4]

Some ICO influencers and advisers, such as Ian Balina, also came under scrutiny from the SEC. Known for his investment strategies and reviews, Balina frequently used his social media platforms to promote various ICOs to his large follower base. The SEC alleged that Balina failed to disclose the compensation he received from ICO projects for promotional services, which constitutes a violation of the anti-touting provisions of the federal securities laws.[5] This lack of disclosure meant that Balina's followers and potential investors were not aware of the financial incentives influencing his promotions, which created a misleading representation of the projects he endorsed.

As a result, Balina faced charges from the SEC. His case underscored the broader issue of the role of influencers in the ICO ecosystem and highlighted the importance of transparency in promotional activities, particularly when influencers and advisors have a substantial impact on investor decisions.

ICO Portals, Aggregators, and Rating Services Providers

During the ICO boom of 2017–2018, ICO portals and aggregators emerged as significant players in the ecosystem. These platforms provided a centralized location for investors to discover, compare, and scrutinize various ICOs. Portals such as ICOBench, ICODrops, ICOAlert, CoinSchedule, and ICO Rating facilitated discoverability of projects, providing much-needed visibility to them. These platforms offered ratings and reviews of ICOs based on a set of criteria, including team experience, technology, market potential, and legal compliance. Investors could leverage these reviews to make more informed decisions about their prospective investments. ICOs with high ratings often benefited from an added layer of credibility, attracting more potential investors.

Another key function of these aggregators was allowing investors to compare multiple ICO projects side by side. This feature made it easier to identify and analyse potential investment opportunities. Furthermore, the costs of listing an ICO on these platforms varied, with some offering free basic listings and others charging for premium listings and additional marketing services.

According to Boreiko and Vidusso (2019), there's a parallel to be drawn between the fixed-income credit rating agencies such as Fitch, Moody's, and Standard & Poor, and the online platforms that started providing listing, analysis, and rating services for ICOs. These platforms emerged as critical sources of information for potential investors, similar to how credit rating agencies assess a borrower's quality or ability to repay.

By the end of 2017, there were 51 such listing platforms. However, the extent of information provided about each ICO varied widely among these platforms. Some platforms offered only rudimentary lists of current and upcoming ICOs with minimal information, while others provided comprehensive reports on specific ICOs. Certain platforms went a step further and rated ICOs, helping investors gauge the relative quality of the ICOs listed.

Despite the intentions of these platforms to reduce information asymmetry about ICO projects, several challenges tainted their effectiveness. The quality of data provided was often subpar, and there was a general neglect of past ICOs in favour of the more trendy and hyped ones. Furthermore, the rules for assigning ratings were often unclear, creating potential bias and misinformation. In addition, due to the business model where the ICO issuers paid to get listed (also known as the issuer-pays model), fraudulent ICOs frequently found their way onto these lists. As a result, there was a prevailing sentiment among investors that these lists and ratings didn't necessarily mitigate the information asymmetry surrounding ICO projects.

Boreiko and Vidusso (2019) conducted an analysis of token sales from 2013 to September 2017 and how these sales were rated or included on major aggregator websites. Their research found a correlation between an ICO's inclusion on multiple aggregators and its subsequent success in raising funds. ICOs listed on several aggregators were more likely to reach their minimum funding goal (min cap) or maximum requested amount (hard cap), irrespective of other factors. However, given the predominant issuer-pays model among ICO aggregators, the authors noted that this success could be attributed to larger marketing budgets and increased publicity rather than the quality or potential of the ICO.

Upon examining ratings from four listing websites, significant discrepancies were discovered across sources, and the overall quality of the ratings was found to be mediocre. While these ratings had some capacity to account for the total funds raised, they didn't provide reliable predictions on whether an ICO would reach its minimum or maximum funding goals. Given the frequent modifications in rating methodologies and the common practice of assigning or adjusting ratings post-ICO campaigns, the authors underscored the shortcomings of these portals in delivering quality service to both investors and ICO teams.

Moreover, while these platforms were beneficial, they also did not escape regulatory scrutiny. Notably, the SEC prosecuted CoinSchedule for failing to disclose compensation it received from ICOs for promotional services.[6] This brought to light a pervasive issue within the ICO ecosystem – the promotion of ICOs, often without due diligence or proper scrutiny, motivated by financial gains. This prosecution underscored the importance of transparency and the need for these platforms to comply with regulatory requirements, highlighting the complexities of navigating the ICO landscape.

ICO platforms, Token Sale Facilitators, and Launchpads

As the ICO industry matured, heightened competition for investor funds led to an increase in both complexity and cost associated with the ICO process. For a successful fundraise, startups found themselves enlisting a broad network of advisors. In response to this growing challenge, intermediaries such as platforms, token sale facilitators, and launchpads stepped into the spotlight, particularly between 2017 and 2018. Known for streamlining the token sale process, these entities deftly managed investor registration, executed KYC and AML checks, oversaw fund collection, and handled the distribution of tokens. By providing a secure and user friendly interface, they ensured that investors enjoyed a seamless experience when participating in ICOs.

One of the first ICO platforms was the Koinify project. Koinify was a platform that hosted token sales (or ICOs) for decentralized projects. The company was launched in 2014 and provided a way for users to participate in crowdsales for projects building on blockchain technology. Their goal at that time was to enable and simplify the process of purchasing tokens in these sales, ensuring that the process was secure and straightforward for users. Koinify was also notable for its diligence in selecting projects; they aimed to list only those projects that were considered viable and had a real use case for the blockchain. However, Koinify closed its operations in late 2015.

CoinList then emerged as an essential player, particularly for high-profile ICOs. This platform provided a broad suite of services, from investor vetting to token distribution, making it a go-to solution for many blockchain projects. StartEngine, another notable platform, was particularly effective for crowd-funding, serving as a launching pad for numerous successful ICOs.

ICO launchpads emerged as another form of platform aimed at facilitating and streamlining the process of conducting token sales. These platforms offered an array of services similar to ICO platforms, but they often integrated additional features designed to improve project success and investor confidence. At their core, ICO launchpads provided a platform for projects to launch their ICOs. This included support for investor registration, KYC/AML checks, fundraising, and token distribution. However, they also offered value-added services, such as project vetting, marketing support, and sometimes even advisory services to ensure the project was well-positioned for success.

One notable aspect of ICO launchpads was their focus on due diligence and investor protection. Projects launching on these platforms were often subjected to rigorous scrutiny to verify their legitimacy and potential for success. This added layer of security helped to build investor confidence and set these platforms apart from the more traditional ICO platforms.

Examples of prominent ICO launchpads include Coin Factory, Coral, Blockstarter, ICOBox, and many more. These platforms not only helped projects raise funds, but also connected them with their respective vibrant communities, leading to better visibility and user adoption. However, the importance and prominence of these ICO platforms have been significantly diminished due to two main developments.

First, the rise of Initial Exchange Offerings (IEOs). These represented a shift in how token sales were conducted, with cryptocurrency exchanges such as Binance and Huobi taking over the role of ICO platforms. Exchanges had several advantages: they could provide immediate liquidity post-IEO, they had a ready base of KYC-approved users, and they commanded substantial marketing power, making them more competitive in this new business model. Second, the advent of decentralized exchanges (DEXs), such as Uniswap and SushiSwap, enabled blockchain projects to launch and list their tokens without the need for an intermediary, further diminishing the role of traditional ICO platforms. By allowing direct, peer-to-peer trading, DEXs have dramatically transformed the token issuance landscape.

Despite these developments, these platforms maintained their significance in the token issuance landscape. They provided projects with a valuable avenue for fundraising and initial distribution, particularly during the later years of the ICO industry's evolution.

Crypto Exchanges and Liquidity Providers

Crypto exchanges emerged as pivotal players in the ICO ecosystem, particularly as the industry developed and evolved from the initial explosion in 2017–2018. They furnished a platform for projects to list their tokens after the ICO, fostering liquidity and enabling price discovery. This platform further helped tokens to garner market visibility and credibility which, in turn, attracted a broader spectrum of investors.

Early crypto exchanges, such as Bitstamp and Kraken, founded in 2011, along with Coinbase and Bittrex, launched in 2012 and 2013 respectively, primarily provided a platform for trading cryptocurrencies. For early ICOs, it was often necessary to negotiate directly with each exchange to determine if their newly issued token would be accepted for trading. Many small crypto exchanges with dubious origins and minimal token turnover emerged in 2015–2016, lacking any reputable standing. Therefore, securing a listing on a respected exchange served as a clear signal to investors of the seriousness and quality of an ICO.

Later, exchanges began to offer token-listing services, granting ICO tokens a venue for price discovery and trading with other cryptocurrencies. This marked the initial step of exchanges widening their reach in the ICO industry. Furthermore, the emergence of IEOs allowed exchanges to manage the token sale process on behalf of projects, providing investors with a more streamlined and secure investment route. The evolution from ICOs to IEOs and the rise of DEXs demonstrated the dynamic nature of the crypto market and the crucial role crypto exchanges played in it. These platforms have navigated the shifting landscape and adapted to changing regulations and market demand, providing crucial services for projects and investors alike.

The complexity of regulatory compliance also fell under the ambit of crypto exchanges. In response to tightening ICO regulations, exchanges undertook KYC/AML checks on ICO participants. This ensured regulatory compliance and significantly curtailed the risk of fraud. Additionally, exchanges broadened their offerings by providing custody and asset management services, ensuring secure storage for ICO funds and managing assets on behalf of projects or investors.

The importance of crypto exchanges in the ICO landscape was underscored by their ability to enhance a project's trustworthiness and credibility. A token's listing on a reputable exchange sent a positive signal to the market about the project's legitimacy and potential, thereby attracting more investors. Simultaneously, exchanges, with their user-friendly platforms, made ICO participation and token trading more accessible and convenient, which broadened the investor base.

In July of 2017, the Parity Wallet Hack occurred, resulting in a significant loss for many ICO projects that stored their funds there. The incident occurred due to a vulnerability in Parity's multi-signature wallet, which resulted in a loss of approximately 150 000 Ether, equivalent to about $30 million at that time.[7] Later, in November that year, the Parity Multisig Hack occurred, when an anonymous user accidentally triggered a function that caused the wallets' funds to be irretrievably locked.[8] This event affected more than 500 wallet addresses, freezing about 514 000 Ether (worth approximately $150 million at the time).

Many ICO projects were among the victims of this incident, as they had collected and stored their funds in Parity multi-signature wallets. The funds locked by this incident remain inaccessible to this day, and recovering them would require a hard fork of the Ethereum blockchain, which is a contentious and complex process that has not been agreed upon by the Ethereum community.

The Parity wallet incidents underscored the potential vulnerabilities associated with decentralized storage options and smart contract usage. As a result, ICO teams started looking for more secure alternatives for fund storage.

Crypto exchanges emerged as a popular option, offering enhanced security features and professional asset management services.

Crypto exchanges, with their robust security infrastructure, provided a safer haven for ICO funds. They have a vested interest in maintaining the highest security standards to keep their users' funds safe, which generally include measures such as cold storage, multi-signature wallets, and two-factor authentication. Cold storage, in particular, is widely used by exchanges to securely store the majority of their assets offline, limiting their exposure to hacking attempts.

Apart from security, exchanges also offered an array of additional services to ICO teams, including custody services and asset management. Custody services entail the safekeeping and management of digital assets, providing ICO teams with the peace of mind that their funds are in safe hands.

However, it is important to note that crypto exchanges were not immune to failures and losses, some of which led to significant impacts on investors. The Mt. Gox incident in 2014, where a massive security breach led to the loss of 850 000 Bitcoins (worth around $450 million at the time), and subsequent bankruptcy, is one such infamous example from early years.[9] This event not only sent shockwaves throughout the crypto industry but also resulted in a prolonged market downturn. Similarly, in 2016, the major altcoin exchange Cryptsy collapsed following a security breach and allegations of fraud, causing users to lose millions of dollars' worth of cryptocurrencies.[10]

Recently, in November 2022, FTX, the third-largest cryptocurrency exchange by volume with over a million users worldwide, collapsed and triggered a massive shock in the crypto market, wiping out billions and plunging the market's valuation below $1 trillion.[11] FTX's CEO, Sam Bankman-Fried, resigned, and the company declared bankruptcy. Shortly after, the exchange suffered a suspected hack with hundreds of millions worth of tokens being stolen. In December that year, Bankman-Fried was arrested in The Bahamas and subsequently extradited to the United States, where he pleaded innocent to all criminal charges in January of 2023.

Just as Amazon and Meta (formerly Facebook) have dominated their respective sectors, several cryptocurrency exchanges have experienced similar trajectories, transforming into giants in the burgeoning crypto industry. Leading platforms such as Kraken, Coinbase, and Binance have not only amassed significant trading volumes, akin to Amazon's dominance in the e-commerce sphere, but have also gained millions of customers and expanded globally, like Meta's wide-reaching influence in the social media landscape. However, much like the scrutiny faced by Amazon and Meta, these crypto behemoths have also attracted the attention of regulators due to their influential roles.

First, in April 2023, the SEC charged Bittrex, a crypto asset trading platform, and its former CEO with operating an unregistered exchange, broker, and clearing agency.[12] This case marked yet another development in the growing regulatory scrutiny of the cryptocurrency sector. Bittrex, which is based in Seattle, decided to cease operations in the United States on 30 April 2023 following these charges. According to a bankruptcy petition filed in Wilmington, Delaware court, Bittrex's assets and liabilities each fell between the range of $500 million and $1 billion. This episode echoes the broader challenges faced by the crypto industry, as it navigates an increasingly complex regulatory landscape akin to those encountered by major tech corporations like Amazon and Meta.

Next, the SEC turned its attention to Binance, the world's largest cryptocurrency exchange, which controlled more than half of the average monthly crypto volume at the start of 2023. In February, New York regulators halted the issuance of a Binance-branded stablecoin, BUSD. Shortly afterward, the US Commodity Futures Trading Commission (CFTC) filed a lawsuit against Binance, claiming that a significant portion of Binance's reported trading volume and profitability stemmed from the 'extensive solicitation of and access to' US customers. The latest setback for Binance occurred in June 2023, when the SEC sued the crypto exchange and its billionaire founder, Changpeng Zhao.[13] The SEC alleged that they had drawn US customers to their unregulated international exchange and had commingled investor funds with their own, violating US securities law.

Furthermore, DEXs have not been exempted from regulatory pressure. In a statement issued in April 2023, the SEC clarified its position on such entities involved in the trade of crypto assets considered as 'securities'.[14] The Commission underscored that any organization, association, or group of persons that fits the definition of an 'exchange' must register accordingly as a 'national securities exchange' or an 'alternative trading system' (ATS).

This mandate extends to the burgeoning sector of decentralized finance (DeFi), which the SEC argues already fits the existing definition of an 'exchange' based on the nature of crypto assets being traded on these platforms. In essence, if the DeFi platforms facilitate the trade of tokens classified as securities, they fall within the regulatory purview and need to adhere to the requisite compliance procedures. This shift underscores the evolving regulatory landscape that DeFi platforms, much like their centralized counterparts, are expected to navigate.

REGULATORS AND JURISDICTION SHOPPING

The previous sections and chapters clearly illustrate the significant influence regulators exert over the ICO ecosystem. In the early stages of its development, around 2015–2016, the ICO market largely flew under the regulatory radar. However, as the market began to grow and mature, regulatory bodies like the SEC started to take notice. By mid-2017, the SEC began actively pursuing violations and prosecuting token sellers on a large scale. For more details on the regulation of ICOs, please refer to the forthcoming chapters.

Regulators in general enforce guidelines and rules designed to protect investors, maintain the integrity of markets, and uphold financial stability. As the ICO market has evolved, so too has the approach to regulation, with different jurisdictions adopting varied strategies. This varied landscape has given rise to a phenomenon known as *jurisdiction shopping*, where ICO projects select a country for their operations based on favourable regulatory climates, tax benefits, or other supportive elements.

Jurisdiction shopping is driven by factors such as regulatory clarity, favourable conditions, tax benefits, and supportive infrastructure. For instance, some countries offer explicit guidance on ICOs, simplifying the compliance process for projects. Others adopt a more lenient approach to ICO regulation, lowering potential barriers to entry. Tax incentives can also be a draw for blockchain and cryptocurrency businesses, including ICOs. Lastly, a strong blockchain ecosystem – with readily available technical expertise, industry partnerships, and resources – can sway projects to choose one jurisdiction over another.

Switzerland, Estonia, Singapore, and Malta are examples of popular jurisdictions for ICOs. Switzerland, with its renowned 'Crypto Valley' in Zug, offers a welcoming regulatory environment alongside a robust blockchain ecosystem. Estonia's innovative environment, bolstered by its e-residency program, draws many ICO projects. Singapore's clear regulatory guidelines and pro-innovation stance have made it a preferred destination for blockchain-based ventures, including ICOs. Malta, often referred to as the 'Blockchain Island', offers comprehensive regulations for blockchain and cryptocurrency, providing a well-defined framework for ICOs and other projects.

The SEC, on the contrary, has been somewhat hesitant to provide clear-cut guidelines for crypto actors, reflecting the complexities and ongoing debates around cryptocurrency regulation. Crypto exchange Coinbase even filed a lawsuit against it in April 2023, requesting the regulator to disclose its response to its one-year-old petition asking whether existing SEC regulatory frameworks would be applicable to the crypto industry. The petition urged the SEC to establish rules for the regulation of securities offered and traded through digital methods, such as cryptocurrencies.

CONCLUSION

Throughout this chapter, we have navigated the complex network of players that constitute the ICO ecosystem. Each of these participants – founders, investors, advisors, industry experts, ICO listing and rating portals, exchanges, wallet providers, auditors, legal advisors, regulatory authorities, and the community – plays an indispensable role in the ICO process.

In the ICO ecosystem's infancy, a direct, decentralized model was used, with early projects like Mastercoin, NXT, Counterparty, NEM, and MaidsafeCoin demonstrating that a successful launch could be achieved without a multitude of intermediaries. However, as projects grew in scale and complexity, the need for additional expertise and support systems became evident. These new intermediaries introduced more sophisticated marketing strategies, more robust security measures, and better navigation of a rapidly evolving regulatory landscape.

The ICO ecosystem's maturation process is an evolution, with the changing landscape requiring ongoing adaptation to balance all stakeholders' interests effectively. These evolutions have not only aided the projects and investors but also enriched the ecosystem as a whole, with each participant contributing to the success and long-term sustainability of the projects.

However, conducting research within this complex and ever-changing ecosystem presents significant challenges. Understanding how the various pieces of the ICO puzzle fit together to ensure a project's success is critical, but it requires employing novel investigative techniques to properly study this innovative space. As we transition to the next chapter, we will delve into the methods and techniques used to research ICOs effectively. We aim to provide an in-depth understanding of the methodologies used in ICO research, a crucial step in furthering our comprehension of this transformative fundraising method.

NOTES

1   bitcointalk.org/index.php?topic=5181153.
2   github.com/bitshares/how.bitshares.works/blob/master/docs/technology/history_bitshares.rst.
3   www.sec.gov/news/press-release/2019-87.
4   www.sec.gov/news/press-release/2018-268.
5   www.sec.gov/news/press-release/2022-167.
6   www.sec.gov/news/press-release/2021-125.
7   http://blog.openzeppelin.com/on-the-parity-wallet-multisig-hack-405a8c12e8f7.
8   medium.com/@Pr0Ger/another-parity-wallet-hack-explained-847ca46a2e1c.
9   www.investopedia.com/terms/m/mt-gox.asp.
10   www.coindesk.com/markets/2016/08/11/cryptsy-ceo-stole-millions-from-exchange-court-receiver-alleges.
11   en.wikipedia.org/wiki/Bankruptcy_of_FTX.
12   www.sec.gov/news/press-release/2023-78.
13   www.sec.gov/news/press-release/2023-101.
14   www.sec.gov/news/statement/uyeda-statement-ats-041423.

REFERENCES

Agrawal, A., Catalini, C., and Goldfarb, A. (2014) 'Some simple economics of crowd-funding', *Innovation Policy and the Economy*, 14(1), pp. 63–97.

Ahlers, G.K., Cumming, D., Günther, C., and Schweizer, D. (2015) 'Signaling in equity crowdfunding', *Entrepreneurship: Theory and Practice*, 39(4), pp. 955–980.

Boreiko, D. and Risteski, D. (2021) 'Serial and large investors in Initial Coin Offerings (ICOs)', *Small Business Economics*, 57, pp. 1053–1071.

Boreiko, D. and Vidusso, G. (2019) 'New blockchain intermediaries: Do ICO rating websites do their job well?' *The Journal of Alternative Investments*, 21(4), pp. 67–79.

Campino, J., Brochado, A., and Rosa, Á. (2021) 'Initial Coin Offerings (ICOs): The importance of human capital', *Journal of Business Economics*, 91(8), pp. 1225–1262.

Dombrowski, N., Drobetz, W., Hornuf, L., and Momtaz, P.P. (2023) 'The financial and non-financial performance of token-based crowdfunding: Certification arbitrage, investor choice, and the optimal timing of ICOs', CESifo Working Paper No. 10393.

Ernst & Young (2018) 'EY research: Initial Coin Offerings (ICOs)'. Available at: https://assets.ey.com/content/dam/ey-sites/ey-com/en_gl/topics/banking-and-capital-markets/ey-research-initial-coin-offerings-icos.pdf (accessed: 1 July 2023).

Fahlenbrach, R. and Frattaroli, M. (2021) 'ICO investors', *Financial Markets and Portfolio Management*, 35(1), pp. 1–59.

Fisch, C. and Momtaz, P.P. (2020) 'Institutional investors and post-ICO performance: An empirical analysis of investor returns in Initial Coin offerings (ICOs)', *Journal of Corporate Finance*, 64(101679), pp. 1–24.

Fisch, C., Masiak, C., Vismara, S., and Block, J. (2021) 'Motives and profiles of ICO investors', *Journal of Business Research*, 125, pp. 564–576.

Giudici, G., Giuffra Moncayo, G., and Martinazzi, S. (2020) 'The role of advisors' centrality in the success of Initial Coin Offerings', *Journal of Economics and Business*, 112(105932), pp. 1–17.

Hackober, C. and Bock, C. (2021) 'Which investors' characteristics are beneficial for Initial Coin Offerings? Evidence from blockchain technology-based firms', *Journal of Business Economics*, 91, pp. 1085–1124.

Howell, S.T., Niessner, M., and Yermack, D. (2019) 'Initial Coin Offerings: Financial growth with cryptocurrency token sales', *Review of Financial Studies*, 33, pp. 3925–3974.

Huang, W., Meoli, M., and Vismara, S. (2020) 'The geography of Initial Coin Offerings', *Small Business Economics*, 55(1), pp. 77–102.

Huang, W., Vismara, S., and Wei, X. (2021) 'Confidence and capital raising', *Journal of Corporate Finance*, 77(101900), pp. 1–23.

Kuppuswamy, V. and Bayus, B.L. (2018) 'Crowdfunding creative ideas: The dynamics of project backers'. In D. Cumming and L. Hornuf (eds.), *The Economics of Crowdfunding*. Cham, Switzerland: Palgrave Macmillan, pp. 151–182.

Mollick, E. (2014) 'The dynamics of crowdfunding: An exploratory study', *Journal of Business Venturing*, 29(1), pp. 1–16.

Momtaz, P.P. (2021) 'CEO emotions and firm valuation in Initial Coin Offerings: An artificial emotional intelligence approach', *Strategic Management Journal*, 42(3), pp. 558–578.

Perez, C., Sokolova, K., and Konate, M. (2020) 'Digital social capital and performance of Initial Coin Offerings', *Technological Forecasting and Social Change*, 152(119888), pp. 1–14.

Roosenboom, P., van der Kolk, T., and de Jong, A. (2020) 'What determines success in Initial Coin Offerings?' *Venture Capital*, 22(2), pp. 161–183.
Schueckes, M. and Gutmann, T. (2021) 'Why do startups pursue Initial Coin Offerings (ICOs)? The role of economic drivers and social identity on funding choice', *Small Business Economics*, 57(2), pp. 1027–1052.

6.   Researching Initial Coin Offerings

INTRODUCTION

When it comes to researching Initial Coin Offerings (ICOs), the task can feel much like navigating uncharted territory. Given my background in empirical corporate finance research, I found this new area surprisingly different, despite the many commonalities. However, as I began exploring this topic in early 2017, I was intrigued to discover the wealth of information available, albeit largely unstructured, akin to big data. This chapter aims to guide you on how to extract and interpret this data effectively.

It is important to underscore, however, that the landscape of ICO research has changed dramatically since I first delved into it. A methodology that was pertinent in the 2017–2020 period may be completely obsolete in 2023. Several data sources have vanished, and companies have shifted their strategies from maximizing transparency about their ICOs to maintaining utmost secrecy, even going to the extent of removing previous publications and statistics.

To start, it is crucial to recognize the major challenges that come with ICO research. Unlike conventional financial markets, there are no standardized reporting or disclosure practices for ICOs, making comparisons and analysis across various projects difficult. In addition, ICOs are a recent phenomenon, meaning that there is limited historical data for assessing long-term performance and success rates of these projects. Furthermore, the quality and reliability of available information can vary dramatically. Some projects provide detailed documentation and regular updates, while others offer scant or misleading data. ICOs also exhibit vast heterogeneity – they range from small to massive, and announced ICOs aren't always actual campaigns, as anyone can publish and run an ICO with ease.

This necessitates focusing on more substantial deals or confirmed cases of collected funds as announced by the firms themselves. The absence of reliable databases adds another layer of difficulty. Nevertheless, blockchain technology can help overcome some of these hurdles, providing a certain level of transparency and immutability that is inherent to the system. Blockchain can help access accurate, real-time information on ICO transactions, token distributions, and fund usage, facilitating a more efficient analysis.

In the earlier days, ICOs were announced on platforms like Bitcointalk and other forums. There was little to no tracking in venture capital databases that collected information on non-blockchain financing. Early aggregators provided patchy data at best, and the reported results lacked consistency. This issue was exacerbated by the high failure rate of ICO projects, leading to the elimination of information online to avoid regulatory scrutiny. Today, tracking social media provides an ongoing source of information on ICOs. Internet archives have become valuable reservoirs of data. Free or subscription databases provided by researchers in the field can be another resource. In the following sections, we delve into the specifics of each of these research methods, equipping you with the necessary tools to navigate this complex, rapidly evolving field.

SEARCHING FOR ICO DATA

The guiding principle in academia, often referred to as *publish or perish*, encourages researchers to continuously produce high-quality, publishable work. The central objective in this pursuit is to identify intriguing research questions and to conduct rigorous scientific analysis. For empirical studies, substantial data is required for statistical analysis. In the conventional finance realm, assuming adequate research funds are available, obtaining relevant data has become relatively straightforward in the current age. Corporate transactions can be sourced from various resources like Refinitiv Eikon. Databases such as DataStream or BankScope provide abundant accounting data, while market data on a plethora of financial instruments is readily available from stock exchanges or numerous other data providers, each catering to specific needs.

Not so long ago, data on venture capital and angel investors was fragmented and difficult to collate. Today, however, comprehensive databases like Crunchbase and Pitchbook have brought order to this chaos, tabulating data in an accessible format. For crowdfunding, the platforms themselves have stepped up, acting as repositories of data, maintained and published online for the convenience of any interested parties. Given the ready availability of this data, it is unsurprising that a wealth of research has emerged, examining various facets of crowdfunding.

In contrast, the early days of ICOs presented a different scenario: there was no database that captured ICO deals. Despite bearing some resemblance to IPOs in being funding operations, ICOs were unique. They were outside the conventional definition of a financial transaction, making them an intriguing object of study. But how could one study something that left no traditional data trail?

The answer, it turns out, was not to be found in a library, a place traditionally associated with research in the pre-digital age. In today's world, especially within the finance field, data is primarily harvested from the internet. ICOs, despite their unconventional nature, were no exception. This shift in data sourcing marks a clear departure from traditional research methodologies, illustrating how researchers have adapted to the ever-evolving financial landscape.

ICO Data in Internet

In the initial stages of research, discovering ICOs of interest is of paramount importance. This task can be accomplished with the aid of various online platforms that serve as aggregators, listing, rating, and summarizing different ICOs. Websites such as ICOBench, ICODrops, CoinSchedule, and ICO Alert, play, or rather played, a crucial role in this regard. They maintain up-to-date records of ongoing, upcoming, and completed ICOs, providing a limited overview to researchers. These platforms not only rate ICOs based on a multitude of factors but also provide project summaries and essential project details. Hence, researchers can leverage these platforms to identify intriguing ICOs that warrant further study, thus providing a rich ground for formulating compelling research questions.

Once you've found some ICOs you're interested in, you can use regular search engines like Google, Bing, or DuckDuckGo to find more information. By searching for the name of the ICO or related keywords, you can find a lot of useful content. You can also search for terms like '[ICO name] review' or '[ICO name] analysis' to find more detailed information and assessments.

Next, it is a good idea to check out the official websites of the ICOs. These websites usually have a lot of detailed information about the project. They tell you about the team behind the ICO, the technology they're using, and specifics about the token sale. Also, look for the project's White paper. This is a document that should give you a thorough understanding of what the ICO is trying to achieve, how the tokens will be used, and how the token economy will work.

Social media and online discussion forums can also be useful sources of information. Places like X (formerly known as Twitter), Reddit, Telegram, and Discord often have discussions and updates about specific ICOs. Reading these discussions can give you insights into what the community thinks about the project and what the latest developments are. However, keep in mind that you should be careful about misinformation or biased views. Industry blogs and news outlets can also be helpful. Websites like CoinDesk, CoinTelegraph, and The Block often write articles and analysis on specific ICOs. These sources can give you an objective view of the ICO, including interviews with the project founders, expert opinions, and market updates.

Lastly, if available, be sure to examine any research reports, analysis, or legal documents connected to the ICO. Some ICOs, depending on their geographic location and local laws, may have public filings or legal documents available online. These documents can provide valuable insights into the legal aspects of the ICO. In the case of later-stage blockchain financing deals, such as STOs, legal documents are often filed with regulators. This is because these offerings are typically structured to comply with existing legislation. However, it is worth noting that these compliant offerings represent only a small fraction of ICOs.

In the early days of ICOs, transparency was the name of the game. Teams behind ICOs made every effort to provide as much information as possible to prospective investors. They sought to reduce information asymmetry and prove the quality and seriousness of their projects. Public disclosure was seen as a mark of credibility and a strategy to attract investors.

However, the ICO landscape began to shift around 2018. The SEC started cracking down on ICOs that allowed US citizen participation, prosecuting several for alleged illegal securities offerings and other violations. This increased scrutiny from the SEC led to significant changes in the ICO environment. Suddenly, conducting an ICO became a high-stakes endeavour. Attracting the attention of regulators, once seen as an opportunity for transparent fundraising, was now viewed as a risk. As a result, ICOs began to operate more discreetly, with many projects becoming less open with their information. The emphasis had notably shifted from maximum disclosure to more guarded operations.

Moreover, as the number of frauds in the ICO space began to rise, security concerns became paramount. ICO campaigns started to take a more secretive approach, making detailed information available only to registered users who had passed KYC checks. This move was a step towards preventing scams, but it also added another layer of complexity to the ICO data landscape. Many ICOs even took the drastic step of deleting their social media publications related to their campaigns. This was done both out of fear of regulatory repercussions and as a measure to protect against potential fraud.

This shift had profound implications for the accessibility of ICO data. What was once a field characterized by transparency and open access became shrouded in secrecy and restrictions. Obtaining historical data on ICOs became a challenging task, as records that were once public and readily available became restricted or were removed entirely.

Moreover, acquiring data on discontinued or unsuccessful ICOs presents a unique set of challenges. Unlike successful projects that maintain an active online presence, these ventures often vanish from the digital landscape, making it particularly difficult to retrieve historical information.

When an ICO project ceases to exist, the first casualty is usually the project's website. It is taken offline as a cost-saving measure or as a result of legal repercussions, making it virtually impossible to access information about the project or its token sale. This is a significant loss of a primary data source, as project websites typically host a wealth of information, including project descriptions, team details, roadmaps, and most importantly, White papers. Similarly, social media accounts associated with unsuccessful ICOs often get deactivated or abandoned. These accounts not only serve as a platform for project announcements, they are also a rich source of community sentiment data. The closure of these channels results in the loss of a key avenue for gleaning insights about the project's history and the factors that led to its failure.

Even more challenging is the loss of access to the ICO's White papers. These documents are essentially the project's blueprint, providing comprehensive details about the ICO's goals, use cases, and tokenomics. When an ICO fails, its White paper often disappears with it, as the links leading to these documents become invalid or the documents are removed from hosting platforms. In some cases, even third-party platforms that list and rate ICOs remove discontinued or unsuccessful projects from their databases. While this is done to maintain the quality and relevance of their listings, it further exacerbates the difficulty of accessing data on these projects.

The ephemeral nature of digital information presents a significant challenge to researchers studying the ICO phenomenon. Without adequate archival practices, valuable data can be lost forever, making it difficult to build a comprehensive understanding of why some ICOs fail. To mitigate this issue, researchers may have to resort to advanced data retrieval methods such as web archiving or use specialized tools that trawl the internet and capture data before it disappears. We turn to these sources next.

Internet Archives

Internet archives have proven to be an invaluable resource when researching ICOs, especially those that have been discontinued or were unsuccessful. These archives offer access to historical information, including older versions of websites, White papers, and other associated documents. This kind of data can be crucial in analyzing the evolution of projects over time, or for understanding the operations and pitfalls of ICOs that did not succeed. My own experience in researching past ICOs suggests that in many instances, these internet archives are the only reliable source of information on smaller projects that have been discontinued or failed in their ICO campaigns.

One prominent example of such an archive is the Wayback Machine (archive.org), provided by the Internet Archive, that stores more than 808 billion webpages saved over time. This digital trove of the World Wide Web allows users to browse and access historical versions of websites, including ICO project websites and their associated documents such as White papers, team biographies, and details of token sales. With the Wayback Machine, you can search using a specific URL, or make use of its search functionality, to find archived pages relevant to a particular ICO. Furthermore, these services enable users to inspect different versions of the same page saved over a specific time period. This feature can be particularly useful in tracking changes and developments in an ICO project over time.

Another useful web archiving service is Archive.is, also known as Archive Today. Much like the Wayback Machine, it stores snapshots of webpages, giving researchers the ability to access historical versions of websites and their content. Whether you are searching for specific URLs or browsing for archived information related to ICOs, Archive.is can be a potent tool in your research arsenal.

Even Google Cache, a feature provided by the Google search engine, can come in handy. Though it might not be as comprehensive as the Wayback Machine or Archive.is, it stores cached versions of webpages which can provide access to older versions of ICO websites or documents. To utilize this feature, search for the specific URL on Google and click on the small downward-facing arrow next to the search result, then click 'Cached' to view the older version of the page.

Reflecting on my own experience in researching past ICOs, these internet archives, in many instances, served as the only sources of dependable information on smaller, failed, or discontinued projects that ran ICO campaigns. After experimenting with all the options mentioned above, the Wayback Machine proved to be the most effective tool for this purpose. Therefore, when embarking on a journey of ICO research, do not overlook the potential of these internet archives. They could very well provide the information you need to understand the full story behind an ICO's life cycle.

For instance, consider the notorious ICO project, The DAO, which was compromised by a hacker who drained its collected funds. This incident not only spotlighted the security vulnerabilities of such projects but also triggered increased scrutiny by the SEC towards ICOs. Today, the original website of The DAO is long gone. A simple internet search yields only general information and third-party posts about its history and legacy. While you can glean some details of the token sales from posts about its ICOs, the majority of sources either delve into the general discussion and history of The DAO or provide links to similarly named ICOs, such as DAO Maker. While it is occasionally possible to find basic information and, in exceptional cases, a working link to the project's White paper, seeking more detailed information, especially the results of the token sales, often proves a futile task.

One of the few remaining active ICO portals in 2023, Icoholder, offers a link to the project's White paper but provides very limited information about the token sale. Luckily, it displays the project's website, which, unsurprisingly, is now defunct, seven years later. However, by using the Wayback Machine, it is possible to access the original token sale webpage from the project's home-page as it appeared in May 2016 (web.archive.org/web/ 20160501124717/ http:/daohub.org). As depicted in Figure 6.1, a substantial amount of informa-tion can be sourced from it, including the results of the sale, the contribution address to which funds were sent, and even links to various useful documents, such as the Terms of Sale.

Source: web.archive.org.

Figure 6.1   *Snapshot of historical webpage of The DAO token sale as in May 2016*

ICO Portals Data

The advent of ICOs as a novel fundraising method immediately necessitated platforms that could provide data on these offerings to investors and research-ers. This demand led to the emergence of ICO portals, aggregators, and rating databases – resources that proved invaluable for studying ICOs. They offered a wealth of data, from basic project details to in-depth reports and analyses. Given the rapid growth of the ICO market, these platforms quickly gained pop-ularity. Because of the nascent nature of ICOs and their associated high risk, these platforms provided a much-needed layer of understanding and analysis. They simplified complex information, aided the decision-making process for potential investors, and served as essential tools for researchers.

The business models of these platforms varied, but most generated revenue through a combination of advertising, sponsored listings, premium services, or consulting. Basic ICO data, such as project summaries, ratings, and token sale details, were often accessible for free. More in-depth data and reports, which required more time and resources to produce, were typically offered for a fee or through subscription-based services.

Many platforms used Application Programming Interfaces (APIs) to provide data. APIs allowed users to access and retrieve data programmatically, simplifying the process of collecting large amounts of data or integrating ICO data into other applications. However, some platforms may have charged for access to their APIs. When an API was not available or did not provide the required data, web scraping became an alternative. Web scraping involves writing scripts or using tools to extract information automatically from webpages. However, it is more complex and time-consuming than using APIs, and some platforms' terms of service prohibited it.

Several prominent ICO aggregators and rating databases emerged during this period, each offering a unique range of services. For instance, ICOBench emerged as one of the most renowned platforms, providing listings, ratings, and analysis. Other platforms such as ICODrops, CoinSchedule, ICO Alert, and ICORating also made substantial contributions to the ICO research landscape. In 2017, during the peak of ICO activity, there were over 50 professional ICO portals (Boreiko and Vidusso 2019), in addition to numerous smaller projects that listed only a select number of ICOs. However, Boreiko and Vidusso (2019) discovered significant discrepancies in the data reported by various portals for the same ICOs. It recommended that investors approach the ratings produced by these portals with caution, considering the variations in rating methodology and the frequent adjustments made post-ICO campaigns.

Despite their offerings, these platforms often provided limited and sometimes incorrect information about ICO campaigns. Moreover, many of them failed to disclose their remuneration for listing certain ICOs and provided misleading information to make these ICOs stand out from the rest. For example, the once-renowned portal, CoinSchedule, served as a valuable tool for researchers, investors, and enthusiasts, listing hundreds of ICOs with extensive details. However, when the SEC began pursuing ICOs for alleged securities law violations, CoinSchedule, like other ICO listing platforms, found itself in a precarious situation. In fact, in 2021, the SEC charged CoinSchedule for failing to disclose that they received compensation from the ICO issuers listed on their platform.[1] The website was consequently shut down, and the project discontinued. Many other popular ICO portals and ICO rating services followed suit, and by 2023, very few remained in business.

INSPECTING BLOCKCHAINS

One distinctive feature that sets ICOs apart from other forms of financing is their utilization of blockchain technology. Although this introduces some additional risks, it simultaneously provides an extra source of data for ICO research. The open nature of blockchain data allows anyone to analyze transactions, the dynamics of wallet balances, timestamps, and other pertinent information. Even though blockchain data is pseudonymous (the identities of the participants are masked yet traceable through their public addresses), a significant amount of information can still be gleaned from it.

Analyzing a blockchain involves inspecting the data contained within the blocks, transactions, and addresses of a specific blockchain network. Numerous sources and tools are available for scrutinizing various blockchain networks, including Bitcoin, Ethereum, and others. Some academic papers have successfully leveraged this blockchain data to extract valuable information about ICOs and their investors. For instance, Boreiko and Risteski (2021) studied the dynamics of contributions from large-balance wallets and those that sent funds to multiple ICO campaigns, deducing the behaviour of large and serial ICO investors from the Bitcoin and Ethereum blockchains.

In a similar vein, Fahlenbrach and Frattaroli (2021) used Ethereum blockchain data to conduct an in-depth analysis of investors and provided some details about the average number of contributors and related statistics. Howell et al. (2019) analyzed the Filecoin ICO using blockchain data, while Lee et al. (2021) used individual investor contribution data to study how swiftly an ICO reaches its soft cap and to test the theory of the wisdom of crowds. This multifaceted use of blockchain data further illustrates its value in providing unique insights into the behaviours and dynamics of ICOs and their participants.

Block Explorers

Block explorers are essentially search engines for blockchains, offering a wealth of detailed information regarding transactions, blocks, and specific addresses within a blockchain. In practice, every blockchain has its own explorer that allows the user to inspect the executed and recorded transactions in the blockchain. These tools are crucial for users to navigate the complexity of the digital ledger technology and access critical data. Notable block explorers like Blockchain.com Explorer, Blockchair, and BlockCypher cater to the Bitcoin network, while Etherscan and Etherchain primarily serve Ethereum users. Blockchair extends its services to multiple networks, including Bitcoin Cash and Litecoin, among others.

With these block explorers, users can delve into a wealth of data, such as transaction specifics like transaction IDs, inputs, outputs, fees, and the number of confirmations. It is also possible to access information about blocks, including the block height, the timestamp, the miner, the size, and the number of transactions contained within. Additionally, they provide visibility into address balances and their respective transaction history.

Analysis of Bitcoin Blockchain

In theory, a researcher herself can download the entire Bitcoin blockchain. This would involve running a full Bitcoin node, which maintains a complete copy of the blockchain's history. But be aware, this is a resource-intensive process and requires substantial storage space, processing power, and some technical knowledge. Nevertheless, it would allow the researcher to inspect transaction data directly without relying on third-party services, such as blockchain explorers.

Blockchain explorers, in essence, serve as user-friendly interfaces to visualize and track activities on blockchain networks. For Bitcoin, popular blockchain explorers like Blockchain.com Explorer, BTC.com, Blockchair (blockchair.com), and BlockCypher (live.blockcypher.com) all provide similar core services but may differ in terms of additional features, user interface, and the specific data points they highlight. These tools parse the Bitcoin blockchain, interpret the data, and present it in a readable format. They let users view transaction histories, block information, and balance of specific Bitcoin addresses. Furthermore, they enable the user to follow the path of a particular transaction by tracing the inputs and outputs, offering a more profound understanding of Bitcoin's transaction flow.

Some of these explorers may be part of a broader service provided by a specific company. For example, Blockchain.com offers a wallet service along with its explorer. BlockCypher mainly offers cloud-based solutions, designed to help businesses develop blockchain applications using web APIs, that allow users to create and decode transactions and deploy contracts. As part of a free service, the company also offers explorer for seven blockchains, including Bitcoin and Ethereum. Many block explorers, however, are open-source projects, meaning that their code is freely available to the public, allowing other developers to understand, contribute to, or create their own versions of the explorer.

The first blockchain explorer for Bitcoin was Blockchain.info, now known as Blockchain.com, established in 2011. The need for more explorers emerged as the crypto space grew in complexity and user base. Different explorers might offer various additional features tailored to the needs of different users.

For instance, some focus more on user privacy, while others might emphasize data analytics capabilities.

In terms of ICOs, blockchain explorers can be a potent tool for researchers. They can be used to scrutinize the investment dynamics and the behaviour of individual addresses associated with specific investors. By examining transaction histories, researchers can gain insights into the movement of tokens from the ICO address to investors, follow their subsequent trajectory, and even identify major players. It can help to study investment patterns, such as hold periods, the speed of selling tokens, or the proportion of tokens an entity controls. Such data can offer valuable insights into the investment behaviour, the perceived value of the token, and the dynamics of token distribution, contributing to an in-depth understanding of the market, invaluable for both academic research and practical investment decision-making.

The Bitcoin blockchain provides an expansive and detailed trove of information that is often utilized for academic research. Foley et al. (2019), for instance, utilized Bitcoin blockchain data to examine the extent of blockchain's use in illicit activities. In another compelling study, Boreiko and Risteski (2021) analyzed 83 Bitcoin contribution contracts related to ICOs to gain insights into investor behaviour during these ICOs. Through their blockchain analysis, they unveiled systematic evidence of the types of ICO investors, their investment patterns, and their impact on the success of campaigns. While the pseudonymous nature of blockchain data did not permit the identification of personal characteristics of investors, it did allow for the detailed reconstruction of the investment history of each contribution address, each presumably linked to a specific investor. Their study resulted in a comprehensive database containing 129 886 contributions from 105 472 individual addresses on the Bitcoin blockchain that had been used to send funds to Bitcoin-accepting ICOs.

The beauty of blockchain technology lies in its transparency and accessibility. It allows anyone to replicate such empirical analyses and learn to use blockchain explorers efficiently. Take, for instance, the first ever ICO of Mastercoin in 2013. The Bitcoin contribution address for its token sale is readily available online for anyone to view. In stark contrast to many other information sources on ICOs, data on the blockchain cannot be altered or removed later on.

The ICO contribution address for Mastercoin was 1EXoDusjGwvnjZUyK-kxZ4U HEf77z6A5S4P. By entering this address into the Blockchair explorer, one can retrieve summary information about this wallet. The results show that a total of 6674 Bitcoins were sent to this address, and 6672 Bitcoins were transferred out from this address (as depicted in Figure 6.2). This level of transparency, detail, and immutability is what sets blockchain technology apart and offers significant potential for various forms of research and analysis.

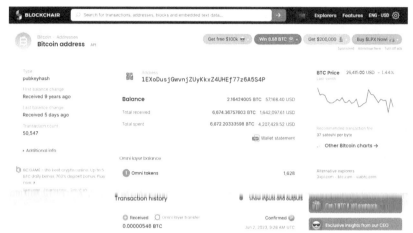

Source: blockchair.com/bitcoin/address/1EXoDusjGwvnjZUyKkxZ4UHEf77z6A5S4P.

Figure 6.2   *Snapshot of Mastercoin ICO contribution address information*

The data extraction process can be refined to include only transactions that occurred during the ICO contribution period. The btc.com explorer is a convenient tool for this, as its free version permits the filtering, sorting, and exporting of all transactions. The explorer reveals that the first contribution to the ICO happened on 31 July 2013, when an individual sent 16 Bitcoins. This initial contribution was followed by two more transactions of 5 and 1 BTC respectively (as shown in Figure 6.3). Furthermore, btc.com explorer provides an export function that enables the user to save all (or a subset of) transactions in a CSV format. This data can then be imported into a spreadsheet or a statistical software for further analysis.

Such data can be used for testing various hypotheses and validating theories. For example, consider the theory of information cascades. In the context of fundraising campaigns, the concept of *investment cascades* refers to the phenomenon where early investments trigger a sequence of subsequent investments. This can be attributed to the theory of informational cascades, where subsequent investors, upon seeing early investments, interpret them as signals of the project's potential success and hence follow suit. These cascades can significantly impact the fundraising dynamics and outcomes of fundraising.

Vismara's 2018 study of investment cascades in crowdfunding yielded valuable insights that can be applied to ICOs and token sales. By examining the timestamps and sizes of contributions, Vismara identified patterns and trends, gaining an understanding of how initial pledges can influence subsequent

Source: explorer.btc.com/btc/ address/1EXoDusjGwvnjZUyKkxZ4UHEf77z6A5S4P.

Figure 6.3   Snapshot of Mastercoin ICO first three contributions

pledging activity. Blockchain data, with its accurate, unchangeable log of each transaction – complete with timestamp and transaction value – provides an ideal resource for conducting similar analyses. By exporting and examining this data, one can monitor how investments flow into an ICO, identifying if and when investment cascades occur, how they evolve, and the effect they have on the overall success of the ICO. This analysis can also illuminate whether large *whale* investments have a disproportionate influence on these cascades.

Furthermore, early-bird bonuses, as discussed in previous chapters, can serve as catalysts for information cascades. These bonuses, which often take the form of additional tokens or discounts for investors who participate in the ICO's early stages, not only encourage early investment but can also stimulate information cascades.

To illustrate, we downloaded all contribution data for the Augur ICO, which took place in 2015 and was the first ICO on the Ethereum blockchain. Augur also accepted BTC contributions, which were gathered from a publicly announced Bitcoin address. We used this information to download all transactions that took place during the ICO period. With the early-bird bonus schedule known, we could create an ICO timeline chart (Figure 6.4), which confirmed the impact of bonuses on the timing and size of the contributions. Indeed, the figure displays clear spikes in the number of investors and total daily contributions right at the end of each bonus tier. Gathering such data for a set of ICOs allows for a statistical analysis that could yield robust confirmation of a causal effect.

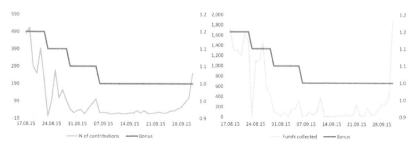

Source: Bitcoin blockchain and author's calculations

Figure 6.4   Daily total contributions on Bitcoin crowdfunding address and number of investors in Augur ICO (left axis) against early-bird tier bonus (right axis)

In theory, Bitcoin wallet addresses can be reused; indeed, a single wallet can generate and control multiple Bitcoin addresses. When one initiates a transaction, they have the option to either send change back to the original address or route it to a new one. However, it is considered good practice to use a new address for each transaction for privacy reasons. This is because all Bitcoin transactions are publicly visible on the blockchain, and reusing addresses can enable someone to track how many Bitcoins are being sent or received from a single address. This practice is standard for the Bitcoin blockchain. This fact was confirmed by Boreiko and Risteski in their 2021 study, which found that only half a per cent of all contributing addresses invested in more than one ICO. Therefore, Bitcoin blockchain data is somewhat limited, precluding any more sophisticated analysis beyond the basic level.

Analysis of Ethereum Blockchain

The Ethereum blockchain differs somewhat from the Bitcoin blockchain in terms of address usage. Unlike Bitcoin, Ethereum does not automatically create a new address for every transaction. Ethereum addresses are typically reused, and there is less of an emphasis on generating new addresses for each transaction. This is partly due to the fact that Ethereum addresses are not intended just for sending and receiving Ether, but are also used to interact with smart contracts on the Ethereum network.

In Ethereum, an address can represent either an external-owned account (EOA), which is controlled by private keys, or a contract account, which is controlled by its contract code and can only be activated by an EOA. Therefore, it is more common in Ethereum for addresses to be reused across multiple transactions. Some Ethereum wallets do provide users with an option to create and manage multiple Ethereum addresses. For privacy-conscious users, these features can provide similar benefits to the address generation systems used in Bitcoin wallets, although they are not as integrated into the standard operation of the network. As a result, the majority of Ethereum accounts are reused and allow for more detailed analysis of ICO investors' behaviour (Boreiko and Risteski 2021, Fahlenbrach and Frattaroli 2021).

There are several commonly used Ethereum explorers, each offering unique features and focus areas. Etherscan (etherscan.io), which was launched in 2015, shortly after the Ethereum network itself was initiated, is perhaps the most widely recognized Ethereum explorer. It presents exhaustive data about transactions, addresses, and blocks. Moreover, it provides a robust set of developer tools, including APIs and contract verification services. A distinguishing feature of Etherscan is its ability to explore Ethereum's *internal transactions*, which are instigated by contract interactions, unique to the Ethereum network.

Another notable Ethereum explorer is Beaconcha (beaconcha.in, formerly Etherchain). While it may not be as feature-packed as Etherscan, Beaconcha provides essential data through a simple, clean interface. It also offers distinctive visualizations, including charts displaying the gas price and network difficulty over time. Blockchair (blockchair.com), although not exclusive to Ethereum and supporting multiple blockchains, is also a valuable tool. It gives detailed information about transactions, blocks, and addresses, and it boasts a variety of advanced search and filtering options. A handy feature of Blockchair is its ability to allow users to download data in various formats, which proves useful for researchers and developers.

The selection of an Ethereum explorer largely hinges on one's specific needs. For those needing advanced developer tools or contract-related data, Etherscan might be the preferable option. However, for individuals interested in network statistics or desiring to download blockchain data, Beaconcha or Blockchair might be better suited. Regardless of the choice, each of these explorers serves as an indispensable tool for anyone interacting with, or studying, the Ethereum network.

As a result, the Ethereum blockchain explorers are often used both in industry and in academia to research various aspects of problems related to token sales. One of the most common uses of blockchain explorers is for transaction verification. Ethereum explorers, like Etherscan, can verify if a particular transaction has occurred and determine its status. This is particularly important for businesses accepting cryptocurrency payments, ensuring the validity and finality of transactions.

Ethereum explorers also facilitate the analysis of smart contracts. They permit users to inspect the details of a smart contract, including its source code if it has been verified. This proves essential for developers debugging their contract code, or for users who need to validate a contract before interacting with it. Market analysis is another area where Ethereum explorers prove beneficial. The data offered by these tools allows market analysts to track trends, such as the number of daily transactions or the most active smart contracts. This valuable information can help identify popular dApps, detect emerging trends, or observe shifts in the Ethereum ecosystem. Moreover, the immutable and transparent nature of the Ethereum blockchain opens the doors for forensic investigations. In cases of illicit activities, such as stolen funds, the transaction trail can be followed using a blockchain explorer.

Lastly, blockchain explorers proved to be invaluable in studying ICOs. As we have previously discussed, both academics and industry professionals routinely employ these explorers for a myriad of analytical purposes. Take, for example, Vitalik Buterin, the creator of Ethereum. He has frequently highlighted the value of using blockchain explorers, such as Etherscan, to gain insights into the dynamics of token sales. In his articles and blog posts, Buterin demonstrates how an Ethereum explorer can assist in identifying patterns and trends within ICOs, selecting the best design for a token sale, and others.[2]

Blockchain Inspection Intermediaries

If one lacks a technical background or does not wish to spend time delving into blockchain transactions, intermediaries can assist individuals and businesses in navigating this intricate ecosystem. These intermediaries can be broadly classified into three categories: full-node wallets or clients, APIs and libraries, and advanced analytics tools and platforms.

Full-node wallets or clients, like Umbrel (umbrel.com) and Bitcoin Core (bitcoin .org/ en/ bitcoin -core) for Bitcoin or Geth (geth.ethereum.org) for Ethereum, serve as bridges connecting users to the blockchain. They permit direct interaction with the network and enable the querying of data stored therein. Users can extract information about transactions, addresses, and blocks through these tools. Furthermore, they can facilitate the submission of new transactions to the network.

APIs and libraries, on the other hand, are tools provided by many blockchain platforms that permit developers to access and interact with blockchain data programmatically. This functionality makes it possible to extract data similar to that available through block explorers. Additionally, developers can utilize

APIs and libraries to create custom applications that interact with the blockchain in innovative ways.

The third category includes advanced analytics tools and platforms. These platforms, such as Nansen (nansen.ai), Dune Analytics (dune.com), and Glassnode (glassnode.com), offer sophisticated data analysis and visualization tools. They provide in-depth insights into the blockchain network, focusing on key metrics like on-chain activities, token flows, and address classifications.

In addition to these, there are cryptocurrency research firms like Messari (messari.io), CoinMetrics (coinmetrics.io), and Delphi Digital (delphidigital.io). These firms provide comprehensive research, market analysis, and insights into the blockchain and cryptocurrency domain. Such information can empower investors to make informed decisions about their investments.

Free Blockchain Data Portals

Despite the prevalence of firms that provide blockchain analytics services for a fee, the industry also hosts many resources that are completely free of charge. These can be invaluable to researchers who may not have extensive financial resources. Numerous data portals, such as CoinMarketCap (coinmarketcap.com), CoinGecko (coingecko.com), CryptoCompare (cryptocompare.com), and Live Coin Watch (livecoinwatch.com), deliver high-quality data extracted from various blockchains.

CoinMarketCap is arguably one of the most popular sources of cryptocurrency market data. It provides a comprehensive overview of thousands of different cryptocurrencies, ICOs, and tokens. By aggregating information from various cryptocurrency exchanges, it provides real-time data on prices, market capitalization, trading volumes, and supply of different cryptocurrencies. Regarding ICOs and tokens, CoinMarketCap offers an abundance of useful information for free. You can find details about ongoing, upcoming, and past ICOs, including their start and end dates, platform, token supply, funds raised, and more. It also provides a brief description of each ICO, its vision, and the problem it seeks to solve, which can be helpful for investors seeking to understand the project's fundamentals.

The platform also lists tokens separately from their parent cryptocurrencies, displaying data such as current price, market cap, circulating supply, volume, and percentage change over a certain period. Tokens are also categorized based on the blockchain they are built upon, such as Ethereum, Binance Smart Chain, etc. This detailed breakdown can be helpful for investors looking to better understand the token market landscape. Additionally, CoinMarketCap provides historical data for price, market cap, and volume, enabling investors to conduct time-series analysis to identify trends and patterns. This can be particularly useful for research and analysis, as it allows for tracking a token's performance over time.

While CoinMarketCap is a well-known and widely used platform for tracking cryptocurrency data, it is not the only resource of its kind. Several other platforms also offer comprehensive and often free data about cryptocurrencies, tokens, and ICOs. CoinGecko is a popular alternative to CoinMarketCap, offering data on a wide range of cryptocurrencies and tokens, including current prices, trading volumes, market capitalization, and more. CoinGecko also includes unique features such as a developer activity index (sourced from GitHub) and a public interest score, which considers factors such as search engine volume. Furthermore, it lists DeFi tokens and yield farming pools, making it popular among DeFi enthusiasts.

CryptoCompare provides real-time and historical data on cryptocurrencies. It features a wide range of cryptocurrencies and offers detailed charts and analysis tools. In addition, CryptoCompare presents reviews, guides, and other educational content that can be beneficial for both novice and experienced investors. Live Coin Watch offers real-time cryptocurrency prices, charts, and market capitalization information. It features a clean, user-friendly interface, and allows users to customize their dashboard to monitor selected cryptocurrencies.

CONCLUSION

As we conclude this chapter on utilizing blockchain data to research ICOs, it is crucial to acknowledge the wealth of resources available at our disposal. Whether you are a researcher, investor, or an enthusiastic learner, you can leverage blockchain explorers, access free data portals on the web, or purchase third-party analytics from a variety of established providers. Each approach has its unique strengths and can provide insightful perspectives into the intricate dynamics of ICOs.

Blockchain explorers like Etherscan and Blockchair offer a direct view into the raw data underlying each transaction on the network. They allow users to dive deep into the specific details of transactions, blocks, and addresses. Free web portals such as CoinMarketCap and CoinGecko serve as comprehensive data repositories, providing real-time and historical data on countless cryptocurrencies and ICOs. For those seeking more detailed and nuanced analytics, firms like Nansen, Chainalysis, and Glassnode offer premium services with sophisticated data visualizations and analysis tools.

The advent of blockchain technology has transformed the field of research significantly, particularly in the realm of ICOs. The transparency and immutability of blockchains mean that data is not only abundantly available but also incredibly reliable. The data is unalterable and comprehensive, providing a full, transparent ledger of transactions.

This unprecedented level of data availability presents both a significant opportunity and a considerable challenge. The large volume of data requires advanced tools and techniques to analyze effectively. However, the rewards for doing so can be enormous. With careful and detailed analysis, researchers can gain a deep understanding of investment patterns, token sale dynamics, investor behaviour, and much more. Therefore, it is only natural to examine what academics have researched so far in ICOs. This will be the focus of the next chapter.

NOTES

1   www.sec.gov/news/press-release/2021-125.
2   vitalik.ca/general/2017/06/09/sales.html.

REFERENCES

Boreiko, D. and Risteski, D. (2021) 'Serial and large investors in Initial Coin Offerings (ICOs)', *Small Business Economics*, 57, pp. 1053–1071.

Boreiko, D. and Vidusso, G. (2019) 'New blockchain intermediaries: Do ICO rating websites do their job well?' *The Journal of Alternative Investments*, 21(4), pp. 67–79.

Fahlenbrach, R. and Frattaroli, M. (2021) 'ICO investors', *Financial Markets and Portfolio Management*, 35(1), pp. 1–59.

Foley, S., Karlsen, J.R., and Putnis, T.J. (2019) 'Sex, drugs, and Bitcoin: How much illegal activity is financed through cryptocurrencies?', *The Review of Financial Studies*, 32(5), pp. 1798–1853.

Howell, S.T., Niessner, M., and Yermack, D. (2019) 'Initial Coin Offerings: Financial growth with cryptocurrency token sales', *Review of Financial Studies*, 33, pp. 3925–3974.

Lee, J., Li, T., and Shin, D. (2021) 'The wisdom of crowds in FinTech: Evidence from Initial Coin Offerings', *The Review of Corporate Finance Studies*, 11(1), pp. 1–46.

Vismara, S. (2018) 'Information cascades among investors in equity crowdfunding', *Entrepreneurship: Theory and Practice*, 42(3), pp. 467–497.

7.   Initial Coin Offerings research

INTRODUCTION

So, what do we know about Initial Coin Offerings (ICOs)? While myriad press articles, posts, and blogs have been published about ICOs in industry literature related to blockchain, discussing various cases and individual token sales, scientific literature takes a different approach. The strength of scientific literature lies in its rigorous statistical analysis, where hypotheses are posited and then either proved or rejected. For instance, it is one thing to highlight that investors earned an annualized return of 170 per cent from the Ethereum ICO to March 2023, or almost 300 per cent to October 2021. However, it is a completely different proposition to demonstrate, through statistically significant results, that a large and diverse sample of ICOs yielded a positive average annual return for subscribers to all of the ICOs in the sample. In other words, while industry literature often focuses on specific, individual cases and narratives, scientific literature provides a broad, statistically validated perspective. This distinction is crucial to understand for anyone looking to draw meaningful conclusions about the performance and impact of ICOs.

ICOs first appeared in 2013 but didn't gain widespread popularity until 2017. Unlike the field of computer science, where new phenomena are researched and published within a span of three to six months, economic academic literature requires a substantial amount of time to accumulate sufficient evidence and conduct meaningful econometric analysis. Consequently, it took a considerable amount of time for the first working papers, let alone published articles, on ICOs to appear. Additionally, in recent times, the entrepreneurial finance literature was primarily focused on crowdfunding as the new hyped method of fundraising, so it wasn't until 2017 that the first empirical work was published on ICOs. As of early 2023, fewer than 300 papers focusing in one way or another on ICOs have been published on the Social Science Research Network (SSRN).[1]

Comparatively, over 1200 papers have been published on the crowdfunding fundraising method and there are more than 4000 published papers on venture capital financing. Clearly, despite the attention it has received in industry literature, the ICO is a considerably less researched phenomenon in academic circles. Still, academics have studied ICOs and tested a lot of hypotheses about

ICO performance, factors affecting their success, the role of entrepreneurs and investors, and so on.

Several comprehensive academic papers have been published to date that provide thorough reviews of the amassed research on ICOs. Notable among these are works by Brochado and Troilo (2021), Watts et al. (2023), and Alshater et al. (2023). These pieces delve deeply into the accumulated evidence surrounding ICOs and offer intricate analyses on various aspects of this novel form of entrepreneurial finance. They examine topics ranging from success determinants and the long-run performance of ICOs, to their impact on the broader financial ecosystem. The authors explore ICOs from various perspectives, integrating findings from different sub-fields of research and drawing connections to broader economic, financial, and sociocultural trends. They meticulously piece together a multifaceted picture of ICOs, reflecting both the opportunities they offer and the challenges they pose.

These papers serve as an excellent resource for those seeking an in-depth understanding of the ICO landscape. They offer valuable insights into the evolution of ICOs and their implications for entrepreneurs, investors, policymakers, and scholars. They also highlight gaps in current knowledge and provide direction for future research. We, instead, only briefly touch upon some of the main issues surrounding ICOs, serving as a primer for those new to the subject and as a refresher for those already familiar with it. For a more comprehensive and nuanced understanding of ICOs, we strongly recommend that interested readers consult the aforementioned review papers. These articles provide a wealth of knowledge that can greatly enhance one's understanding of the complexities and potential of ICOs in the modern financial landscape.

The empirical research on ICOs has primarily focused on two central themes. Firstly, the legal literature, which despite its non-empirical nature, provides vital insights into the legal status of tokens and regulatory approaches, mostly within the US system, but with some exploration of European regulations. This body of work also often interacts with the research on frauds associated with ICOs. Secondly, much of the academic discourse has investigated the metrics of ICO success, drawing parallels with Initial Public Offerings (IPOs) and crowdfunding.

This chapter dissects the determining factors for ICO success as presented in industry reports and academic studies while underscoring the distinction between short-term and long-term performance. The broader performance of ICOs is also scrutinized to assess whether they underperform on average as often thought. Furthermore, the chapter analyses tokenomics and examines the market performance of ICOs. It also situates ICOs within the broader landscape of entrepreneurial finance and economics and looks at the papers that studied the role of ICO intermediaries. Finally, the chapter concludes by identifying areas that academic literature has yet to sufficiently explore.

LEGAL RESEARCH

Research into the legal aspects of ICOs primarily revolves around the foundational question of how these offerings should be classified under law. At the heart of the legal debate is whether tokens issued in an ICO should be categorized as securities. This designation holds substantial implications, as securities are subject to specific legal frameworks and regulatory guidelines that govern their issuance, sale, and trade.

In the US, the Howey Test has emerged as a significant factor in these discussions. The Howey Test, derived from a Supreme Court case, provides a standard for determining whether certain transactions qualify as *investment contracts* – a type of security. When applied to ICOs, the test is used to ascertain whether a token demonstrates the characteristics of an investment contract, such as an investment of money in a common enterprise with a reasonable expectation of profits primarily derived from the efforts of others. ICOs that pass the Howey Test are, therefore, considered securities and subject to Securities and Exchange Commission (SEC) regulation.

For example, Gurrea-Martínez and Remolina (2019) discuss the varied global regulatory responses to ICOs. They explore the controversies around classifying tokens issued during ICOs, under securities law. The paper also notes other challenges posed by ICOs from multiple legal perspectives, including accounting, finance, corporate governance, data protection, anti-money laundering, and insolvency law.

Henderson and Raskin (2018), in turn, aim to bring clarity to the process of identifying which digital assets can be classified as securities by suggesting the use of two new tests. The *Bahamas Test* investigates whether a digital asset's decentralization level makes it non-securitized; the *Substantial Steps Test* evaluates if an investment was made with the anticipation of profit. The article proposes a structured approach to foster a clearer understanding and encourage discussion about developing more predictable laws and regulations in this field.

Hacker and Thomale (2017) propose a detailed method that classifies tokens into three main categories: currency, investment, and utility tokens. They examine the different impacts of these types and their mixed forms under EU securities regulation. Although the wide range of tokens requires individual analysis, the study finds that certain types and mixed forms of tokens fall under EU securities regulation. Generally, pure investment tokens are seen as securities, while pure currency and utility tokens are not supposed to be regulated as securities in the EU.

Boreiko et al. (2020) suggest moving away from the current classifications of tokens, as they believe the distinctions can be confusing. They argue that *utility tokens*, which are used for customer payments and can also be traded on secondary markets, blur the lines between currencies, financial assets, and goods. The authors also highlight the growing role of online crypto exchanges, which sometimes act as intermediaries and oversee Initial Exchange Offerings (IEOs). They suggest that the crypto market is beginning to resemble a segment of the capital market. The paper also argues that, because tokens have an investment component, they should be considered tradable securities under the Prospectus Regulation. The authors compare European and US securities regulations, noting that differences make Europe less friendly to blockchain startups.

While the question of whether ICOs qualify as securities is a central theme, other legal topics of interest have emerged in academic discussions around ICOs. For example, the potential for fraud in ICOs has been another focal point of research. As a relatively new and somewhat unregulated domain, ICOs could potentially be used as vehicles for fraudulent activities, such as Ponzi or pyramid schemes. These concerns have prompted calls for more robust regulatory measures to protect investors.

In the context of frauds, Park and Park (2020) examine how the SEC tackles the issue of unregistered sales of digital tokens using a strategy called *Regulation by Selective Enforcement*. Instead of penalizing numerous violators, the SEC has chosen to set precedents by handling a small number of significant cases. This approach has been facilitated by other enforcers of securities laws, such as state regulators and private plaintiffs, allowing the SEC to concentrate on nationally important issues. While this strategy has seen some success, the authors highlight that the SEC's selective enforcement may create misleading perceptions of legal clarity, potentially confer unfair advantages to early players like Ethereum, and lead to varying interpretations and outcomes in similar cases, posing significant challenges to the overall regulatory landscape.

Furthermore, there is an ongoing academic discourse around consumer and investor protection in the context of ICOs. The lack of transparency and the highly technical nature of blockchain technology may make it difficult for the average investor to fully understand the risks involved in participating in an ICO. This has sparked debates about the role of regulatory authorities in ensuring adequate disclosure and the appropriate balancing of innovation against investor protection. Zetzsche et al. (2019) argued that many ICOs lack sufficient disclosure of information, with over half of the ICO White papers reviewed not mentioning the project initiators or backers, providing contact information, nor detailing the applicable law, client funds management, or the involvement of an external auditor. As a result, the article concludes that decisions to invest in them can rarely be based on logical calculations. Signs of a typical speculative bubble are apparent, thus presenting a significant challenge for regulatory bodies.

Finally, ICOs have sparked conversations regarding their influence on conventional financing approaches. These discussions encompass an evaluation of how ICOs align with current securities laws, a debate on the suitability of existing regulations, and contemplation over the necessity for new legal structures specifically designed for this innovative fundraising method. A few papers, including works by Barsan (2017) and Kaal (2018), among others, examined the emerging strategies towards ICOs in various jurisdictions. Overall, these discussions reflect the complex and evolving legal landscape around ICOs, indicating that they are at the intersection of technology, law, and finance. This ongoing discourse emphasizes the need for a nuanced understanding of ICOs, robust regulatory frameworks, and measures to ensure investor protection.

STUDYING ICO SUCCESS

Determining the success of a fundraising campaign, such as an ICO, is not as straightforward as it might initially seem. One might instinctively think that the amount of funds raised is a clear measure of success. However, this may not necessarily be the case. Drawing a parallel with countries, we can observe that the biggest countries are not always the richest, nor do they guarantee the happiest population. Therefore, using the volume of funds raised as the sole measure of success may not always yield accurate conclusions.

The complexities involved in defining success have prompted researchers to examine various facets of token sales, using multiple dimensions as proxies for success. It is crucial to note that we are focusing on the success of the ICO itself, not the ultimate success of the startups involved – that will be dealt with in the next section. Even startups that manage to raise substantial funds during their ICO can fail when it comes to executing their business ideas.

Academic research on ICOs has introduced and debated various measures for evaluating the success of these campaigns. This includes factors such as the achievement of funding goals, successful token listing on an important crypto exchange, the volatility of the token price post-ICO, and the progress of the project as outlined in the roadmap, among others. Every such factor offers a different perspective on success and, when taken together, these factors provide a more nuanced and comprehensive evaluation of an ICO's success. These multiple dimensions of success are essential in providing a balanced view of an ICO's outcome. They take into consideration both the financial aspects and the broader impacts, such as advancements in technology, market growth, and contributions to the blockchain ecosystem. In the following sections, we will discuss these measures of success and explore how they are utilized in academic research on ICOs.

Funds Raised

One of the primary objectives of an ICO is to raise capital for the development and growth of a project. As such, the total amount of funds raised serves as a critical indicator for evaluating an ICO's success. Generally, an ICO that raises a substantial amount of funds is considered more successful than one that falls short of its fundraising goals. However, the context of the fundraising and the specific needs of the project should be considered when interpreting this metric. No empirical paper on ICOs omits the analysis of the funds raised. This measure is probably the most widely used technique to study the success of ICOs. Alshater et al. (2023) identified 31 academic articles with more than ten citations that examined ICO success, and virtually all of them used funds raised as one of the measures.

The total funds an ICO can amass can be impacted by a variety of factors, including the overall appeal of the project, the credibility of the team behind it, the thoroughness of the White paper, and the efficacy of their marketing campaigns. Take, for example, the ICO of Filecoin, a decentralized storage network. This project raised over $250 million in 2017, marking it as one of the most significant ICOs in history. Filecoin's impressive fundraising accomplishment was largely credited to its revolutionary approach to decentralized data storage, as well as the sterling reputation of its parent company, Protocol Labs. However, a closer look at the figures reveals an interesting story. A significant portion of the funds, a quarter to be exact, was raised from 150 institutional investors during the pre-sale. The remaining funds came from 2100 investors during the public sale (Howell et al. 2019). This prompts the question: did the ICO truly resonate with the broader community given the relatively small number of contributors?

Additionally, while Filecoin continues to persist as an active project that regularly shares updates, its market performance raises doubts about its valuation during the ICO. As of May 2023, Filecoin's token price stood at $4.5, lower than its public sale price, and a staggering 98.5 per cent less than its all-time high reached during the peak of the cryptocurrency market. Hence, we find ourselves questioning the disparity between the initial hype, large funds raised, and the current performance of the project. Was it truly worth it?

Various cases show that a large amount of funds raised does not always guarantee long-term success. For example, Tezos, a blockchain platform for smart contracts, raised over $230 million in its 2017 ICO but faced numerous challenges and legal disputes that hampered its progress. Another prominent example, the one-year-long ICO of EOS that ended in the middle of 2018, certainly made a splash when it arrived on the scene, amassing a record-breaking sum in its ICO. However, the fundraising campaign was not without its controversies. There were allegations of price manipulation, resulting in inflated values that drew the attention of investors worldwide (Griffin 2021). This led to a significant legal confrontation with the SEC, resulting in a settlement.

Although the EOS project was enveloped by substantial hype and expectations due to its high-profile ICO and the ground-breaking claims of its developers, its actual outcome has so far been somewhat underwhelming, as we can observe in 2023. Despite its initial promise and grand aspirations, EOS has struggled to maintain its early momentum and realize its full potential. The massive fundraising campaign and the subsequent legal issues appear to have overshadowed the project's tangible achievements, leading to a modest performance in the broader context of the crypto ecosystem.

Thus, while the funds raised can serve as an initial indicator of an ICO's success, it should be considered alongside other indicators for a more comprehensive assessment. In an academic context, researchers often examine the relationship between funds raised and other factors, such as the project's technical innovation, team expertise, and market conditions. By analysing these relationships, academics aim to identify patterns and trends that can inform future ICOs and help investors make more informed decisions.

Community Engagement and Network

Another essential indicator for assessing ICO success is the level of community engagement and the growth of the project's network. A strong and active community can significantly contribute to the long-term success of a project by providing valuable feedback, promoting the project, and driving demand for the token. In addition, a large and engaged user base can enhance the project's network effects, which are critical for the success of many blockchain-based platforms.

The concept of network effects stems from Metcalfe's Law,[2] which posits that the value of a network is proportional to the square of the number of its users. In other words, as the number of users in a network increases, the value of the network grows exponentially. This principle can be applied to blockchain projects, where the value of the platform and its native token often depend on the size and activity of its user base. A larger user base translates into increased utility, adoption, and demand for the token, ultimately driving its value.

Community engagement can be measured through various metrics, including the number of social media followers, forum discussions, and developer contributions on platforms such as GitHub. A project with a high level of followers demonstrates that it has captured the interest of users and investors, which can contribute to its long-term success. Boreiko and Sahdev (2018), Belitski and Boreiko (2022), Campino et al. (2022), among many other studies, have shown its importance for ICO success using various measures of community engagement listed above.

Crowdfunding, a popular method of raising funds for early-stage projects, shares similarities with ICOs in terms of community engagement. Both fundraising methods rely on a broad base of supporters who contribute small amounts of capital in exchange for future rewards or benefits. In the context of crowdfunding, a large community of backers can help to validate a product or idea, create a loyal customer base, and generate word-of-mouth marketing. Similarly, a robust and engaged ICO community can provide valuable feedback, attract new users, and support the project's growth.

One notable example of strong community engagement in an ICO is the Basic Attention Token (BAT) project. BAT, a digital advertising platform, successfully raised $35 million in its 2017 ICO within 30 seconds. The project's success can be partly attributed to its strong community support, which continues to drive its adoption and development. The BAT community actively participates in discussions, contributes to the project's codebase, and promotes the platform to new users.

An interesting, albeit indirect, measure of the BAT project's popularity is found in the usage statistics of the Brave browser. Developed by the same team behind BAT, this browser ingeniously employs BAT tokens to reward its users. Even when juxtaposed with Chrome, Safari, or Opera browsers, the Brave browser holds its ground. As of 2023, Brave commands approximately 1 per cent of the global browser market share, with more than 50 million users turning to it on a monthly basis. A noteworthy statistic reveals that nearly 31 per cent of users between the ages of 25 and 34 prefer the Brave browser to its alternatives.[3] Furthermore, as of May 2023, the BAT token finds itself in the top 100 tokens by market capitalization, according to reports by CoinMarketCap. These factors collectively attest to the project's popularity within the community and the extensive network of participants that it enjoys.

However, it is important to underscore that community engagement, despite its significant influence, is not the sole determinant of success. In some instances, a project might rapidly swing in and out of favour, underscoring that hype, in and of itself, does not necessarily translate to long-term viability for a project. An endeavour must not only deliver on its promises and demonstrate consistent progress, but it must also provide tangible value to its users.

For instance, consider the trajectory of Dogecoin, a cryptocurrency project that garnered widespread attention and a large community owing to its humorous branding and meme-centric marketing approach. Although the project initially experienced a period of rapid growth, it subsequently grappled with maintaining this momentum due to its limited technological innovation and lack of clear use cases. A significant change transpired when Elon Musk expressed his interest in it, although this attention came after Dogecoin had already regained some of its initial popularity. However, a subsequent drop in price might suggest that Dogecoin does not maintain a leading position, especially with the emergence of newer meme coins that have quickly become the centre of attention, such as Shiba Inu and many others. Yet, the extreme volatility of these meme coin prices may not necessarily reflect community support, but they could potentially signal the speculative interest to capitalize on this community intrigue.

Token Listing and Liquidity

Token listing and liquidity are undeniably critical aspects contributing to the eventual success of an ICO. These factors directly influence the capacity of investors to acquire, liquidate, and trade the issued tokens. A successful ICO often culminates in its tokens being listed on reputable cryptocurrency exchanges, amplifying the project's visibility and enhancing the token's liquidity. As a measure of success, token listing takes the second spot in terms of frequency, as illustrated by numerous research studies (Boreiko 2019, Momtaz 2021a, Ante and Meyer 2021).

In the nascent stage of ICOs, project founders often paid considerable sums to get their tokens listed on popular exchanges. They were acutely aware of the pivotal role that liquidity and market accessibility played in the success of their projects. The listing fees charged varied from one exchange to another, with some commanding hundreds of thousands – or even millions – of dollars.[4] Generally, these fees were settled in the form of the project's native tokens or other cryptocurrencies, such as Bitcoin or Ethereum. However, the dynamics of this practice have evolved over time. Today, many exchanges have instituted more stringent listing criteria, emphasizing regulatory compliance, project quality, and community support. This transition has ushered in a more merit-based approach to token listing. Projects must now prove their worth and long-term potential to earn a place on reputable exchanges.

The notion of token listing as a measure of success is not without controversy. On one hand, token listing facilitates investor exits, allowing them to earn substantial returns by subscribing to tokens and selling them. This strategy mirrors that used in IPOs, where offerings often exhibit significant price growth on the first day of trading – a phenomenon known as IPO underpricing. This phenomenon can inflate interest in a project during an ICO, which can subsequently lead to a sudden price collapse after listing.

One example of an ICO that saw a substantial initial price increase followed by a sharp decrease is Augur (REP). Augur is a decentralized prediction market platform built on the Ethereum blockchain. Following its ICO in 2015, Augur's REP token saw a considerable increase in price upon listing. However, in the months and years following its listing, the price of REP has seen significant volatility and overall decline. Another example is Bancor (BNT), a blockchain protocol that enables users to convert different virtual currency tokens directly instead of exchanging them on cryptocurrency markets. After raising about $150 million in an ICO in 2017, Bancor's BNT token experienced a significant surge in price on its first day of trading. However, similar to Augur, the value of BNT has seen considerable volatility since its initial listing and has generally trended downwards in subsequent years.

Nevertheless, the process of listing an ICO project on a cryptocurrency exchange brings along a multitude of benefits. First, it is a gateway to liquidity, making the tokens easier to buy and sell for investors. This ease of trading can draw a larger pool of participants to the project, enhancing its growth trajectory. An ICO listing is not just about liquidity, though. It is also a significant step in increasing a project's visibility and credibility. When a token gets listed on a reputable exchange, it becomes exposed to a wider audience.

One notable example of a successful ICO with robust token listing and liquidity is Chainlink, a decentralized oracle network that managed to raise a relatively small amount, around $30 million, in 2017. The native token of Chainlink, LINK, was subsequently listed on several leading exchanges, including Binance and Coinbase, enhancing its visibility and liquidity substantially. Following this, the project witnessed significant growth and has since emerged as a forerunner in the decentralized oracle arena. As of May 2023, the LINK token holds the 23rd position by market capitalization, and it ranks among the top 20 tokens by average daily trading volume. Furthermore, the project surpasses its competitors on various performance metrics, maintaining its leading position even six years post-ICO.

Investor confidence can also get a significant boost from a token listing. Investors often view a token's presence on a recognized exchange as an assurance that the project has met specific standards and is less likely to be a scam. Moreover, listing on an exchange is also a way for projects to raise additional funds. It serves as a stamp of approval that can aid in future funding rounds, and in some cases, the token can even be used as collateral, or reserve tokens may be sold easily to obtain any quick financing needed.

A lesser-known benefit of an ICO listing is the ability to tap into the exchange's existing community. Exchanges have their own clusters of traders and investors, and a listing opens the door to this community, helping projects build a wider user base. Lastly, the opportunity for global reach cannot be underestimated. When a project is listed on an international exchange, it gains access to markets that might be difficult to penetrate otherwise.

Interestingly, several projects that were deemed successful across multiple dimensions saw their tokens listed only after a significant period post-ICO. SAFTs, or Simple Agreements for Future Tokens, are one such example. It is common for these SAFTs to be successfully completed, but for the associated tokens to only be listed on exchanges after considerable time has passed. Apart from the already discussed SAFT of Filecoin, some other projects followed a similar route. The Blockstack project (stacks.co, USA), for instance, used SAFTs to raise funds and became one of the first projects to receive clearance from the SEC to conduct a token offering in the USA, albeit with some restrictions on who could participate. Their native token, STX, was listed two years later on exchanges such as Binance and KuCoin.

Long-run Performance of ICO

Understanding the long-term success of an ICO requires more than just examining the funds raised or its listing on exchanges. Indeed, these factors can be viewed as mere proxies for success. What truly matters is the long-term performance of the ICO project, akin to how the operating performance (measured by returns on equity (ROE), returns on assets (ROA), or generated operating cash flows), matters in traditional companies. Yet, for ICOs, many of which are at a nascent startup stage, conventional metrics such as these have little relevance. There are no financial reports, no revenues, only a pilot project in many cases. So how do we gauge long-term performance in this context?

Evaluating an ICO's long-run performance is crucial as it sheds light on the project's ability to fulfil its promises, create value for token holders, and adapt to the rapidly evolving landscape of blockchain technology. However, this task is not straightforward due to the unique characteristics of these projects and the often-intangible nature of their deliverables. To tackle this, researchers have developed alternative ways of assessing the success of ICOs in the long run.

One such method is observing the token price's abnormal returns over a longer timeframe, such as six months or even longer. In the short term, following a token's listing, prices may surge due to a variety of factors, even for projects that lack sound fundamentals. However, over the long term, it is challenging to maintain such artificially inflated values. The market is, more often than not, a harsh adjudicator of value, swiftly penalizing those projects that do not deliver real, tangible results. Therefore, examining the abnormal return over an extended period can provide a more accurate picture of an ICO project's genuine success.

One common approach used within the industry to measure the long-term performance of an ICO is to analyse the price appreciation and return on investment (ROI) of its native token. Consistent price appreciation and positive ROI over an extended period may indicate that the project is creating value for its investors and that it harbours potential for future growth. However, it is crucial to consider the broader market context, as factors such as market cycles and overall sentiment can significantly impact token prices.

Many ICO portals provide summary statistics on a vast range of ICO tokens' ROI and other measures. Often, this data presents a picture of exceptional performance, potentially leading one to feel they are missing an opportunity to invest and amass wealth. For instance, the portal Icolistingonline.com show-cases the top ten ICOs with the highest returns, boasting an ROI ranging from 10 000 to 11 million per cent.[5] However, such figures can be very misleading.

Firstly, there is the issue of survivorship bias, with the majority of ICOs rendering their tokens worthless, equating to a negative 100 per cent return. This fact is often overlooked by naïve investors. Secondly, these lucrative returns are one-off events and provide no guarantee that an average ICO investment would yield even a remotely similar return – they are not representative of the norm. The concept of risk also comes into play: extreme returns do not account for risk and volatility. High returns often come hand in hand with high risk, therefore, if one only looks at high returns, they may underestimate the risk associated with these investments. Lastly, market conditions also play a role: extreme returns could be the product of specific market conditions that may not be replicable in the future. These outliers could be a result of a *bubble* or a unique market event.

In our study of the topic, we have obtained data on ICO ROIs from the DropStab.com portal and will briefly discuss it here to provide an overview of overall returns on ICOs. The portal presents ROI data for 1571 ICO tokens as of March 2023. The data shown is not annualized and represents the ROI from the final ICO price, which is somewhat misleading as it does not account for the different time periods used to calculate ROIs.

Various methods can be used to display ROI for an investment. Here, we adhere to the industry convention of calculating ROI as the current price over the ICO price, expressed as a multiple. With this convention, an ROI of 1.0x signifies that the current price of the token is exactly equal to the ICO price, indicating an overall ROI of zero per cent. ROI values less than one suggest a loss on investment, whereas values above one indicate a positive return. For instance, an ROI of 2.0x implies that the total buy-and-hold return from acquiring the token at ICO price and selling it now is 100 per cent.

Figure 7.1 displays the distribution of ICO ROIs across various bins. It is clear from the data that almost half of the sample tokens resulted in a complete loss of investment, with current values below 1 per cent of the ICO price. Another fifth of the ICOs show a loss of half of the total investment, and only 16 per cent of all ICOs demonstrate substantial investment gains (ROI above 2.0x, or a 100 per cent return). Given the inherent risks of investment, this picture is rather bleak. It suggests that ICOs might be a poor investment. Furthermore, this data does not include fraudulent cases where the ROI would clearly be null.

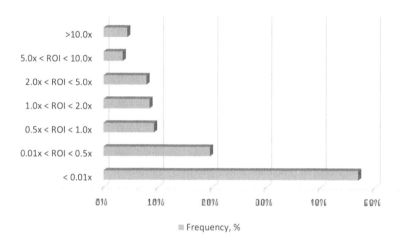

Source: The data comes from 1571 ICOs listed on Dropstab.com ICO portal (accessed: 10 March 2023).

Figure 7.1   Distribution of ICO ROIs

Figure 7.2 provides more detailed information about ICO ROIs. It plots the ROI against the total market capitalization of the token. As expected, there is a clear positive correlation: more successful projects have a higher market capitalization and provide a higher overall return from investing in their ICOs. Given the substantial variability in both market capitalization and ROI data, we use logarithmic scales here to produce a more meaningful picture. Thus, an ICO with a log ROI of 2 and a log market cap of 4, displays an ROI of 7.39x and a market capitalization of $54.6 million.

Aside from a few large and very successful projects (some of which are annotated on the chart), the majority of ICOs (three-quarters) do not yield a positive return. When compared to the Ethereum ROI of 6,136x (equating to a 613 500 per cent total return) or the Binance BNB token ROI of 2,226x (or a 222 500 per cent total return), these figures demonstrate that success stories in ICOs are relatively rare.

Several academic studies have attempted to measure the long-run performance of ICO projects. For instance, Hu et al. (2019) analysed the secondary market returns of 222 cryptocurrencies, finding a strong correlation with Bitcoin performance. In another study, Dittmar and Wu (2018) compared the performance of ICOs with non-ICO cryptocurrencies and discovered that ICOs tended to outperform their counterparts. Furthermore, Momtaz (2021b) investigated the pricing and performance of over 1400 ICOs. The study found

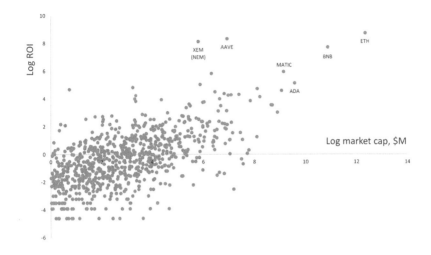

Source: The data comes from 1 571 ICOs listed on Dropstab.com ICO portal (accessed: 10 March 2023).

Figure 7.2   *ICO ROIs vs tokens market capitalization*

that, on average, ICOs are underpriced by 15 per cent, although 40 per cent of ICOs are overpriced. Overall, however, the author found that ICOs significantly underperform in the long run, confirming our visual inspection of the available data.

ICOs AND ENTREPRENEURIAL FINANCE

The advent of ICOs has opened a new avenue in the landscape of entrepreneurial finance, and a dozen research papers have studied this aspect. The general idea is that ICOs, as an alternative channel of fundraising, along with crowdfunding, hold the potential to fully democratize the process of raising funds for blockchain and digital ventures. Researchers have been drawing comparisons between ICOs and traditional early-stage financing options, such as crowdfunding and venture capital, as the ICO market continues to expand (Tonnissen et al. 2020). These comparisons offer insights into the strengths and weaknesses of ICOs as a financing mechanism allowing entrepreneurs, investors, and regulators to make more informed decisions (Fisch et al. 2022).

Schueckes and Gutmann (2021) delve into the economic and behavioural drivers that persuade entrepreneurs to ICOs as a mechanism to fund their startup ventures. In an effort to illuminate the motivating factors behind this decision, the authors engaged in thorough interviews with founders or senior management of startups that had secured funding through ICOs. The analysis unearthed four central themes that seem to significantly influence the decision to pursue ICO funding: the funding dynamics, the building of a community, the role of tokenomics, and personal and ideological motivations. In terms of funding, the unique advantages that ICOs offer, such as rapid access to a global pool of investors, were identified as key driving factors. The ability of ICOs to build and engage a community of supporters and future users was another critical component. The utility of tokens within the ecosystem of the startup, or *tokenomics*, also emerged as a central consideration in the decision to opt for an ICO. Lastly, personal and ideological drivers, particularly the entrepreneur's alignment with the ethos of decentralization and democratization embodied by blockchain technology, played a pivotal role in this choice.

Interestingly, the findings suggest an interplay between the entrepreneur's social identity and the blockchain technology's facilitative attributes in shaping entrepreneurial strategies and financing decisions. The social identity of entrepreneurs, as members of the blockchain community with its unique culture and values, was found to align with and reinforce the choice of ICOs as a funding mechanism. The blockchain technology, in turn, enabled these entrepreneurs to translate their values and visions into practice by providing a new model of raising capital that resonates with their social identity. This study offers valuable insights into the multifaceted reasons behind entrepreneurs' adoption of ICOs as a funding tool and underscores the complex interplay of technological, economic, and sociocultural factors at play.

Together, various streams of entrepreneurial finance research provide a comprehensive understanding of the role of ICOs in this setting. They highlight the transformative potential of ICOs while also drawing attention to the challenges and risks that they pose. This burgeoning area of research continues to evolve as the ICO market matures and as researchers gain a more nuanced understanding of this innovative form of finance.

CONCLUSION

The ICO landscape has been subject to extensive research over the past decade since the first token sale was launched. However, a significant amount of the phenomenon remains unexplored. Given the gradual pace at which academic research progresses, often reliant on substantial data to yield meaningful results, it is anticipated that more studies are forthcoming. These future investigations will benefit from a historical perspective, distancing themselves from the hype surrounding blockchain and ICOs during the peak years of 2018–2019.

Still, as Alshater et al. (2023) pointed out, academic production on ICOs peaked in 2021 and began declining in 2022, possibly indicating diminished interest in the topic. However, whether this decrease is due to a comprehensive understanding of ICO success determinants and long-run performance, or other factors, remains to be seen. Despite the considerable knowledge amassed, certain mysteries persist, and areas remain unexplored.

Pivotal questions linger, such as how ICOs will transcend geographical, ethnic, and gender boundaries to democratize entrepreneurial finance? How can they provide startup financing opportunities irrespective of the entrepreneurs' geographical location, ethnicity, and gender? Further, the role of artificial intelligence (AI) and machine learning (ML) in surmounting moral hazards in ICOs' quality signalling is another area ripe for exploration. The potential impact of regulatory frameworks on accelerating the integration of ICOs into entrepreneurial finance is also worth investigating.

Future research must also address whether ICOs will become integral to pre-angel stage entrepreneurial finance for creative ventures, and which traditional businesses are likely to adopt and benefit from ICO financing. The factors influencing entrepreneurs' choice between ICOs and traditional startup financing options also warrant further study. In the context of cybersecurity, researchers need to explore what factors can alleviate the negative impact of cyber risks. The role of regulation, institutional frameworks, and voluntary disclosure in enhancing ICOs' role in entrepreneurial development and economic growth also demands further attention.

As the ICO landscape evolved and mutated to Security Token Offerings (STOs) and IEOs, addressed later in the book, it will be critical to understand how ICOs and their successors can be shielded from regulatory intervention, what kind of disclosure is required to mitigate fraud risks, and whether tokens will emerge as alternative investment assets for individual and institutional investors.

In conclusion, while significant strides have been made in ICO research, much remains to be discovered. Continued exploration of these and other uncharted areas will provide a more comprehensive understanding of the role and potential of ICOs in entrepreneurial finance. The future of ICO research is promising and will undoubtedly yield insights critical to entrepreneurs, investors, regulators, and academic scholars. However, many agree that one of the most intriguing themes that ICOs have brought about is the matter of widespread frauds with which ICOs have become associated. We look into this in great detail in the next chapter.

NOTES

1   The Social Science Research Network is a repository for preprints devoted to the rapid dissemination of scholarly research in the social sciences, humanities, life sciences, and health sciences, among others.

2   en.wikipedia.org/wiki/Metcalfe%27s_law.
3   Data sourced from bravebat.info and earthweb.com/brave-market-share.
4   www.investopedia.com/news/how-much-does-it-cost-list-ico-token.
5   www .icolistingonline .com/ ico -101/ the -10 -icos -with -the -highest -return -on -investment.

REFERENCES

Alshater, M.M., Joshipura, M., Khoury, E.R., and Nasrallah, N. (2023) 'Initial Coin Offerings: A hybrid empirical review', *Small Business Economics*, 61, pp. 891–908.

Ante, L. and Meyer, A. (2021) 'Cross-listings of blockchain-based tokens issued through Initial Coin Offerings: Do liquidity and specific cryptocurrency exchanges matter?' *Decisions in Economics and Finance*, 44(2), pp. 957–980.

Barsan, I.M. (2017) 'Legal challenges of Initial Coin Offerings (ICO)', *Revue Trimestrielle de Droit Financier*, 3, pp. 54–65.

Delitski, M. and Doroiko, D. (2022) 'Success factors of Initial Coin Offerings', *The Journal of Technology Transfer*, 47, pp. 1690–1706.

Boreiko, D. (2019) *Blockchain-based Financing with Initial Coin Offerings (ICOs): Financial Industry Disruption or Evolution?* Mantova: Universitas Studiorum.

Boreiko, D. and Sahdev, N.K. (2018) 'To ICO or not to ICO – Empirical analysis of Initial Coin Offerings and token sales', SSRN. Available at: https://ssrn.com/abstract =3209180 (accessed: 1 July 2023).

Boreiko, D., Ferrarini, G., and Giudici, P. (2020) 'Blockchain startups and prospectus regulation', *European Business Organization Law Review*, 20(4), pp. 665–694.

Brochado, A. and Troilo, M.N. (2021) 'Initial Coin Offerings: An emergent research area', *Digital Policy, Regulation and Governance*, 23(2), pp. 113–131.

Campino, J., Brochado, A., and Rosa, A. (2022) 'Initial Coin Offerings (ICOs): Why do they succeed?' *Financial Innovation*, 8(17), pp. 1–35.

Dittmar, R.F. and Wu, A. (2018) 'Returns to Initial Coin Offerings: An empirical examination', SSRN. Available at: https://ssrn.com/abstract=3259182 (accessed: 1 July 2023).

Fisch, C., Meoli, M., and Vismara, S. (2022) 'Does blockchain technology democratize entrepreneurial finance? An empirical comparison of ICOs, venture capital, and REITs', *Economics of Innovation and New Technology*, 31(1–2), pp. 70–89.

Griffin, J.M. (2021) 'Were ETH and EOS repeatedly recycled during the EOS Initial Coin Offering?' White Paper. Available at: https://www.scribd.com/document/52 2992453/Eos# (accessed: 1 July 2023).

Gurrea-Martinez, A. and Remolina, N. (2019) 'The law and finance of Initial Coin Offerings'. In C. Brummer (ed.), *Cryptoassets: Legal, Regulatory and Monetary Perspectives*. Oxford: Oxford University Press, pp. 117–156.

Hacker, P. and Thomale, C. (2017) 'Crypto-securities regulation: ICOs, token sales and cryptocurrencies under EU financial law', *European Company and Financial Law Review*, 15(4), pp. 645–696.

Henderson, M.T. and Raskin, M. (2018) 'A regulatory classification of digital assets: Toward an operational Howey test for cryptocurrencies, ICOs, and other digital assets', Coase-Sandor Working Paper Series in Law and Economics, No. 858.

Howell, S.T., Niessner, M., and Yermack, D. (2019) 'Initial Coin Offerings: Financial growth with cryptocurrency token sales', *Review of Financial Studies*, 33, pp. 3925–3974.

Hu, A.S., Parlour, C.A., and Rajan, U. (2019) 'Cryptocurrencies: Stylized facts on a new investible instrument', *Financial Management*, 48(4), pp. 1049–1068.

Kaal, W.A. (2018) 'Initial Coin Offerings: The top 25 jurisdictions and their comparative regulatory responses', *CodeX Stanford Journal of Blockchain Law & Policy*, U of St. Thomas (Minnesota) Legal Studies Research Paper No. 18–07.

Momtaz, P.P. (2021a) 'Initial Coin Offerings, asymmetric information, and loyal CEOs', *Small Business Economics*, 57(2), pp. 975–997.

Momtaz, P.P. (2021b) 'The pricing and performance of cryptocurrency', *The European Journal of Finance*, 27(4–5), pp. 367–380.

Park, J.J. and Park, H.H. (2020) 'Regulation by selective enforcement: The SEC and Initial Coin Offerings', *Washington Journal of Law and Policy*, 99, pp. 98–132.

Schueckes, M. and Gutmann, T. (2021) 'Why do startups pursue Initial Coin Offerings (ICOs)? The role of economic drivers and social identity on funding choice', *Small Business Economics*, 57(2), pp. 1027–1052.

Tonnissen, S., Beinke, J.H., and Teuteberg, F. (2020) 'Understanding token-based ecosystems – A taxonomy of blockchain-based business models of start-ups', *Electronic Markets*, 30(2), pp. 307–323.

Watts, S., Joshi, M., and Singh, S. (2023) 'Initial Coin Offerings: Current trends and future research directions', *Quality and Control*. DOI: 10.1007/s11135–023–01701-z.

Zetzsche, D.A., Buckley, R.P., Arner, D.W., and Foehr, L. (2019) 'The ICO gold rush: It's a scam, it's a bubble, it's a super challenge for regulators', *Harvard International Law Journal*, 60(2), pp. 267–315.

8. Initial Coin Offerings pitfalls: Scams, flops, and security breaches

INTRODUCTION

It is a common yet inaccurate presumption that the term 'Initial Coin Offering' (ICO) is synonymous with *scam* or *fraud*. Indeed, a cursory Google search of 'Initial Coin Offering' yields roughly three million hits; when paired with 'scam' or 'fraud', the results equate to two-thirds of all ICO-related pages, which are at least partially devoted to fraudulent activities surrounding token sales. Contrastingly, a similar search for 'credit card fraud' or 'financial industry fraud' reveals only a third and a fifth of the pages are focused on fraud, respectively.

It is vital to clarify that not all ICOs are scams. ICOs are innovative fundraising mechanisms utilized by startups, especially those in the blockchain and cryptocurrency sectors, aiming to raise capital through issuing their native tokens or coins. Although instances of fraudulent ICOs and scams have occurred, a plethora of legitimate ICO projects have successfully secured funds and delivered on their promises.

Nevertheless, the early days of ICOs were characterized by low entry barriers and limited regulatory oversight. These factors proved a potent lure for unethical individuals who exploited the fervour surrounding cryptocurrencies to defraud investors. Scammers exploited ICOs as a platform for making false promises, inflating the potential of their projects, or simply absconding with the raised funds. This led global regulators to intensify their focus on ICOs, implementing stringent rules and guidelines to safeguard investors and validate the legitimacy of the projects. The cryptocurrency community has also become more prudent when investing in ICOs, highlighting the need for rigorous research and due diligence.

In this chapter, we will scrutinize the contentious claim that *all* ICOs are scams. Initially, we will delve into the risks confronting ICO investors and juxtapose the levels of fraudulent activity with conventional finance – a sector where fraud levels are surprisingly high despite strict regulation, public scrutiny, and its established status. Subsequently, we will examine the issue of ICO scams, provide a classification, and discuss some of the most infamous cases.

This chapter will also address ICO flops and failures that, while not fraudulent per se, resulted in substantial investor losses. Lastly, we will touch upon security breaches and hacks leading to significant losses of ICO funds, affecting both investors and founding teams. Through this comprehensive exploration, we aim to offer a balanced perspective on the controversial subject of ICOs and their association with fraudulent activities.

INVESTMENT RISKS IN THE ICO LANDSCAPE

Investing in ICOs can be highly rewarding but also entails several risks. The ICO setting is characterized by numerous factors that elevate investment risks. First, the lack of consistent regulation and oversight leads to a higher potential for fraudulent or poorly managed ICOs. Second, future legal challenges or regulatory restrictions can introduce unforeseen complications for project functionality and investment viability. Even if the ICO project is successful, investors may face substantial losses if the token's value declines due to market fluctuations. Moreover, tokens issued in an ICO may not be immediately tradable on cryptocurrency exchanges, compelling investors to wait for an extended period before they can liquidate their investments. Furthermore, the trading volume for some tokens may be low, making it challenging for investors to sell their holdings at a fair market price.

Journal articles and social media platforms are replete with warnings and dramatic stories of investors losing their funds due to security breaches, failures of ICO startups, or outright frauds and scams. Indeed, one of the most significant risks in the ICO landscape is the potential for fraudulent schemes. Scammers may craft convincing White papers and websites to lure investors into contributing funds, only to disappear with the collected money without delivering on their promises.

Even if an ICO is not a scam, the project may still fail to achieve its goals or deliver the promised product or service. Startups, especially those in the highly competitive blockchain and cryptocurrency space, often face significant challenges, and many projects do not survive. Moreover, as most ICOs are related to blockchain and cryptocurrency projects, they inherently carry technological risks. These risks can include software bugs, security vulnerabilities, and potential issues with the underlying technology, all of which can adversely impact the project's success and the value of its tokens.

The inherent risks associated with ICO investments were evident to many from the onset. Typically, in such situations, regulators are quick to intervene to protect investors. Historical examples abound in the financial industry to illustrate this point. A notable instance is the introduction of the Securities Act and the establishment of the Securities and Exchange Commission (SEC) in the 1930s, in response to frauds and investor abuses in the American stock market. Another example is the introduction of the Sarbanes-Oxley Act in 2002 following the spectacular collapse of Enron. However, regulating ICOs proved unusually challenging due to the need for coordinated efforts across multiple countries. This was primarily due to the global nature of crypto assets and the fact that token sales were conducted almost entirely outside the traditional financial system.

Consequently, investors in the burgeoning ICO market from 2017–2018 were largely left to fend for themselves in identifying legitimate campaigns and managing the accompanying investment risks. This was met with mere recommendations or warnings from regulators in developed countries, or outright bans on ICO activity in some nations, such as China. Sensing an opportunity, fraudsters flooded the ICO market with various types of scams, exploiting naïve crypto investors. Accordingly, the subsequent sections of this chapter will delve deeper into the possible classification of illicit ICO activities, including frauds, failures, and security breaches.

ICO SCAMS AND FRAUDS

As previously mentioned, one of the most significant risks within the ICO landscape is the potential for fraudulent schemes. Media outlets often highlight the various methods that fraudsters employ to deceive naïve investors under the guise of ICOs. They create convincing White papers and websites to attract contributions, only to disappear with the funds without fulfilling their promises. Whether through Ponzi schemes, where initial investors are paid high returns from later investors' contributions, outright scams where criminals fabricate a legitimate project, or traditional scam schemes using the ICO disguise to entice the greedy, the result is usually the same: disillusioned investors and claims that all blockchain, cryptocurrency, and ICO initiatives are nothing but scams.

Numerous media articles echo these concerns. For instance, Grobys et al. (2022) report that 56.8 per cent of ICOs were involved in scams, accounting for 65.8 per cent of the relevant market capitalization, or an estimated $15.38 billion. Similarly, Sapkota et al. (2020) suggested that half of all ICOs were pure scams. However, more rigorous studies, while acknowledging that some ICOs are indeed scams, refrain from making such sweeping assertions. Hornuf et al. (2022) conducted an extensive investigation of fraudulent ICOs and found that they represented only a fraction – less than 20 per cent – of all ICOs under study. Our hand-collected data on ICOs from 2014 to the end of 2017 aligns with these findings, showing that scam ICOs do not constitute the majority of token sales. Even though the number of scams is significant, most were easily identifiable as frauds – exhibiting numerous red flags – and failed to raise significant funds before vanishing.

ICOs vs. Common Financial Industry Frauds

Even though professional and sound studies of ICO frauds never confirmed the claims that ICOs showed an extreme level of scams, mainstream media was filled with scary stories about crypto investing, even labelling Bitcoin an elaborate scam, comparing it to the tulip bubble in Holland in the past. Strangely, while decrying each ICO scheme that deceived investors, even when such fraud had very little to do with the crypto universe and token sales, the media turned a blind eye to the continuous crime and loss of investors' funds in various sectors of the financial industry.

Take, for example, credit card fraud, a form of identity theft that involves unauthorized use of another person's card information to make purchases or access funds. This has been, and still is, a significant and wide-ranging issue with severe implications for individuals, businesses, and the broader economy. Credit card fraud can occur in various ways, including card theft, phishing, skimming, and data breaches. The statistics are quite sad. In a well-established, heavily regulated industry, with elaborate investor protection and maximum cybersecurity, 65 per cent of US credit card holders in 2022 have been fraud victims at some point in their lives.[1]

The level of fraud remains resilient and consistently high, despite all regulatory efforts and investments in customer protection. According to the Nilson Report, which specializes in the international payment card sector, global losses due to payment card fraud exceeded $32 billion in 2021.[2] This is a striking figure that illustrates the scope of the problem, emphasizing that fraud is not a unique issue to the ICO landscape, but a systemic risk present in all facets of the financial industry. The US bore a significant portion of this loss, nearly $12 billion, representing a surge of 14 per cent in global fraud losses compared to the previous year. More alarmingly, the industry anticipates sustained substantial losses due to fraud in the coming decade. The projected cumulative loss worldwide is estimated to reach a staggering $397 billion, with the US expected to account for a sizable $165 billion of that total.

Frauds are equally widespread in the conventional investment industry, with some notable cases truly staggering in their scope. The scale of these spectacular failures and the number of investors involved is mind-boggling. These massive frauds run for years undetected, stripping investors of vast sums of money, rendering ICO frauds pale and insignificant in comparison. Table 8.1 lists the most infamous investment scams and provides a brief description of each.

Table 8.1   *Ten notorious investments frauds in the last 25 years*

No.	Fraudster	Year	Type	Est. losses	Description
1	Waste Management	1997	Falsified results	$6b	A massive financial fraud with systematically falsified and misreported financial statements to meet predetermined earnings targets.
2	Bre-X Minerals	1997	Falsified results	$3b	Falsification of sample cores made a worthless mine in Indonesia appear to have extensive gold deposits, leading to a market capitalization of CAD$6 billion for Bre-X, before the fraud was exposed and the company's stock became worthless
3	Stratton Oakmont	1998	Pump-and-dump	$0.2b	notorious 'pump-and-dump' scheme in the 1990s, artificially inflating the prices of owned stocks through misleading statements, then selling them off at these artificially high prices for immense profits.
4	Enron	2001	Falsified results	$74b	Use of accounting loopholes and special purpose entities to hide debt and inflate profits, giving a false impression of financial health, which eventually led to its bankruptcy.
5	Qwest Communications International	2002	Falsified results / insider trading	$3b	A massive accounting scandal between 1999 and 2002, where it fraudulently reported over $3 billion in revenue, leading to inflated stock prices.
6	WorldCom	2002	Falsified results	$11b	One of the largest accounting frauds in history in which the company's assets were falsely inflated by approximately $11 billion, leading to its bankruptcy in 2002 and significant losses for investors.
7	Bayou Hedge Fund Group	2005	Ponzi scheme	$0.4b	A US Ponzi scheme that defrauded investors by fabricating the fund's performance to attract new investments, which were then used to pay earlier investors.
8	Bernie Madoff	2008	Ponzi scheme	$65b	Largest Ponzi scheme in history, defrauding investors of billions of dollars by promising consistently high returns and using new investors' money to pay old investors, creating the illusion of genuine profits.

No.	Fraudster	Year	Type	Est. losses	Description
9	Wirecard	2022	Falsified results	$32b	The German fintech company admitted that €1.9 billion (about $2.1 billion) listed in their accounts likely did not exist, following which it filed for insolvency.
10	FTX	2022	Misuse of funds	$8b	A Bahamas-based cryptocurrency exchange that misused investor funds from FTX for Alameda Research and personal expenses, including beach house purchases.

Note: This data is derived from open sources and describes the most notorious cases of fraudulent activities in the investment industry.

In recent years, one of the most infamous Ponzi schemes in the investment world was orchestrated by Bernie Madoff. Convicted in 2009, Madoff ran the largest Ponzi scheme in history. His investment firm, Bernard L. Madoff Investment Securities LLC, defrauded thousands of investors out of billions of dollars. He accomplished this by using the funds of new investors to pay returns to existing clients, creating the illusion of a profitable business. Madoff's Ponzi scheme spanned decades, and its ultimate collapse profoundly impacted the financial industry and the lives of those who lost their investments. Interestingly, while this debacle caused significant concern, regulators did not consider banning investment firms outright. In contrast, such drastic measures were seriously considered for ICOs in many countries.

Types of ICO Scams

While it is difficult to provide exact numbers or relative frequencies of ICO scams due to the rapidly evolving landscape and limited data, we can classify common types of ICO scams into several large groups. These are exit frauds that include fake (or clone) ICOs, pump-and-dump schemes, Ponzi schemes, and to some extent, market manipulation activities can also be included.

Exit scams are a significant risk associated with ICOs. In an exit scam, the organizers set up an ICO for a new cryptocurrency, complete with an attractive website, a detailed White paper, and often ambitious promises of the revolutionary technology their project will offer. As a less intricate alternative, the scammers may clone the information from the legitimate ICO or fake it completely from the start. The idea is to entice as many investors as possible with the promise of high returns. Once the funding round begins, investors buy the new cryptocurrency, usually with well-established cryptocurrencies like Bitcoin or Ethereum. The organizers might generate considerable hype around the ICO to attract a significant number of investors.

However, once the fraudsters have gathered enough money, they abruptly abandon the project: the website is taken down, social media accounts are deleted, and any attempts at communication are ignored. The tokens promised to the investors may never come into existence, or, if they do, they typically hold no real value and are not listed on any exchange. As a result, the investors are left at a significant loss. It must be said that it is the anonymous nature of cryptocurrency transactions and the subsequent difficulties in tracing funds in the crypto universe, not the nature of ICOs as a fundraising mechanism, that attracted fraudsters to ICOs in a seemingly disproportionate size.

Despite some instances of exit scams being prosecuted, the process of legal redress can be challenging due to several factors. First, cryptocurrency fraudsters often use a variety of techniques to conceal their identities and stolen funds. They might use privacy-focused cryptocurrencies like Monero or Zcash, which are designed to obscure the identities of transaction participants, making tracking funds extremely difficult. Second, they may also use services known as *mixers* or *tumblers*, which intermingle potentially identifiable or tainted cryptocurrency funds with others, further obscuring the origins of the funds. Third, another method used to hide stolen funds involves moving the funds through numerous addresses. This technique, often referred to as *chain-hopping* or *crypto laundering*, can make the transaction trail incredibly complex and hard to follow. Additionally, fraudsters may use *over-the-counter* (OTC) brokers, which can provide further anonymity as these brokers do not tend to implement strict Know Your Customer (KYC) procedures.

Finally, fraudsters might also use cryptocurrency to fiat money exchanges, especially those with lax regulations, to convert their stolen assets into traditional currency, which can then be withdrawn and used more freely. Despite these techniques, the advent of advanced blockchain analysis tools has made tracking such activities increasingly possible, and regulatory entities worldwide are tightening their procedures to prevent such fraudulent practices.

Ponzi schemes, in turn, involve the promise of high returns on investment, where early investors are paid using the funds of new investors. The scheme eventually collapses when there are not enough new investors to pay the existing ones. As it was shown in the previous section, Ponzi schemes are not exclusive to ICOs, however, in the context of ICOs, here is how a Ponzi scheme would usually work:

1. A new cryptocurrency is created, and its ICO is launched with significant marketing hype, promising high returns.
2. Early investors in the ICO receive returns, not from any actual profit earned by the organization, but from the contributions made by new participants. This can lead to positive testimonials and create a sense of legitimacy around the ICO.

3. As long as new investors continue to invest in the ICO, the scheme can keep running. The high returns that are promised to, and initially paid out to, the early investors are usually funded by the money from new investors.
4. However, when the inflow of new investors slows down (or stops), the scheme collapses. The organizers cannot pay the promised returns to older investors as they are out of money, and they often disappear with whatever is left of the investment capital.

The ICO environment has been a fertile ground for Ponzi schemes due to a combination of factors, including the global nature of the audience, lack of regulation, investor enthusiasm for blockchain technology, and the potential for high returns. Later on, we will discuss some spectacular cases of Ponzi schemes that robbed ICO investors of millions of dollars. Nonetheless, these pale in comparison to the Ponzi schemes in the conventional investment industry, as shown in the previous section.

Pump-and-dump schemes in ICOs involve artificially inflating the price of a token through coordinated buying and spreading false or misleading information about the project by the founders. Once the price reaches a high point, the scammers sell their tokens, causing the price to plummet and leaving investors with substantial losses. While not unique to cryptocurrencies, pump-and-dump schemes have found a fertile ground in this arena due to its relatively unregulated nature and the ease with which information (and misinformation) can spread among investors.

Such a scheme works as follows: in an ICO, a company or individual introduces a new cryptocurrency to the market. Investors buy these tokens during the ICO phase in the hope that the coin will gain popularity and increase in value after the official launch, as has often happened with many ICO tokens. A pump-and-dump scheme can occur in an ICO when the creators or insiders artificially inflate the value or promise of the project to entice investors. They *pump* the ICO by spreading hype and excitement about the project, often using misleading or exaggerated claims about the project's potential.

Once the ICO has concluded and the creators have sold a significant amount of tokens to the public, they may *dump* their own tokens on the market, leading to a drastic drop in price. This is often facilitated by the lack of regulation and transparency in the crypto space. After the dump, the creators walk away with the money raised during the ICO, leaving investors with worthless (or near-worthless) tokens. This kind of activity is illegal in many jurisdictions due to its fraudulent nature, but the global and somewhat anonymous nature of cryptocurrency transactions can make it difficult to track and prosecute the perpetrators. Moreover, with crypto tokens it is very hard to identify the correct value of the token, so it might be difficult to prove that the founders indeed engaged in pump-and-dump activities rather than merely miscalculating the tokens' worth.

Apart from these categories of scam ICOs, other schemes exist, for example bounty scams and crypto market manipulation. In bounty scams, ICO projects offer bounties or rewards for promotional activities such as sharing posts on social media, translating materials, or writing blog articles. However, after the contributors have completed the tasks, the scammers refuse to pay the promised rewards. Given the absence of any contractual relationship between the parties, enforcing the bounty agreement is often a futile task.

Crypto market manipulation, in turn, envisages activities on the part of the founders or connected entities conducted on the open market to inflate token price. Although there is no direct evidence of such activities, it is believed that these methods were used in some ICOs that were conducted over an extended period of time, where good market performance is vital to continue attracting new ICO investors.

For example, the paper by Griffin (2021) raises concerns about possible manipulation during the EOS one-year-long ICO, conducted by Block.one between 2017 and 2018. The paper alleges that EOS tokens were wash-traded on the Binance and Bitfinex cryptocurrency exchanges, a process where the same entity acts as the buyer and seller for the same asset to artificially boost volume or manipulate prices. This could have given an illusion of high demand, pushing up the token's price, and potentially attracting more investors to the ICO. Although Block.one itself is not accused of wrongdoing, the research identifies 21 accounts that may have recycled EOS tokens during the ICO. Funds linked to these accounts equate to 1.2 million Ether, or approximately $815 million at the time.

Red Flags and Warning Signs

With so many ICO offerings turning out to be scams that ran away with investors' money, and increased media coverage tarnishing the overall image of ICOs as fraudulent, it became apparent that there was a pressing need to identify these frauds to avoid investing in them. Regulators were not much help as they merely issued general warnings about the high risks of investing in ICOs. ICO portals were not eager to search for and list fraudulent ICOs, as nobody was willing to pay for such services. This left the investor community to its own devices.

Blockchain enthusiasts, bloggers, and industry experts soon began to notice that there were common features present in the majority of fraudulent token sales. These warning signs were termed *red flags*, and the community actively started to study ICOs to hunt for signs of wrongdoing. Among the most obvious indicators of a potentially risky or fraudulent ICO were the following factors.

Inadequate or vague White paper
The White paper is an essential document outlining the project's details, objectives, and technical aspects. A poorly written, unclear, or overly generic White paper can be a sign that the project is not well thought out, or that it lacks substance. If the White paper does not convey a clear and detailed roadmap, outlining the various development stages and timelines, and if it provides a very blurred vision of its future plans, it definitely is a clear warning sign. Moreover, with the advent of new technologies, it has become easier to spot plagiarism when fraudsters simply copy parts of legitimate ICO White papers. As a result, a thoughtful analysis of a project's White paper has become a must for any careful ICO investor.

Recently, a paper by Meoli and Vismara (2022) employed machine learning (ML) techniques to analyse ICOs. The researchers applied this novel methodology to a sample of 383 ICOs launched between August 2014 and December 2019. The results showed a significant improvement in forecast accuracy of ICO success, with an increase from 54 per cent using conventional Logit models, to 73 per cent when using ML techniques. The study introduced an innovative algorithm-based approach, which enables individual investors to analyse the content of ICO White papers. A notable finding of the research is that the structure of ICO White papers, which has often been overlooked in past studies, plays a crucial role in determining the success of ICOs. It is highly likely that employing such algorithms to identify fraudulent ICOs will also be quite effective.

Unrealistic promises and guarantees
Promises of guaranteed high returns are one of the most prominent red flags indicating potential investment fraud. This is particularly true in the case of ICOs, due to their volatile nature and the considerable risks associated with investing in them. When a project or investment opportunity guarantees high returns, it often means that the promoters are trying to lure unsuspecting investors with the promise of quick and easy profits. In reality, investments carry inherent risks and returns are never guaranteed. The higher the promised returns, the higher the risk generally is.

Legitimate projects and investment opportunities understand this fact and are typically transparent about the risks involved. They avoid making overly optimistic promises or guarantees, and instead provide realistic expectations based on sound business models, technology, market research, and analysis. Ponzi schemes or exit frauds, on the other hand, rely on these unrealistic promises and guarantees as a means to entice and trap unsuspecting investors. These types of fraud heavily depend on a constant influx of new investments to deliver returns to earlier investors, creating a cycle of deceit. This pattern starkly contrasts with legitimate projects, which generate returns through actual business activities and growth.

Anonymous, inexperienced, or fake team

The team behind an ICO project is indeed a crucial aspect to consider when determining its credibility. Legitimate projects often have a transparent and experienced team steering the venture. If the team members remain anonymous, lack relevant experience, or do not have verifiable qualifications, it could indeed be a potential warning sign. While it is true that in the early days of ICOs, the teams were often anonymous or known only by their online pseudonyms, and many of these projects were indeed legitimate and even successful, the ICO market matured and investors became more discerning. Human capital, the people and talent behind the project, emerged as a critical factor that signalled the project's potential for success.

As investors started to look beyond just the White paper and technical aspects of the project, the team's experience, credibility, and reputation became a significant consideration. A strong team with a proven track record in relevant fields lent credibility to the project and instilled confidence in potential investors. Recognizing this shift, fraudsters quickly adapted. The anonymity, which initially was commonplace and acceptable, started becoming associated with fraudulent activities. To bypass this suspicion and continue attracting investments, fraudsters began to falsify team identities. They created fake biographies and professional profiles, fabricated social media accounts with minimal activity, and even used stolen or stock photos from the internet to represent team members.

Lack of a working product or prototype

ICO projects with a working product or prototype are generally more trustworthy than those without one. Be cautious of projects that rely solely on concepts and ideas without any tangible evidence of progress. A legitimate ICO project should have an open-source code repository, such as GitHub, where investors and developers can review the project's progress. A lack of a visible code repository may indicate that the project is not actively being developed, or that it has something to hide. Of course, not every open-source project necessarily has to be a fraudulent one, as attracting professional investors might require proprietary codes or algorithms to be able to commercialize it. Nevertheless, coupled with other red flags, the absence of a working product or open-source code certifying the project's validity and progress, is a clear sign of potential fraud.

Limited or no community engagement

A strong and active community is a positive sign for ICO projects. Community engagement is a crucial factor in the success and credibility of an ICO project. In the decentralized world of blockchain and cryptocurrency, a robust and active community often serves as the backbone of a project. It not only provides valuable support, but also fosters an environment of trust, transparency, and collaborative effort.

A strong community typically manifests itself in various forms: active social media channels, lively discussions on online forums such as Reddit or Bitcointalk, regular updates from the project team, ongoing developer activity, and a responsive customer or investor support. These all contribute to building a vibrant ecosystem around the project. Active community engagement signifies that there is an interest and belief in the project. It indicates that people are not only willing to invest their money but also their time and energy. This is particularly important in the blockchain world, where projects are often open-source and depend on their community for development, testing, troubleshooting, and promoting the project.

If an ICO project has limited or no presence on social media, lacks a dedicated forum for discussions, or shows no signs of a vibrant and engaged community, it might be a red flag for potential fraud. Fraudulent projects might not invest time and effort into building a community or engaging with users because their primary goal is to raise funds quickly and then disappear. However, this is not necessarily the case, as a lack of community engagement could also suggest that the project has failed to garner interest or trust and is simply unsuccessful.

Unverified claims and partnerships

Claims of partnerships, endorsements, or affiliations with well-known entities are often used by ICO projects to increase their credibility and attract investors. While these connections can indeed be a positive sign if they are genuine, they can also be exploited by unscrupulous actors as a means to lend an undeserved air of legitimacy to their projects. Fraudulent ICO projects often make grandiose and unverified claims to create an illusion of being well-connected within the industry. They might falsely claim to be partnering with well-known companies, to be endorsed by prominent industry figures, or to be affiliated with reputable institutions. These deceptive tactics can make the project seem more reputable and successful than it really is, thereby luring unsuspecting investors.

Unfortunately, due to the decentralized nature of the cryptocurrency market and the lack of stringent regulatory oversight, it can be relatively easy for fraudsters to make such false claims with impunity. Hence, potential investors should be extremely wary of any ICO project that makes bold claims about partnerships, endorsements, or affiliations. It is important to independently verify any such claims before investing. This can include reaching out directly to the claimed partners, checking for official announcements from the partners themselves, or seeking confirmation from third-party sources. Any suspicious fact here is definitely a warning sign of potential fraud.

Identification of ICO Scams

The issue of scam ICOs very much concerned the blockchain industry from the start. In the absence of regulation or clearly defined rules, various solutions were tried from the supply side to instil trust into ICOs and limit the quantity and damage done by fraudsters. For example, Vitalik Buterin, Ethereum's co-founder, advocated the wider use of smart contracts in token sales. In essence, his idea was that instead of individuals placing unwavering trust in a particular project, they would secure their tokens within a smart contract. These funds would then be directed into a Decentralized Finance (DeFi) solution that generates a specified interest rate, which in turn, funds the project's future activities.

This concept is particularly intriguing as it minimizes the risk for investors. With their funds securely locked in a smart contract, it eliminates the possibility of the project's team vanishing unexpectedly, as Buterin metaphorically suggests, 'to Indonesia or something'.[3] This mechanism ensures a level of safety and security for investors' funds that was not available in the earlier stages of ICOs. Indeed, some ICOs in 2017–2019 extensively used smart contracts to run token sales, where the contributed funds were made available to the founders only after the investors had received their tokens, or some milestones were reached. Still, this did not become standard practice and the issue of identifying false campaigns remained.

As mentioned above, it was left to ICO investors to identify fraudulent ICOs themselves. Many bloggers and industry experts published various articles that attempted to educate investors on how to be vigilant. They listed the various red flags discussed above and how to spot them.[4] Some blockchain or ICO portals set up databases to be filled by the community that listed dead, abandoned, or fraudulent projects.[5] Even dedicated websites such as scam-alert. io were created that listed various types of crypto-scams, among them, ICO frauds.

Individuals and blockchain enthusiasts also participated in fraud identification. For example, Bitcointalk.org portal set up a special board dedicated to scam accusations, where users could discuss, alert, and get information about potential frauds. Some users there attempted to collect all fraud alerts and maintain curated lists of identified scams that were quite extensive. For example, a thread 'SCAMS of our BitcoinTalk' meticulously listed all identified scams advertised on the portal with clear proof and red flags spotted.[6] Many more threads did a similar service for the blockchain community.

The SEC and other regulators have indeed taken several measures to educate investors about the potential risks associated with ICOs. They have employed a multifaceted approach, which includes providing traditional educational resources, issuing public warnings, creating a mock ICO to illustrate the potential for fraud, and even prosecuting some ICO founders for fraud or non-compliance with existing securities regulations.

One of the key ways the SEC has educated investors about ICO risks is through its Office of Investor Education and Advocacy (OIEA – investor.gov). The OIEA regularly publishes investor alerts and bulletins designed to provide the public with information about the risks associated with investing in certain asset classes, including ICOs. In these publications, the SEC highlights the many potential risks associated with ICOs. They warn investors about the lack of regulatory oversight, the potential for fraud, the high degree of volatility in the cryptocurrency market, and the possibility of losing all invested capital.

Another significant step that the SEC took was the launch of a mock ICO, called *HoweyCoins*, designed to educate investors and show how easily ICO scams can appear legitimate.[7] The HoweyCoins website was intentionally designed to have many of the hallmarks of fraudulent ICOs, including promises of guaranteed returns and a countdown clock to create a sense of urgency. However, when users attempted to purchase the fictitious 'HoweyCoins', they were redirected to an SEC webpage educating them about ICO scams.

Notwithstanding all the efforts of regulators, industry experts, and blockchain communities, ICO scams proliferated and managed to steal quite a substantial amount of money from millions of investors worldwide. In the next section we turn to the analysis of the most notorious ICO scams of all time.

Case Studies: Notorious ICO Scams

Even though the media is brimming with harrowing stories of billions of dollars stolen from ICO investors, leading some to claim that all cryptocurrencies, including Bitcoin, are outright scams,[8] creating a definitive list of ICO scams presents challenges. The data is inconsistent, estimates of investors' losses are imprecise, and various sources often conflate all crypto-related frauds, failing to distinguish investment scams from ICO-related ones.

Take, for example, the 2017 ICO of COSS that utilized investors' funds to establish a comprehensive Singapore-based platform offering exchange services, a marketplace, e-wallet services, and a variety of other crypto-related services. The platform operated for three years before abruptly locking all users' funds without warning, under the pretence of migrating to a new platform, and subsequently disappeared from the radar. This is undeniably a crypto-scam that initially financed itself through an ICO. However, it does not fit the typical mould of a fraud that leverages the ICO mechanism to steal investors' money.

Consider another example: the Petro cryptocurrency, launched by the Venezuelan government in 2017. It reportedly raised $735 million on the first day of the ICO alone, with President Nicolas Maduro claiming the total had exceeded $5 billion by March 2018. However, Venezuelan Congress declared the Petro illegal, arguing that borrowing against the country's oil reserves was unconstitutional. Furthermore, the US government banned its citizens from trading in Petro due to concerns about potentially aiding a repressive regime. Some sources have labelled it a pure scam, but we cannot include it in our list. It significantly deviates from typical cases and could be considered an outlier, if not an entirely different category to a conventional ICO.

As a result, we have spent considerable time identifying the top ten biggest pure ICO-related frauds of all time that (see Table 8.2). Compared with the investments frauds, these are, except for the top three, relatively small by industry standards and rather short-lived schemes that involve either a Ponzi pyramid scheme or an exit scam. The scams are not limited to one country and very often represent international elaborated schemes that operated across continents and defrauded thousands of investors.

Table 8.2   Top ten ICO frauds

No.	Fraudster	Year	Country	Type of fraud	Est. losses	Description
1	OneCoin	2017	Bulgaria	Ponzi scheme	$4b	Massive global cryptocurrency Ponzi scheme that defrauded investors of billions of dollars by falsely promising high returns and perpetuating the illusion of a legitimate cryptocurrency platform.
2	Bitconnect	2021	USA	Ponzi scheme	$2.4–4b	Lending and exchange crypto platform that would yield up to 40 per cent returns per month.
3	Pincoin and Ifan	2018	Vietnam	Ponzi scheme	$660–870m	Promised investors up to 40 per cent in monthly profits and issued cash withdrawals in the form of their own token, iFan.
4	ACChain	2017	China	Exit scam	$80m	Platform that would tokenize real-world assets.

No.	Fraudster	Year	Country	Type of fraud	Est. losses	Description
5	Bitcoiin	2018	USA	Ponzi scheme	$75m	Project promised substantial returns to investors, promoted by the actor Steven Seagal.
6	Centra Tech	2017	USA	Exit scam	$32m	Debit card project promoted by boxer Floyd Mayweather and music producer DJ Khaled.
7	Plexcoin	2017	Canada	Ponzi scheme	$15m	The founders of the project promised investors over 1300 per cent return on investment per month.
8	Opair and Ebitz	2016	Unknown	Exit scam	$2.9m	Debit card project based on XPO coin. The developer, only known as Wasserman, was anonymous.
9	Pure-Bit	2018	South Korea	Exit scam	$2.8m	Cryptocurrency exchange project.
10	Benebit	2017	Unknown	Exit scam	$2.7m	System for keeping track of customer rewards points, discounts, promotions, and other loyalty program rewards.

Notes: Definitions of the types of fraud are discussed in the previous sections of the chapter. Data in this table comes from public internet sources deemed reliable, however, accuracy cannot be fully guaranteed.

Let us look at the famous OneCoin fraud that is claimed to have pulled up to $4 billion from 2014 to 2016, relying on false promises and a multi-level marketing (MLM) scheme, where earlier users were paid to recruit new ones. However, OneCoin's claims were entirely false; the cryptocurrency did not have a real blockchain, its price was artificially controlled, and the profits paid out were merely the money invested by newer members. As authorities began to investigate in 2017, Ignatova, one of the founders, disappeared and remains at large. In the aftermath, several key figures involved with OneCoin have been arrested and charged, and the hunt for Ignatova, dubbed *Cryptoqueen*, continues.

The OneCoin scam indeed serves as a stark warning about the potential dangers of investing in the cryptocurrency space. However, upon closer inspection, this case does not represent a conventional ICO from that period. OneCoin was not a true blockchain, but merely a façade and a catchy name designed to parasitize on the crypto hype of the time. Investors mostly contrib-uted fiat money, and overall, the operations were highly inscrutable and suspicious. Yet, it did tarnish the image of token sales in many countries and likely marked a turning point when public opinion began to label all ICOs as frauds.

A couple of similar schemes were run in other countries. BitConnect in the USA and Pincoin in Vietnam rank as the second- and third-largest ICO frauds, respectively. These top three ICOs share striking similarities in their operational dynamics. Each of them enticed investors with the promise of unusually high, guaranteed returns. For instance, BitConnect pledged returns of up to 40 per cent per month, while OneCoin and Pincoin promised substantial value growth and profits. Moreover, all three schemes used a Ponzi or pyramid structure, where older investors were paid with funds from new investors, creating a cycle of dependency. In terms of the authenticity of their so-called cryptocurrencies, both OneCoin and Pincoin did not operate on a genuine blockchain. Similarly, BitConnect's volatility software was never explained transparently nor verifiably.

Apart from these three fraud cases, the remaining entries in the top scam league are significantly smaller in size. ACChain, a Chinese exit scam, raised and absconded with *only* $80 million in 2017, before Chinese authorities banned all national ICOs altogether. A similar scheme in the US, Centra Tech, raised $32 million before it was shut down by regulators. Another US-based ICO Ponzi scheme, Bitcoiin, got away with $75 million. The three smallest ICOs from the top ten are all exit scams, each having stolen under $3 million. Indeed, as many researchers have acknowledged, the distribution of scam ICO sizes is heavily skewed to the right – the vast majority of frauds fortunately involve small sums of money. Moreover, their numbers are relatively small compared to the widespread belief cultivated by the media.

SECURITY BREACHES IN ICOs

As we have seen in the previous section, ICO investors faced substantial risks of losing their contribution due to the high number of scam schemes that proliferated during the peak times of ICO activity. Moreover, even when investors participated in a legitimate token sale, the risks were still high. The popularity of ICOs made them a prime target for cybercriminals, leading to numerous security breaches. This section examines common security vulnerabilities, the consequences of these breaches, and notable case studies of major ICO security incidents.

Common Security Vulnerabilities

Phishing attacks have consistently posed a significant risk in the realm of ICOs, presenting substantial dangers to potential investors. In a typical scenario, scammers imitate legitimate ICO projects by disseminating meticulously crafted emails or messages to potential investors. The content of these messages is usually designed to induce recipients into transferring funds to the scammer's cryptocurrency address rather than to the project's official wallet. This fraudulent tactic preys upon both the intricacies of the blockchain system and the frequently less-than-robust cybersecurity measures employed by many ICO projects.

Indeed, cryptocurrency addresses, including Bitcoin and Ethereum, are essentially alphanumeric sequences. They do not inherently possess identifying information linking them to a particular individual or entity. As a result, a user might inadvertently transfer funds to a hacker's address, effectively resulting in a loss. In the context of ICOs, this type of phishing has occurred quite frequently, largely due to a combination of factors. One factor is the often-inadequate understanding and implementation of cybersecurity measures by ICO project founders. In the nascent, fast-paced world of blockchain technology and ICOs, there can be a misguided rush to launch a project without adequately considering or comprehending the array of cyber risks. The absence of proper cybersecurity frameworks and measures leaves these projects, and subsequently their investors, vulnerable to attacks.

Additionally, many people psychologically do not treat cryptocurrencies as real money. This mindset may stem from the digital, somewhat abstract nature of cryptocurrencies, making individuals more likely to act carelessly when transacting with these assets. The sense of urgency created during an ICO can exacerbate this tendency, causing potential investors to transfer funds without thoroughly verifying the legitimacy of the destination address.

As a more general alternative, hacking of ICO websites and social media channels also represents a significant vulnerability. These attacks, instead of directly targeting individual investors, are more pervasive, aimed at affecting a larger group of people by manipulating the source of communication and information about the ICO. Hackers often exploit weaknesses in the website security to gain unauthorized access. Once inside, they might replace the authentic wallet address for contributions with their own, effectively redirecting all incoming funds. This method is particularly sinister as it targets not a single investor but all those who visit the website and decide to contribute to the project. As the wallet address shown on the website is considered the official one, potential investors usually have no reason to doubt its authenticity.

The same can be said for social media channels. ICOs often use platforms such as X (formerly known as Twitter), Facebook, or Telegram to communicate with their potential and current investors. Hackers might gain control of these accounts and send out misleading messages, either providing a fraudulent wallet address or posting false information to manipulate the token price.

Smart contract vulnerabilities have also been a common issue, particularly in the early stages of broader smart contract usage in ICO campaigns.

Smart contracts are essentially self-executing contracts with the terms of the agreement directly written into lines of code. However, they are not devoid of risk. Flaws in the code can lead to unintended consequences such as funds being locked, stolen, or exploited by hackers. The coding language Solidity, designed for Ethereum smart contracts, while relatively straightforward and similar to other programming languages, still necessitates professional expertise. Notwithstanding its relative simplicity, the creation of secure and efficient smart contracts in Solidity requires an understanding of both the specifics of the language itself and the underlying blockchain infrastructure.

Unfortunately, many project founders overlooked this crucial aspect. Opting for cheaper alternatives in smart contract development, they were not entirely aware of how devastating a coding mistake could be once identified by malicious hackers. This cost-cutting decision often led to security breaches and consequent loss of funds. It is important to note that once the funds are stolen due to a smart contract breach, there is often no straightforward way to recover them.

Following several high-profile cases of funds being lost due to smart contract exploits and hacks, ICO founders began to recognize the importance of creating secure smart contracts for raising funds. They also realized the value of engaging respected audit firms to review these contracts for vulnerabilities and mistakes. A number of firms have emerged as leaders in this field. One notable example is OpenZeppelin (openzeppelin.com), a technology company that provides security audits for smart contracts. OpenZeppelin's audits are well-regarded in the industry and are used by many ICOs to ensure their smart contracts are secure.

In addition to OpenZeppelin, there are several other notable firms providing similar services such as Quantstamp, ConsenSys Diligence, and Hashlock. These firms, among others, play a critical role in enhancing the security landscape of ICOs. By conducting thorough audits and assessments, they help to identify and fix vulnerabilities in smart contracts, reducing the risk of costly exploits and hacks.

Alongside phishing and website hacking, another category of security breaches commonly associated with ICOs involves Distributed Denial of Service (DDoS) attacks, wallet vulnerabilities, and various other malicious exploits. DDoS attacks, specifically, pose a significant threat to ICOs. In these types of attacks, hackers overwhelm a network by flooding it with traffic, rendering the service unavailable. This can be particularly harmful during a token sale event, where any downtime can lead to lost potential funds and erode investor trust. Concurrently with phishing attacks, DDoS can create a chaotic environment, in which investors are more prone to fall victim to misinformation or fraud.

Wallet vulnerabilities constitute another area of concern. The private keys of a cryptocurrency wallet, which allow the owner to access and manage their funds, must be kept secure. Any lapse in this area, such as storing them improperly, transmitting them insecurely, or failing to use secure wallets, can lead to these keys falling into the wrong hands, resulting in theft of the funds. Additionally, various other forms of attacks such as exploits and malware have been used to compromise ICOs. For example, hackers may take advantage of vulnerabilities in a project's code or system to gain unauthorized access or control. They may also use malware to infiltrate an investor's computer to steal sensitive information, such as wallet keys or login credentials.

The repercussions of security breaches in ICOs can be both immediate and far-reaching, impacting various stakeholders. Financially, these breaches can lead to substantial losses for both the project and its investors. Funds raised during the token sale can be siphoned off by hackers, effectively evaporating the capital meant to bring the proposed product or service to life. Investors, attracted by the potential return on their investments, could find their contributions vanished in the blink of an eye. This abrupt loss of funds can be devastating, especially for those who may have invested a significant portion of their savings.

Moreover, beyond the immediate financial losses, the reputational damage caused by such breaches can have long-lasting effects on the ICO's success and the broader crypto space. A security breach can greatly undermine investor confidence, making it harder for the project to raise further funds and casting a cloud of suspicion over its future prospects. The loss of trust can also ripple out to the larger ICO market, discouraging potential investors and stymieing the growth of the crypto ecosystem. Furthermore, these incidents could attract legal consequences, with potential lawsuits and regulatory actions against the ICO team. They could even prompt regulatory bodies to impose stricter rules on ICOs, which could stifle innovation in the cryptocurrency sector. Having discussed these ramifications, we will now review some case studies of major ICO security breaches.

Major ICO Security Breaches

The Decentralized Autonomous Organization (DAO) remains one of the most notorious cases of a security breach in an ICO, not only for its magnitude but also for the profound implications it had on the regulatory and technical landscape of the cryptocurrency space. The DAO was launched in 2016 with the ambitious aim of revolutionizing how organizations are managed and governed. Using smart contracts on the Ethereum blockchain, the DAO sought to create a completely automated organization with no central authority. However, in June 2016, a significant flaw was exploited in the DAO's smart contract code, leading to the theft of around 3.6 million Ether – equivalent to approximately $50 million at the time. The attacker was able to siphon off this vast sum due to a recursive calling vulnerability in the DAO's smart contract. Instead of the intended functioning, whereby DAO token holders would get their share of the remaining funds when splitting the DAO, the hacker was able to repeat the process multiple times before the transaction could be registered.

This incident triggered a heated debate within the Ethereum community about the most appropriate response. Ultimately, the decision was made to conduct a hard fork of the Ethereum blockchain to restore the stolen funds to their original owners. This decision was not without controversy, with some arguing that it contradicted the immutability principle of the blockchain. It led to a split in the Ethereum community, resulting in the creation of Ethereum Classic, which maintains the original blockchain without the implemented hard fork.

The DAO incident served as a stark reminder of the potential vulnerabilities in smart contract code and the need for robust security measures. It also brought regulatory attention to ICOs, with the SEC later determining that the DAO tokens were, in fact, securities that should have been registered as such. Thus, the DAO hack had far-reaching consequences, both in terms of shaping the Ethereum community and influencing the regulatory stance on ICOs.

The CoinDash ICO hack in 2017 offers another clear example of a security breach, this time involving a website compromise. CoinDash, a platform aimed at making managing cryptocurrency portfolios easier, was in the process of conducting its ICO when disaster struck. At the time of the ICO, potential investors visited the CoinDash website to participate. However, a malicious actor managed to gain unauthorized access to the website. Once inside, they replaced the official Ethereum address for contributions with their own. As a result, investors who thought they were participating in the CoinDash ICO were, in fact, sending their Ethereum directly to the hacker.

In this unfortunate event, CoinDash's lack of website security resulted in approximately $7 million worth of Ether being diverted away from the project and into the hands of the attacker. The hack occurred within minutes of the ICO's launch, and although CoinDash immediately warned users about the breach, the damage had already been done. Despite the setback, CoinDash decided to proceed with the project, pledging to provide tokens to investors who were victims of the hack as if their Ethereum had gone to the correct wallet.

The Enigma ICO hack in 2017 is another illustrative case of cybersecurity shortcomings in the crypto space. Enigma, a platform specializing in data-driven cryptocurrency investment, suffered an embarrassing breach during its ICO, particularly ironic given the company's focus on security and data safety. The incident started when hackers managed to gain access to the Enigma CEO's account. It has been reported that the CEO had been a user of the Ashley Madison website, a service that had previously suffered a high-profile data breach.[9] The Enigma CEO had reportedly neglected to change his passwords following the Ashley Madison breach, and the same credentials were used to gain access to Enigma's vital systems.

Once inside, the attackers seized control of the company's website, Slack account, and mailing list. This enabled them to launch a large-scale phishing attack. Emails, cleverly designed to resemble official Enigma communications, were sent to over 9000 potential investors, directing them to a bogus ICO address. Investors who fell for the scam sent their funds to this address, diverting approximately $500 000 worth of Ether to the hacker's wallet. The Enigma team quickly caught on and attempted to warn investors, but for some, the warning came too late.

The list of these incidents is long and concerning. Other significant examples include the KickICO and Bancor hacks. In each of these instances, the common denominator was a lackadaisical attitude towards security, underscoring the urgent need for a comprehensive security culture in the blockchain sector. KickICO, a blockchain platform for fundraising in cryptocurrencies, experienced a major breach in 2018 when hackers managed to take over the project's smart contract. They destroyed and created tokens at their discretion, stealing approximately $7.7 million before the attack was detected and halted. Bancor, a decentralized cryptocurrency exchange, likewise fell prey to a security breach in 2018. In this instance, hackers stole approximately $23.5 million by exploiting a vulnerability in a wallet used to update smart contracts.

Other notable cases involve the Veritaseum and Etherparty ICOs, both targeted by hackers. Veritaseum, an open-source blockchain platform, lost $8.4 million to hackers during its ICO. Etherparty, a user-friendly smart contract creator, saw its ICO website hacked within a mere 45 minutes of the ICO launch, with the hacker replacing the official address with their own. These incidents all reveal a common theme: a failure to sufficiently consider potential risks and the importance of robust security measures. The complex, technical nature of ICOs and blockchain technology, coupled with high-stakes financial implications, make them attractive targets for cybercriminals.

The Parity Wallet hack in 2017 underscores that even if an ICO project adopts all necessary security measures, threats can still emerge from external sources. Parity, a popular Ethereum wallet, fell victim to a major security breach when a vulnerability in its multi-signature contract was exploited. This flaw allowed the perpetrator to steal over 150 000 Ether, equivalent to approximately $30 million at the time. It was not only individual Parity Wallet users who were victims of this attack, but also several ICO projects that had chosen to store their freshly raised funds in the wallet. Their trust in Parity's reliability and security led to severe consequences as they incurred substantial financial losses due to the breach.

ICO FLOPS AND FAILURES

In the world of ICOs, investor losses are not limited to fraudulent schemes or malicious hacking attacks. There are also numerous cases of significant ICO flops and failures, which have led to substantial financial setbacks for investors. These terms refer to token sales that, while not fraudulent or scams, did not proceed as planned or failed to deliver on their promises or achieve their intended goals. This can occur due to a variety of reasons, such as missteps, poor management, lack of a viable product, an overinflated market valuation, or regulatory changes in the sector. It is crucial to remember that behind the allure of quick returns and revolutionary technology, there lies a volatile and largely unregulated market that can lead to significant losses, even when investing in non-fraudulent ICOs.

Many factors can contribute to the failure of ICOs. One of the main issues is a low level of crypto literacy amongst project teams who start their ICO journey with more enthusiasm than technical or financial knowledge. Technological inadequacies, such as poorly constructed smart contracts or insecure blockchain frameworks, can further complicate matters. Another common pitfall is a poorly defined value proposition, where the project fails to articulate the unique benefits and functionalities of the proposed token, or to demonstrate a clear market need for the project. Lack of due diligence, often stemming from the lack of regulatory oversight in the ICO market, is another key factor. This can lead to investors placing their trust and capital into projects without fully understanding the risks or assessing the project's legitimacy. Lastly, mismanagement of funds is a frequent contributor to ICO failures – without proper financial governance, funds raised during the ICO can be used ineffectively, depleting resources and leading to the project's premature demise.

The mid-2010s saw a surge of interest in ICOs, leading many entrepreneurs to jump on the trend. However, numerous examples have shown the challenges faced by teams lacking the requisite knowledge and skills in blockchain technology, crypto economics, and financial management. The Tezos project in 2017 raised $232 million through their ICO, making it one of the largest fundraisers in the sector at the time. However, despite this successful capital raising, the project was plagued by disagreements among the founders, internal legal disputes, and significant technical delays. This resulted in a significant drop in the value of the Tezos tokens and a struggle to restore investor confidence.

The Bancor project provides another stark example of the complexities and potential pitfalls associated with conducting an ICO. As a decentralized liquidity network, Bancor attracted considerable attention and raised over

$153 million in its ICO in June 2017. However, the project faced controversy and criticism due to its complex token sale structure, which led to confusion and apprehension amongst potential investors. To add fuel to the fire, Bancor's token price experienced a significant drop shortly after the ICO due to market pressures and concerns about the platform's centralization.

Sirin Labs is another illustrative example. The company conducted an ICO in 2017, raising approximately $157 million with the aim of developing and marketing the first blockchain-based smartphone, *Finney*. Despite the substantial funds raised, Sirin Labs encountered several obstacles, leading to a drastic plunge in the value of the Sirin token.

However, even with the best practices and careful planning in place, human errors and unforeseen mishaps can still occur. Prodeum, a blockchain startup aiming to disrupt the agricultural industry, provides a striking example. During their ICO in 2018, a typographical error in the Ethereum smart contract address listed on their website led to a significant loss of investor funds.

The story of Polkadot, however, provides a compelling example of resilience in the face of adversity. Despite losing $98 million of the $145 million they raised in their first ICO due to an unfortunate error, the team managed to carry on with the remaining funds. They successfully ran another ICO 18 months later. Today, in 2023, Polkadot continues to grow and develop. Its token holds a commendable position, ranking 13th by market capitalization. With the official release of Polkadot 1.0, the project has reached a significant milestone in the evolution of blockchain technology, demonstrating the importance of perseverance and adaptability in this dynamic landscape.

CONCLUSION

The narratives of ICO flops, scams, and security breaches often portray a more dramatic image than the actual situation. Indeed, the unregulated landscape of the ICO market has opened the door for a higher incidence of scams and some notable cases of fraud. However, it is essential to remember that this is not a phenomenon exclusive to the crypto world. As we have previously discussed, traditional investment markets have experienced their fair share of schemes that are far larger and more elaborate.

One crucial factor that determines an investor's susceptibility to such schemes is their level of financial literacy. Understanding that the rapid wealth promised by Ponzi-like structures is an illusion akin to a perpetual motion machine is key. Such schemes may be tempting, but they can only operate sustainably for a limited period. As the industry has matured, both investors and founders have grown more knowledgeable and cautious, making them less likely to fall victim to fraudsters. The role of fraudsters in this ecosystem can be likened to that of vultures in the wild: while they pose a threat, they also contribute to the health of the ecosystem by forcing all participants to stay vigilant and robust.

Security is undoubtedly a matter of utmost importance in this field. Over time, recognition of this fact has increased, and protective measures have been enhanced. However, it is worth noting that the evolution of the industry's landscape has also been significantly influenced by regulatory reactions to these security breaches. In many cases, the initial lack of regulatory oversight, followed by arguably overzealous regulatory reactions, has had considerable consequences. The role of regulatory response in shaping the evolution of this industry is crucial, and we will discuss this in greater depth in the next chapter.

NOTES

1   www.security.org/digital safety/credit card fraud report.
2   www.globenewswire.com/en/news-release/2022/12/22/2578877/0/en/Payment -Card-Fraud-Losses-Reach-32-34-Billion.html.
3   cryptopotato.com/vitalik-buterin-in-ethereal-this-is-how-i-eliminate-scams-in -icos.
4   www.investopedia.com/tech/how-identify-cryptocurrency-and-ico-scams.
5   www.coinopsy.com/dead-coins or 99bitcoins.com/deadcoins.
6   bitcointalk.org/index.php?topic=4701035.0.
7   www.investor.gov/ico-howeycoins.
8   fortune.com/2023/01/19/jpmorgan-ceo-jamie-dimon-bitcoin-hyped-up-fraud -cryptocurrencies-waste-of-time-but-blockchain-deployable-technology.
9   en.wikipedia.org/wiki/Ashley_Madison_data_breach.

REFERENCES

Griffin, J.M. (2021) 'Were ETH and EOS repeatedly recycled during the EOS Initial Coin Offering?', White Paper. Available at: https://www.scribd.com/document/522 992453/Eos# (accessed: 1 July 2023).
Grobys, K., King, T., and Sapkota, N. (2022) 'A fractal view on losses attributable to scams in the market for initial coin offerings', *Journal of Risk and Financial Management*, 15(12), pp. 1–18.
Hornuf, L., Kück, T., and Schwienbacher, A. (2022) 'Initial Coin Offerings, informa- tion disclosure, and fraud', *Small Business Economics*, 58, pp. 1741–1759.
Meoli, M. and Vismara, S. (2022) 'Machine-learning forecasting of successful ICOs', *Journal of Economics and Business*, 121(106071), pp. 1–15.
Sapkota, N., Grobys, K., and Dufitinema, J. (2020) 'How much are we willing to lose in cyberspace? On the tail risk of scam in the market for Initial Coin Offerings', SSRN. Available at: https://ssrn.com/abstract=3732747 (accessed: 1 July 2023).

9. Approaches to Initial Coin Offering regulation: Who's in charge?

INTRODUCTION

This book's journey through the intricate world of ICOs has persistently led us back to a central, pivotal theme: the role and influence of regulators in this burgeoning market. As we have seen, the ICO landscape has undergone significant metamorphosis over the years, moving from largely ad hoc and unregulated offerings to more organized structures such as Initial Exchange Offerings (IEOs) and Decentralized Exchange Offerings (IDOs). Given this rapid evolution, the pressing need for a robust, clear, and effective regulatory framework to protect investors, ensure market integrity, and foster innovation has never been more vital.

This chapter delves into the complex and crucial topic of regulation. It grapples with the question of who should regulate ICOs and their successors, and how to establish rules in this fast-paced market while maintaining a balance between protecting investors, upholding market integrity, and fostering innovation. It is important to note that at the time of writing, the regulatory landscape is like a canvas still being painted, with new developments, discussions, and draft regulations appearing at a rapid pace.

This chapter takes readers on a journey through the global history of ICO regulation, exploring the multifaceted roles of various regulatory bodies, the inherently international nature of ICOs, and the hurdles that regulators encounter in trying to keep pace with this rapidly evolving marketplace. Furthermore, it probes into existing regulatory approaches around the world, assessing their effectiveness and identifying best practices. It also peers into the future, speculating about potential developments in this ever-evolving regulatory landscape.

Initially, the chapter focuses on the accumulated experience of investment industry regulation, looking at examples from established financial markets such as equity and derivatives trading. These markets have also been the stage for competition in regulatory approaches and have, on occasion, fallen victim to fraudsters, market bubbles, and more. Subsequently, key topics are addressed, including the roles and responsibilities of different regulatory bodies in overseeing ICOs worldwide, the need for international cooperation in ICO regulation, industry-led initiatives, and the challenges inherent in creating a comprehensive regulatory framework for ICOs. The discourse continues by examining current regulatory approaches in various jurisdictions and potential future developments in the ICO regulatory landscape, along with the role and impact of technological advancements on regulatory enforcement.

By the end of this chapter, the goal is for readers to have gained a deeper understanding of the current state of ICO regulation, the complexities involved in regulating this innovative market, and the potential future directions of regulatory frameworks in this dynamic arena. It should be noted that while this chapter provides the latest insights into regulatory approaches as they stand in the first half of 2023, it does not claim to have the final word on the matter. The regulatory saga is far from concluded. So, let's get started.

HISTORICAL CONTEXT OF ICO REGULATION

It is true that when the first ICO campaigns were initiated between 2014 and 2016, they operated in a regulatory vacuum. The new crypto tokens sold and subsequently traded had no legal status (Pilkington 2018). Many regarded them as either scams or harmless trinkets, merely tokens, that crypto enthusiasts traded amongst each other in a vast online game within the crypto universe. However, many other innovative financial instruments, diverging from the conventional dichotomy of bonds (fixed income) versus shares (equity capital), were also created in a similarly regulatory-free environment, with regulation often following later, sometimes with a considerable lag.

Take, for instance, derivative instruments such as options. Nowadays, they are standard financial instruments essential for risk management. However, they were once an unusual innovation based on principles different from those of shares or bonds. The issue of valuing such instruments was only resolved in the last century. Modern options began to take shape in the early 17th century in Amsterdam with the establishment of the Amsterdam Stock Exchange, regarded as the world's first formal stock exchange (Gelderblom and Jonker 2004). Traders on the exchange began dealing in forward contracts and options on shares of the Dutch East India Company, the first publicly traded company. In those early days, there was no standardized pricing model for options, and regulation was minimal. Trading often occurred informally, with contracts negotiated directly between buyers and sellers. Consequently, the market was marked by inefficiencies and a lack of transparency (Poitras 2009).

It wasn't until the 20th century that the options market began to evolve into a more organized and regulated environment. The establishment of the Chicago Board Options Exchange (CBOE) in 1973 represented a significant milestone, as it introduced standardized option contracts and a centralized marketplace for trading options (Millo 2004). Over time, options markets have become increasingly regulated to protect investors and ensure market integrity. Nowadays, options are traded on regulated exchanges, and their issuance and trading are overseen by financial regulators such as the US Securities and Exchange Commission (SEC) and the Financial Industry Regulatory Authority (FINRA).

Convertible securities, which allow investors to convert their debt or preferred stock into common shares, have been around since the 19th century. The first recorded issuance of convertible bonds occurred in the United States in the 1850s (Calamos 1998). Railroad companies, eager to raise capital for their rapid expansion, issued convertible bonds to attract investors. The convertible feature made the bonds more appealing by offering potential for capital appreciation if the company's stock price increased. Convertible preferred shares, another type of convertible security, were introduced later. Like convertible bonds, convertible preferred shares offer investors the option to convert their preferred stock into common stock at a predetermined conversion rate.

The introduction of convertibles enabled companies to raise capital more easily by offering an attractive combination of fixed-income security and potential capital appreciation. Simultaneously, it provided investors with some degree of downside protection through regular interest or dividend payments, coupled with the potential for upside participation through the conversion option. Still, regulation of convertibles was not enacted until 1934, under the Securities Exchange Act.

More recent examples of financial innovation include collateralized debt securities (CDSs) and crowdfunding instruments. Initially, the CDS market was largely unregulated, with trades conducted as privately negotiated transactions between parties (Tavakoli 2008). The lack of transparency and standardization contributed to the financial crisis of 2007–2008. In response, regulators have introduced measures to increase transparency, reduce counterparty risk, and standardize contracts. Today, CDSs are subject to more stringent regulation, with many transactions cleared through central counterparties and reported to trade repositories.

The regulation of crowdfunding is a more recent development, following the proliferation of crowdfunding platforms. Crowdfunding, as we know it today, began to gain popularity in the late 2000s and early 2010s with the rise of platforms such as Kickstarter and Indiegogo. However, in the United States, regulation around crowdfunding was primarily addressed in 2012 with the Jumpstart Our Business Startups (JOBS) Act (Stemler 2013). Title III of the JOBS Act, also known as the CROWDFUND Act, provided a legal framework for equity crowdfunding, allowing small businesses to solicit investments from the general public. Furthermore, the SEC did not finalize its rules on equity crowdfunding under the JOBS Act until 2015. These regulations retrospectively established a framework enabling small businesses and startups to raise capital from a large pool of investors, each of whom invests a small amount of money.

In essence, regulatory frameworks typically trail behind innovation. As new practices emerge and gain traction, regulators must then scramble to establish rules that protect investors, ensure fair markets, and facilitate capital formation. ICOs were no different in this respect. Not surprisingly, they developed in their early years without guidance, regulation, or any limitations, due to the unbounded nature of the crypto universe. The exponential growth of the ICO market in 2016–2017 necessitated the creation of regulations to ensure investor protection and maintain the stability of financial markets. The next section will delve into the historical context of ICO regulation, starting with investor protection in financial markets, the early days of ICOs, and the evolution of regulatory approaches.

INVESTOR PROTECTION IN THE ICO MARKET

General investor protection is considered a critical aspect of financial markets regulation, as it fosters trust and stability in the financial system. Historically, regulatory bodies have been established to ensure transparency, prevent fraud, and maintain fair practices in the financial industry. The Great Depression, for instance, prompted the creation of the SEC in 1934 to regulate securities markets and protect investors (Duca 2017). Regulatory frameworks have evolved over time to address new financial products and services, as well as to adapt to the global nature of financial markets. One such example is the European Union's Markets in Financial Instruments Directive (MiFID), which aims to improve the competitiveness of European financial markets while safeguarding investor interests.

In general, investor protection regulations aim to provide a secure environment for the investment of capital. These safeguards are designed to reduce the risks associated with investing, thereby promoting trust and encouraging further investment. Key principles include providing investors with accurate and timely information, ensuring fair and transparent market practices, and preventing fraud, manipulation, and abusive practices. Regulations also often include provisions for redress in cases where investors suffer losses due to non-compliance with these standards. Thus, investor protection regulations play a crucial role in the functioning of financial markets, underpinning market confidence, fostering investment, and facilitating economic growth.

Early Days of ICOs

During the early days of ICOs, the regulatory landscape was sparse and often unclear. Regulators were slow to react to such a novel and unconventional way of raising funds for startups. Historically, financial innovation had come at a much slower pace, and many regulators likely thought they had ample time to address the ICO phenomenon. However, this lack of regulation allowed for rapid growth, but it also resulted in several high-profile scams and fraudulent activities. The previous chapter discussed this phenomenon in detail.

The regulators' reaction to the development of token sales could be likened to the early days of complex derivatives related to subprime mortgages. Regulation was limited, and in many instances, it was introduced post-factum. These complex derivatives, such as mortgage-backed securities (MBS) and collateralized debt obligations (CDO), were financial instruments created by pooling mortgages and other debt, which were then sold to investors. These products gained popularity in the early 2000s, as they were seen as a way to diversify risk and generate attractive returns.

Regulatory oversight was limited for several reasons. Firstly, many of these complex derivatives were traded on the over-the-counter (OTC) market, which is less regulated compared to exchange-traded markets. Similarly, ICOs were conducted in the crypto space, completely out of reach of national authorities. Secondly, there was a general belief in the efficiency of markets and a reliance on credit rating agencies to accurately assess the risk of these products. Likewise, the blockchain community firmly believed in the principles of decentralization and the ability of blockchain to ensure trust and the smooth functioning of financial markets without any intermediaries. Finally, financial innovation outpaced regulatory frameworks, as regulators struggled to understand and keep up with the rapid development of these complex instruments. This argument fully applied to the idea of tokens, their role, and functions.

This lack of regulation and oversight in the mortgage derivative markets contributed to the subsequent financial crisis of 2007–2008 (Kumar and Singh 2013). The limited regulation allowed financial institutions to take on excessive risk, as there was a lack of transparency and understanding of the underlying risks associated with these complex derivatives. Additionally, the reliance on credit rating agencies proved to be flawed, as many of these products received high credit ratings despite the high levels of risk involved. When the US housing market started to decline, the value of these complex derivatives plummeted, leading to significant losses for financial institutions and investors. The resulting financial crisis exposed the weaknesses in the regulatory framework and prompted calls for reform.

In response to the crisis, regulators introduced several new regulations to address the issues that had been revealed. These regulations included the

Dodd-Frank Wall Street Reform and Consumer Protection Act in the United States, and the European Market Infrastructure Regulation (EMIR) in the European Union. These regulations aimed to increase transparency, reduce systemic risk, and improve oversight of complex derivatives and the financial institutions involved in their creation and trading.

However, the regulators' approach towards ICOs was much slower. In fact, from 2014 to 2016, the ICO market was still relatively new, and the amounts being raised were small compared to what would follow in 2017. Most regulators around the world were not yet fully aware of this new fundraising method, and it did not attract much regulatory attention.

In the United States, the SEC did not issue any specific guidance or regulation on ICOs until 2017, after the explosive growth of the ICO market. Similarly, European regulatory bodies such as the European Securities and Markets Authority (ESMA) and the UK's Financial Conduct Authority (FCA) did not provide specific guidance on ICOs until 2017. In Asia, where some of the earliest ICOs originated, there was similarly little regulatory attention from 2015 to 2016. Regulatory bodies in countries such as Singapore and Japan began issuing guidance on ICOs only in 2017.

Overall, the years from 2014 to 2016 can be seen as a *grace period* for ICOs, where regulatory attention was limited. It was not until the ICO market grew significantly in size and scope in 2017 that regulators around the world began to take notice and formulate responses (Kaal 2018).

Evolution of Regulatory Approaches

As ICOs gained popularity in 2017, regulators around the world began to pay closer attention to this emerging market. The regulatory response to ICOs has evolved over time, reflecting a balance between promoting innovation and protecting investors from potential risks. Early regulatory responses were limited to warnings and guidelines. In 2017, the SEC released the DAO Report, which stated that tokens issued in ICOs could be considered securities under the Securities Act of 1933, and therefore subject to SEC regulation.[1] Similarly, the ESMA in Europe issued a statement warning investors about the risks associated with ICOs and highlighting the need for regulatory compliance.[2]

At the same time, following the release of guidelines, regulators started taking enforcement actions against ICOs that violated securities laws. In 2017, the SEC initiated its first enforcement action against an ICO, targeting a project called PlexCoin, which had raised $15 million through an allegedly fraudulent offering.[3] Subsequent enforcement actions have targeted other fraudulent ICOs and non-compliant projects. At the same time the European authorities took a more cautious approach, with some countries (such as Switzerland, Malta, Gibraltar, and Estonia) swiftly adopting ICO-friendly regulations, while other countries delayed taking a clear stance. Similar developments were observed in Asia, except for a drastic move to ban all national ICO activity in China in September of 2017.[4]

As ICOs continued to evolve, regulators sought to provide more clarity on the classification of tokens and applicable regulations. The SEC's 2019 Framework for 'Investment Contract' Analysis of Digital Assets provided additional guidance on determining whether a digital asset is a security, using the Howey Test as a reference. This test evaluates whether a transaction involves an investment of money in a common enterprise, with the expectation of profits derived from the efforts of others. The framework helped market participants better understand the regulatory implications of their ICOs and token offerings.

Still, the US regulatory response is considered by many as hesitant and fluctuating. In the DAO report, the SEC determined that DAO tokens were securities and therefore subject to federal securities laws but did not suggest that all ICOs constituted securities offerings. The key conclusion was that the determination depends on the facts and circumstances of each individual ICO. However, as ICO activity proliferated and attracted a wider spectrum of participants, the SEC began to voice concerns about potential investor harm. In a public statement in December 2017, SEC Chairman Jay Clayton emphasized that merely calling a token a utility token, or structuring it to provide some utility, does not prevent the token from being a security.[5] In this statement, Clayton suggested that most ICOs are likely securities offerings due to their resemblance to traditional investment contracts.

Later, in 2018, the same Chairman started to assert that the majority of ICO tokens were securities. His catchy phrase, 'Every ICO I've seen is a security', soon became an internet meme.[6] Later on, his successor, the next Chairman Gary Gensler, echoed this view, expressing his belief that the vast majority of crypto tokens and ICOs violate US securities laws. Interestingly, many media sources misquoted him as saying that 'Every ICO is a security', which, in reality, he never stated. Instead, his words could be interpreted to imply that 'everything other than Bitcoin' could potentially be classified as a security from the SEC's perspective.[7]

Indeed, the SEC's actions align with this viewpoint. Apart from enforcement actions taken against ICOs deemed fraudulent, the SEC continuously updated its list of crypto tokens it considered to be securities, consistently expanding it to include additional entities. In December 2020, Ripple Labs, the company behind the XRP token, became the first established and credible project to be sued by the SEC. The regulator alleged that Ripple had conducted an unregistered securities offering by selling XRP to raise funds, sparking a landmark case in the regulatory treatment of cryptocurrencies.[8] As of June 2023, the SEC's list of alleged securities has expanded to include 67 different coins.

Furthermore, the SEC has shifted its focus to cryptocurrency exchanges. In June 2023, the SEC initiated charges against leading cryptocurrency Binance[9] and Coinbase[10] for operating its crypto asset trading platforms as unregistered national securities exchanges, brokers, and clearing agencies.

In summary, it should be noted that after an initial delay, US regulators significantly stepped up their efforts to halt apparent fraud and sought to bring all tokens and cryptocurrency exchanges under their jurisdiction, firmly regarding all crypto assets as securities under US regulations. This stance sharply contrasts with an alternative, more radical approach – outright banning all ICO activity within national borders. This latter method was adopted by China and South Korea in September 2017, and by India in April 2018, which prohibited all dealings in virtual currencies altogether. Surprisingly, this decision was reversed by the Supreme Court of India in March 2020, allowing banks to handle cryptocurrency transactions from exchanges and traders. Furthermore, South Korean authorities announced prospective regulations in August 2022 that would once again permit ICOs.[11] At the time of writing this book, the Digital Assets Framework Act has not yet been enacted, and South Korean authorities are still investigating the matter.

Several countries have adopted a more favourable or open stance towards ICOs and cryptocurrencies, seeing them as opportunities to attract technological innovation and foster a new sector in the economy. These countries provide legal clarity and supportive regulatory frameworks to help these emerging types of businesses navigate legal requirements. For instance, in 2018, the Swiss Financial Market Supervisory Authority (FINMA) issued guidelines outlining how it would treat ICOs under existing securities regulations, based on the characteristics of the tokens being offered. These guidelines classified tokens into three categories: payment tokens, utility tokens, and asset tokens, each subject to different regulatory requirements.

Among other countries is Singapore, where the Monetary Authority of Singapore (MAS) has been relatively open to ICOs and cryptocurrencies, provided they adhere to anti-money laundering (AML) and counter-terrorism financing (CTF) regulations. ICOs are permitted, but tokens can be classified as securities and should comply with relevant regulations. Estonia, known for its e-residency program and digital initiatives, generally supports ICOs and blockchain-based enterprises. The country has implemented a licensing system for cryptocurrency businesses to ensure compliance with AML and CTF regulations.

Known as *Blockchain Island*, Malta has established a comprehensive regulatory framework for distributed ledger technology, including ICOs. This has made it a popular destination for blockchain startups. Gibraltar has also taken steps to attract blockchain businesses, including ICOs. It introduced a regulatory framework for distributed ledger technology in 2018, aiming to protect consumers and Gibraltar's reputation while encouraging innovation.

The small European nation of Liechtenstein has proposed a Blockchain Act, aiming to provide comprehensive regulation for the token economy. The law seeks to provide legal clarity for businesses using blockchain technology. Luxembourg, a global hub for financial services, has a forward-thinking approach towards blockchain and crypto assets. The country's regulators have issued various licences to cryptocurrency and blockchain companies, and they are actively exploring regulatory frameworks for ICOs.

Instead of outright banning or permitting ICOs, some countries have implemented so-called sandbox and pilot approaches. These allow startups and other market participants to test their products and services in a controlled environment under regulatory supervision. Examples include the United Kingdom's FCA sandbox and the MAS fintech sandbox. These initiatives foster innovation while allowing regulators to gather insights and tailor their regulatory approaches to the unique challenges posed by ICOs and digital assets.

In conclusion, the evolution of regulatory approaches to ICOs has been characterized by an increased focus on providing clarity, enforcing compliance, and promoting international cooperation, as opposed to banning all ICO activity outright. Regulators have sought to strike a balance between fostering innovation and ensuring investor protection and market stability. As the ICO market continues to develop and new challenges emerge, regulatory frameworks will likely continue to evolve, reflecting the need for adaptability and responsiveness in this rapidly changing landscape.

ICO REGULATION BY JURISDICTION

In the previous section, we demonstrated that different jurisdictions around the globe have adopted varying stances – from outright bans and discouragement to open encouragement and support. The diverse attitudes reflect differing economic conditions, legal frameworks, and cultural attitudes towards technological innovation and financial risk. These multifaceted strategies result in a complex mosaic of regulatory landscapes for ICOs worldwide. In this section, we survey the most recent regulatory initiatives and events up to June 2023, painting a picture of the current global environment for ICOs. We survey a range of jurisdictions, examining their unique regulatory postures and delving into the specificities of their approaches to provide a nuanced understanding of the challenges and opportunities presented by these dynamic markets.

United States

In the United States, the SEC is the primary regulatory authority responsible for overseeing ICOs. The SEC has taken the position that most ICOs involve the issuance of securities, and as such, they are subject to federal securities laws. This stance was taken in the DAO Report, released in 2017, which concluded that tokens issued in ICOs could be considered securities under the Securities Act of 1933.

Since then, the SEC has issued further guidance and taken enforcement action against non-compliant ICOs. The 2019 Framework for 'Investment Contract' Analysis of Digital Assets provided additional clarity on when digital assets may be considered securities, using the Howey Test as a reference.[12] The SEC actively asserted that anything happening in the crypto world falls under their supervision, and continuously reinstated their viewpoint. However, as many crypto parties have complained, the SEC was never absolutely clear in expressing their stance. Instead of halting the ICO activity in 2017–2018, it tacitly subpoenaed a considerable number of ICO founders, which intimidated a lot of market participants. As a result, many planned ICOs were cancelled, and many completed ones returned money to investors just to avoid becoming the next target of the SEC's attention.[13]

As the ICO landscape continued to evolve, the SEC found itself thrust into the spotlight due to several high-profile cases. This shift signalled an era of heightened scrutiny and increased regulatory oversight in the world of ICOs. One of the notable instances involved Ripple Labs, the creators of the XRP cryptocurrency. In December 2020, the SEC filed a lawsuit against Ripple Labs, alleging that Ripple's sale of XRP constituted an unregistered securities offering worth over $1.38 billion.

Around the same period, the SEC had another high-profile case with Telegram, a popular messaging app. In 2018, Telegram raised $1.7 billion through an ICO for its TON blockchain platform and the associated *Gram* tokens. However, the SEC intervened in October 2019, halting the launch of the network and the delivery of the tokens by filing an emergency action and obtaining a temporary restraining order.[14] The SEC alleged that the Gram tokens were securities and that the ICO was, therefore, an unregistered securities offering. In March 2020, a federal court sided with the SEC and issued an injunction, which effectively shut down the project.

Facebook's (now Meta) proposed Libra project (later renamed Diem) was another major development that attracted the attention of regulators worldwide. Announced in June 2019, the project aimed to create a stablecoin backed by a basket of currencies and government bonds.[15] However, regulators, including the SEC, expressed concerns over potential issues, including money laundering, financial stability, and the challenge of regulating an entity that could potentially become a globally systemic financial institution. Amid growing scrutiny and several key partners withdrawing their support, Facebook scaled back its plans in December 2020, and ultimately cancelled the project altogether in 2022.[16]

The SEC also targeted crypto exchanges Binance and Coinbase, accusing them of being venues that sell unregistered securities, i.e., all cryptocurrencies excluding Bitcoin. The most recent proposal, in the form of the currently debated bipartisan bill titled the Crypto-Asset National Security Enhancement Act of 2023, would require decentralized finance (DeFi) protocols to impose bank-like controls on their user base. This has shifted the focus onto decentralized exchanges (DEXs), where new coins are listed in a way that somewhat resembles the old-fashioned ICOs.[17]

However, this situation is not a one-sided battle. In April 2023, the crypto exchange Coinbase proactively filed a narrow action in federal court to compel the SEC to respond to Coinbase's pending rulemaking petition, which sought overdue guidance for the crypto industry. It is estimated that more than 1700 entities and individuals submitted comments in support of Coinbase's petition, emphasizing the need for clarity.[18] In a surprising twist for many observers, on 13 July 2023, the United States Southern District Court of New York ruled that Ripple's tokens (XRP) were not a security when sold to the public, but were considered unregistered securities offerings when sold to institutional investors. This decision was seen by many as a victory for Ripple, as it implies that XRPs can be freely traded on any cryptocurrency exchange.[19] The ongoing battle between the SEC and other major exchanges such as Binance and Coinbase is still unfolding, and while the outcome is uncertain, we await it without the presumption that the SEC will necessarily prevail.

European Union

In the European Union, ICO regulation is primarily overseen by individual member states, as there is no EU-wide regulatory framework specifically for ICOs. However, existing EU regulations, such as the Markets in Financial Instruments Directive (MiFID II) and the Prospectus Regulation, may apply to ICOs depending on the nature of the tokens being offered and the jurisdiction in which the offering takes place. The ESMA has issued statements and guidelines on ICOs, stressing the need for compliance with existing regulations and warning investors about the risks associated with ICOs. ESMA has also called for a common EU approach to regulating ICOs and digital assets. Some EU countries have implemented their own regulatory frameworks for ICOs. For instance, France introduced the PACTE law in 2019, which includes a voluntary regulatory framework for ICOs, allowing issuers to seek a 'visa' from the French Financial Markets Authority (AMF) if they meet specific requirements.

In May 2023, there was a recent development in which the European Council adopted the world's first comprehensive set of rules for crypto assets regulation (MiCA). MiCA, which was already approved by EU member states and the European Parliament, requires crypto firms to be authorized by the EU to serve customers in the bloc and to comply with safeguards against money laundering and terrorism financing. In the view of many, MiCA is a politically acceptable and workable compromise, building on existing rules frameworks, offering entrepreneurs certainty, and providing some guidance to the crypto markets.[20]

Asia

ICO regulation in Asia varies greatly by jurisdiction, with some countries taking a more restrictive approach, while others are more open to the market. In 2017, China banned ICOs outright, citing concerns about financial risk and fraud. The Chinese government has maintained a strong stance against cryptocurrencies and ICOs, shutting down domestic exchanges and prohibiting financial institutions from engaging in crypto-related activities. At the time of writing, there has been no change in their views. However, some progress in Hong Kong's development of a regulatory framework for stablecoins hints at a potential shift in China's stance on cryptocurrencies in the near future.[21]

Japan, on the other hand, has a relatively open approach to cryptocurrencies and has implemented regulations for crypto exchanges. However, ICO regulation remains unclear. The Japanese Financial Services Agency (FSA) has indicated that some ICOs may fall under existing securities laws, depending on the nature of the tokens being offered. On 1 May 2020, Japan's new crypto asset regulations, promulgated in April 2019, officially came into effect. The new legislation that amends Japan's Payment Services Act (PSA) and Financial Instruments and Exchange Act (FIEA) will be enforced by FSA. Under the new regulation, electronically recorded transferable rights were expanded to include Security Token Offerings (STOs) and ICO tokens.

After initially banning ICOs in 2017, South Korea has gradually softened its stance. The country is considering the introduction of a regulatory framework for ICOs, which would require issuers to register with the Financial Services Commission (FSC) and comply with specific requirements. In contrast, The MAS has issued guidelines for ICOs, stating that if tokens constitute capital market products under the Securities and Futures Act (SFA), they will be subject to regulation. The MAS has also introduced a fintech sandbox, allowing companies to test their products and services in a controlled environment.

CONCLUSION

In the United States, the SEC is the primary regulatory authority responsible for overseeing ICOs. The SEC has taken the position that most ICOs involve the issuance of securities and, as such, they are subject to federal securities laws. This stance was taken in the DAO Report, released in 2017, which concluded that tokens issued in ICOs could be considered securities under the Securities Act of 1933. Since then, the SEC has issued further guidance and taken enforcement actions against non-compliant ICOs. The 2019 Framework for 'Investment Contract' Analysis of Digital Assets provided additional clarity on when digital assets may be considered securities, using the Howey Test as a reference.

This has led to the SEC actively taking the stance that anything that happens in the crypto world falls under their supervision. However, many in the crypto community have complained that the SEC was never absolutely clear in expressing their views. Instead of halting ICO activity during 2017–2018, the SEC has tacitly subpoenaed a considerable number of ICO founders. This move scared quite a few market participants, resulting in many planned ICOs being cancelled and many completed ones returning money to investors just to avoid being the next target of the SEC's attention.

As the ICO landscape continued to evolve, the SEC found itself thrust into the limelight due to several high-profile cases. This shift signalled an era of intensified scrutiny and increased regulatory oversight in the world of ICOs. Notable instances involved Ripple Labs, creators of the XRP cryptocurrency, and Telegram, a popular messaging app. In both cases, the SEC filed lawsuits, alleging that their token offerings were unregistered securities offerings.

The SEC also took action against crypto exchanges Binance and Coinbase, suing them for allegedly selling unregistered securities, i.e., all cryptocurrencies excluding Bitcoins. The most recent proposal, in the form of the currently discussed bipartisan bill titled the Crypto-Asset National Security Enhancement Act of 2023, would require DeFi protocols to impose bank-like controls on their user base. This has shifted the focus onto DEXs, where new coins are listed in a manner that somewhat resembles the old-fashioned ICOs.

The European Union and Asia, in contrast, have taken varied approaches to ICO regulation. While individual EU member states primarily govern ICO regulation, existing EU regulations may also apply to ICOs depending on the nature of the tokens being offered. In Asia, regulatory stances range from China's outright ban on ICOs to Japan and South Korea's more open approaches and existing regulations for crypto exchanges.

Throughout all of these developments, the common theme is clear: the global ICO frenzy dwindled under increasing regulatory pressure. By 2019,

ICOs had fallen out of fashion. The US market was effectively closed to them, investors grew wary of scams and mediocre token performance, and the advent of the COVID-19 era slashed financial asset valuations, including crypto. However, the need and desire for funding from blockchain projects persisted and so, the industry innovated once again. Instead of ICOs, investors were offered similar products, either compliant with existing regulations or backed by new intermediaries that guaranteed the legitimacy and soundness of the businesses offering their tokens to the public. The era of STOs and IEOs had arrived. The following chapter discusses them in turn.

NOTES

1   www.sec.gov/litigation/investreport/34-81207.pdf.
2   www.esma.europa.eu/press-news/esma-news/esma-highlights-ico-risks-investors-and-firms.
3   www.sec.gov/litigation/litreleases/2019/lr24635.htm.
4   www.cnbc.com/2017/09/04/chinese-icos-china-bans-fundraising-through-initial-coin-offerings-report-says.html.
5   www.sec.gov/news/public-statement/statement-clayton-2017-12-11.
6   www.coindesk.com/markets/2018/02/06/sec-chief-clayton-every-ico-ive-seen-is-a-security.
7   nymag.com/intelligencer/2023/02/gary-gensler-on-meeting-with-sbf-and-his-crypto-crackdown.html.
8   www.sec.gov/news/press-release/2020-338.
9   www.sec.gov/news/press-release/2023-101.
10   www.sec.gov/news/press-release/2023-102.
11   www.forbesindia.com/article/crypto-made-easy/south-korean-central-bank-announces-future-regulations-to-allow-icos-again/79403/1.
12   www.sec.gov/corpfin/framework-investment-contract-analysis-digital-assets.
13   www.nytimes.com/2018/02/28/technology/initial-coin-offerings-sec.html.
14   www.sec.gov/news/press-release/2019-212.
15   www.theguardian.com/technology/2019/jun/18/libra-facebook-cryptocurrency-new-digital-money-transactions.
16   techmonitor.ai/technology/emerging-technology/facebook-diem-stablecoin-cryptocurrency.
17   www.coindesk.com/policy/2023/07/19/new-us-senate-bill-wants-to-regulate-defi-like-banks.
18   www.coinbase.com/blog/coinbase-takes-another-formal-step-to-seek-regulatory-clarity-from-sec-for.
19   www.investopedia.com/sec-vs-ripple-6743752.
20   www.coindesk.com/consensus-magazine/2023/04/20/is-europes-mica-a-template-for-global-crypto-regulation.
21   beincrypto.com/china-lift-crypto-ban-hong-kong-regulatory-progress.

REFERENCES

Calamos, J. (1998) *Convertible Securities*. New York: McGraw-Hill Professional Publishing.

Duca, J.V. (2017) 'The Great Depression versus the Great Recession in the US: How fiscal, monetary, and financial polices compare', *Journal of Economic Dynamics and Control*, 81, pp. 50–64.

Gelderblom, O. and Jonker, J. (2004) 'Completing a financial revolution: The finance of the Dutch East India trade and the rise of the Amsterdam capital market, 1595–1612', *The Journal of Economic History*, 64(3), pp. 641–672.

Kaal, W.A. (2018) 'Initial Coin Offerings: The top 25 jurisdictions and their comparative regulatory responses (as of May 2018)', *Stanford Journal of Blockchain Law and Policy*. Available at: stanford-jblp.pubpub.org/pub/ico-comparative-reg (accessed: 1 July 2023)

Kumar, N. and Singh, J.P. (2013) 'Global financial crisis: Corporate governance failures and lessons', *Journal of Finance, Accounting and Management*, 4(1), pp. 21–34.

Millo, Y. (2004) 'Creation of a market network: The regulatory approval of Chicago Board Options Exchange (CBOE)', Discussion Paper 23, Centre for Analysis of Risk and Regulation, London School of Economics and Political Science, pp. 1–32.

Pilkington, M. (2018) 'The emerging ICO landscape – Some financial and regulatory standpoints', SSRN. Available at: https://ssrn.com/abstract=3120307 (accessed: 1 July 2023).

Poitras, G. (2009) 'From Antwerp to Chicago: The history of exchange traded derivative security contracts', *Revue d'histoire des sciences humaines*, 20(1), pp. 11–50.

Stemler, A.R. (2013) 'The JOBS Act and crowdfunding: Harnessing the power – and money – of the masses', *Business Horizons*, 56(3), pp. 271–275.

Tavakoli, J.M. (2008) *Structured Finance and Collateralized Debt Obligations: New Developments in Cash and Synthetic Securitization*. Hoboken, NJ: John Wiley & Sons.

10. Evolution of Initial Coin Offerings

INTRODUCTION

The realm of fundraising through digital assets continues to evolve, with new innovations and developments constantly reshaping the landscape. As regulators and market participants increasingly understand the potential benefits and risks associated with Initial Coin Offerings (ICOs) alternative forms of digital asset fundraising have emerged to address some of the issues and limitations associated with traditional ICOs. One such innovation is the Security Token Offering (STO), which has gained traction as a viable alternative to ICOs, offering a more regulated and compliant method of raising capital.

However, STOs, despite being touted as a good alternative to ICOs, lacked certain appealing features, leaving them somewhat grounded. The missing gap was filled by cryptocurrency exchanges, which found themselves in an advantageous position. They could select only the best projects, lend their credibility, and organize post-offering trading in tokens, providing much-needed liquidity to investors. The era of Initial Exchange Offerings (IEOs) was ushered in.

In this chapter, we delve into the evolution of ICOs, with a focus on STOs and IEOs as significant developments in the digital asset fundraising space. We will explore the definitions and mechanisms of both STOs and IEOs, discuss their advantages and disadvantages, examine notable examples, and analyse the regulatory landscape surrounding these alternatives to ICOs. In doing so, we aim to provide a comprehensive understanding of these emerging fundraising methods and their implications for the future of digital asset financing.

STOs

As the digital asset landscape continued to evolve, it became clear to the blockchain industry that merely renaming an ICO as a crowdfunding campaign, token sale, or public token sale, and claiming that the offered token is a pure utility token, devoid of any security features or functions, would not deter regulatory attention (Boreiko et al. 2019). As a response, the industry tested a solution in the US, by acknowledging that the tokens offered represent some form of securities and that the token sale should be conducted in compliance with regulations. Consequently, STOs emerged as a more regulated and compliant alternative to ICOs. By issuing security tokens, companies can raise capital while adhering to existing securities laws, enhancing investor protection, and mitigating regulatory uncertainty (Wang 2023).

Definition and Mechanism

An STO is a fundraising method in which a company issues digital tokens that represent ownership in an underlying asset, such as equity, debt, or real estate. These tokens, known as security tokens, are subject to securities laws and regulations, and their issuance and trading must comply with the relevant legal framework. Security tokens differ from utility tokens, which are typically issued in ICOs and provide access to a product or service rather than represent- ing ownership or investment rights (Maas 2019). By being subject to securities laws, security tokens offer increased transparency, investor protection, and regulatory compliance compared to utility tokens. The mechanism of an STO is similar to that of an ICO, with investors purchasing tokens during the offering in exchange for fiat currency, cryptocurrency, or other digital assets. However, unlike ICOs, STOs must comply with strict regulatory requirements, including registration, disclosure, and reporting obligations.

The regulatory landscape for STOs varies by jurisdiction, with different countries adopting different approaches to these offerings. For example, in the US, to avoid registration of the offered securities with the Securities and Exchange Commission (SEC), three main exemptions exist (Mendelson 2019). The most commonly used exemption for securities offerings, Regulation D, has several rules that provide exemptions from the registration requirements, allowing some companies to offer and sell their securities without having to register the securities with the SEC:

1. Rule 506(b) allows an unlimited amount of capital to be raised from an unlimited number of accredited investors and up to 35 other purchasers. However, general solicitation or advertising to market the securities is not permitted. Moreover, the definition of the accredited investor is rather restrictive, effectively limiting the investor base to institutional investors and very large net worth individuals.
2. Rule 506(c) allows for general solicitation or advertising, but all sales must be to accredited investors, and the issuer must take reasonable steps to verify the accredited investor status of all purchasers.

Regulation A+, often referred to as a 'mini-IPO' exemption, permits smaller companies to raise up to $75 million in a 12-month period from the general public. However, under this regulation, companies are obligated to file an offering statement with the SEC, which must be qualified, and to maintain regular reporting. Meanwhile, Regulation Crowdfunding enables companies to accumulate up to $5 million over a 12-month period from both accredited and non-accredited investors, facilitated through an online funding portal registered with the SEC.

In the European Union, security tokens are subject to similar securities regulations, with guidance provided by the European Securities and Markets Authority (ESMA) on the application of EU laws to STOs (Momtaz 2023). Some jurisdictions have adopted a more proactive approach to STO regulation, developing specific frameworks for STOs. For example, in Switzerland, the Swiss Financial Market Supervisory Authority (FINMA) has issued guidelines on the treatment of security tokens and clarified the applicable regulatory requirements. In Malta, the government has enacted a comprehensive legal framework for digital assets, including provisions for STOs and the licensing of security token exchanges.

Despite increasing clarity in some jurisdictions, the regulatory landscape for STOs remains complex and fragmented, with ongoing debates regarding the classification and regulation of security tokens. As the market for STOs continues to grow and evolve, it is likely that regulators will continue to refine their approaches to security token regulation, seeking to strike a balance between promoting innovation and protecting investors (Takahashi 2019).

Notable STOs

STOs have been used across the globe by various companies as a vehicle for raising capital. As per a study by Lambert et al. (2022), the STO market has witnessed the launch of around 280 offerings in 34 different nations. Excluding 86 deals that were marketed as STOs but were actually selling utility tokens within the confines of regulations, a third of these STOs originated in the US, with approximately 10 per cent from Switzerland and the UK, and 4 per cent from Singapore. Other nations hosted a minimal number of STOs.

Although the genesis of STOs cannot be precisely traced due to their gradual emergence, one of the early significant STOs is attributed to Blockchain Capital, who issued Blockchain Capital (BCAP) tokens in April 2017. BCAP tokens represented indirect economic interests in the Blockchain Capital III Digital Liquid Venture Fund, thereby granting token holders a share in the fund's profits. The STO managed to raise $10 million in a mere six hours, selling the tokens as securities under Regulation D to accredited investors, which absolved it from SEC registration (Chaisse and Kirkwood 2022).

Over time, the fund showcased commendable performance. As of the end of 2022, the BCAP portfolio's value, initially established with the raised $10 million, had grown by 1700 per cent, reporting a net Internal Rate of Return (IRR) of 65.6 per cent. However, the tokenized fund constituted an infinitesimal proportion of the company's total assets under management, amounting to $2 billion. The company has since abstained from raising funds via another STO.

tZERO, a subsidiary of Overstock.com, is one of the most renowned entities that executed an STO in the United States. In 2017, tZERO initiated its STO with an aim to issue tokens symbolizing real securities, i.e., preferred equity in tZERO. To ensure legal compliance, the STO was carried out under Regulations D and S for accredited investors in two phases: a pre-sale, or Simple Agreement for Future Tokens (SAFT) phase, and a general sale. tZERO's STO stands out because of the substantial $134 million funds raised and its compliance with US securities laws.

Not all US-based STOs are focused on accredited investors. Some STOs have welcomed retail investors. One such instance is the INX Limited STO, which took place in 2020. Another significant instance is Blockstack PBC, which got SEC qualification to conduct a token offering under Regulation A+ in July 2019. This allowed them to conduct the token sale to a broader audience, raising approximately $23 million from over 4500 investors. Similarly, in 2021, Lottery.com conducted its STO under Regulation A+ of the JOBS Act, offering its security tokens to both accredited and non-accredited investors in the US.

Globally, STOs have been successfully conducted outside the US, adhering to the securities laws of the respective countries. Germany witnessed its first regulator-approved STO by Bitbond, a blockchain-driven lending platform, which raised $3.9 million in 2019 (Henker et al. 2023). Switzerland, known for its progressive stance towards blockchain regulation, has seen about 20 STOs in recent years, with companies like Mt Pelerin leading the way (Kondova and Simonella 2019). The UK also entered the STO scene in 2019 with Smartlands, a blockchain-based platform for tokenizing real-world assets. Singapore's DBS Bank conducted the first national STO worth approximately $15 million in digital bonds in 2021.

While these STOs managed to accumulate significant funds, the STO market size still pales in comparison to the traditional securities market or the ICO market during its peak. The stringent regulatory requirements limiting STO participation to accredited investors can curtail the potential investor base for these offerings. Moreover, with the decline of the crypto frenzy in the second half of 2018, investor interest in ICOs and subsequently in STOs also dwindled, further diminishing the number of firms willing to raise funds using STOs.

Advantages and Disadvantages of STOs

STOs were indeed considered the next step in the evolution of ICOs. The critical factor that underscored this progression was their regulatory compliance. Unlike their predecessor, the ICO, STOs were designed and developed with a clear aim to conform to existing securities laws. This approach not only reduced the risks of regulatory enforcement actions that consistently loomed over ICOs, but also offered a safer and more secure environment for investors. In addition, a significant advantage of STOs was the heightened level of investor protection. This was achieved through stringent adherence to securities regulations, which mandated comprehensive disclosure requirements, robust anti-fraud measures, and several other safeguards. This practice provided a level of security and transparency that was often missing in ICOs, instilling greater confidence in potential investors.

The regulatory compliance of STOs paved the way for the attraction of institutional capital. The regulated and compliant framework of STOs was likely to entice institutional investors, a demographic that was previously hesitant about participating in ICOs due to noticeable regulatory uncertainties. By creating an environment that institutional investors found familiar and safe, STOs could have facilitated the flow of substantial capital into the blockchain sector.

Finally, one of the most compelling benefits of STOs over ICOs was the potential for enhanced liquidity. Security tokens could be traded on regulated exchanges, unlike many tokens issued through ICOs. This opportunity for trading increased liquidity for investors, granting them easier access to secondary markets. The ability to buy and sell these securities on regulated platforms could have given investors more confidence and could have stimulated more active participation in STOs.

In presenting these advantages over ICOs, STOs aimed to bridge the gap between traditional financial markets and the rapidly growing world of blockchain technology. Their goal was to create opportunities for broader participation and innovation in the digital asset space. However, despite these intentions, STOs never truly gained widespread acceptance. To date, after the cooling of the crypto hype and several *crypto winters*, the number of STOs remains small. Few STOs have been conducted since 2021. This trend can be attributed to several reasons.

First and foremost, the costs and complexities associated with compliance can be prohibitively high for smaller companies or projects. The need to adhere strictly to securities laws can render STOs less attractive as a fundraising method, given the associated time and financial resources required for due diligence, legal counsel, and ongoing reporting.

Moreover, the pool of potential participants in STOs is often limited due to stringent regulatory requirements. In many instances, participation is restricted to accredited or qualified investors. This limitation not only reduces the universality that was a hallmark of ICOs, but it also narrows the potential for capital formation. Adding to these concerns is the uncertain regulatory landscape. While STOs are designed to be compliant with current securities laws, these laws and regulations continue to evolve. Future changes in regulation may impact the market, creating an unpredictable operating environment for STO issuers and investors alike.

The promise of enhanced liquidity, a touted advantage of STOs, has also been called into question. The reality is that liquidity does not arise spontaneously as a consequence of conducting an STO. Achieving meaningful liquidity, especially in private markets and with small and micro-cap issuers, is a complex and challenging process. Compounding this issue is the limited number of secondary markets available for trading security tokens. Despite a few platforms facilitating such trade, they often lack substantial volume, undermining their establishment's purpose. The scarcity of such exchanges is attributed to the complicated, expensive, and risky process of obtaining necessary licences and maintaining compliance across multiple jurisdictions. Traditional stock exchanges are also not yet equipped to accommodate security tokens due to infrastructure limitations for blockchain-based digital assets.

Moreover, there is a stark lack of liquidity providers, a crucial component in the creation of real liquidity. The mere existence of several exchanges does not guarantee adequate liquidity. It requires a supporting infrastructure of market makers and other liquidity providers. Another challenge lies in the overstated demand from retail investors. The allure of global access to unaccredited retail investors, a significant selling point of STOs, may not hold up in reality. Even if we suppose it does, it is not necessarily true that retail investors are clamouring for security tokens. Most people do not invest in traditional equity markets despite the relatively straightforward access to popular companies.

Lastly, contrary to popular belief, STOs do not provide easy access to a global pool of investors. Compliance with securities regulations in one jurisdiction does not permit a company to offer its security tokens worldwide or even nationwide. In summary, STOs have not made fundraising significantly easier or cheaper – a key incentive that drove the proliferation of ICOs as a new way to quickly raise funds while avoiding traditional venture capital or banks. In this light, it is evident why STOs have not gained the traction initially expected, and other methods like exchange offerings have gained popularity instead.

IEOs

As the digital asset fundraising landscape continues to evolve, new methods have emerged to address the challenges and limitations associated with ICOs,

SAFTs, and STOs. One such development is the rise of exchange offerings, which have gained traction as an alternative fundraising method. This section will focus on IEOs, exploring their definition, mechanism, advantages, disadvantages, and notable examples.

An IEO is a fundraising method in which a cryptocurrency exchange facilitates the sale of tokens on behalf of a project. IEOs combine aspects of ICOs and traditional exchange listings, with the exchange acting as an intermediary between the project and the investors. In an IEO, a cryptocurrency exchange takes on the role of an intermediary between the project team and investors, managing the token sale and providing a range of services, such as due diligence, marketing support, and compliance. IEOs represent a shift in the digital asset fundraising model, transferring the responsibility of managing the token sale process from the project team to the exchange. This arrangement offers several benefits to both projects and investors. For projects, partnering with a reputable exchange can boost their credibility and enhance their public profile, while also streamlining the fundraising process by leveraging the exchange's existing user base and compliance infrastructure. Investors, on the other hand, can benefit from the exchange's due diligence and vetting of projects, reducing the risk of participating in fraudulent or low-quality token sales.

However, IEOs also introduce new challenges and potential drawbacks. For instance, the reliance on a single exchange for the token sale can create a degree of centralization, potentially exposing the project and investors to the risks associated with the exchange's security, management, and regulatory compliance. Additionally, the fees associated with hosting an IEO can be substantial, potentially making this fundraising method less accessible for smaller or less well-funded projects (Anson 2021).

Despite these challenges, IEOs have gained popularity as a fundraising method in recent years, with numerous high-profile exchanges launching dedicated IEO platforms, such as Binance Launchpad, Huobi Prime, and OKEx Jumpstart. The growth of the IEO market reflects the continued evolution of the digital asset fundraising landscape, as projects and investors seek more reliable, efficient, and compliant ways to raise capital and invest in the emerging blockchain ecosystem.

Definition and Mechanism

IEOs emerged as a distinctive evolution in the digital asset fundraising space, particularly addressing some of the perceived shortcomings of ICOs. In an IEO, the cryptocurrency exchange takes centre stage, serving as the primary platform for the offering. The exchange manages the process of the token sale, conducts due diligence, and vets the projects that seek to raise funds through its platform.

Contrary to the traditional ICO model where projects issue tokens directly to investors, in an IEO, the projects issue tokens – generally utility tokens – via the exchange platform. The exchange not only facilitates the sale but also often handles Know Your Customer (KYC) and Anti-Money Laundering (AML) procedures, ensuring that investors meet the necessary requirements for participating in the token sale. This further adds a layer of compliance and security to the process. Once the IEO is completed, the tokens are typically made available for trading on the same exchange, which offers immediate liquidity to investors.

In a way, this evolution signifies a return to a form of financial intermediation that blockchain technology initially aimed to eliminate. Traditional lending models rely heavily on intermediaries like banks or venture capitalists to make the process more efficient, secure, and trustworthy. These intermediaries perform various useful functions, such as risk assessment, due diligence, and regulatory compliance, to facilitate the lending process.

Interestingly, the evolution of ICOs into IEOs has witnessed a similar trend, with cryptocurrency exchanges stepping in to fulfil the role of intermediaries. These exchanges, through their due diligence and compliance procedures, seek to mitigate the problems of information asymmetry and moral hazard that have plagued the ICO model. These issues, which often resulted in reckless investments with uncertain outcomes, deterred many potential participants from engaging with ICOs.

While the concept of crowdfunding kickstarted with regulated platforms coordinating the process, ICOs initially operated without such intermediaries. However, by 2020, the model had mutated into a platform-based approach, with cryptocurrency exchanges taking up intermediary roles. These exchanges performed similar functions to traditional financial intermediaries – vetting projects, conducting due diligence, managing regulatory compliance, and providing a platform for trading – thereby helping to restore trust and efficiency in the process of blockchain-based fundraising.

Advantages and Disadvantages of IEOs

IEOs possess some notable advantages that have contributed to their popularity as an alternative to ICOs or STOs. A paramount advantage of an IEO is the enhanced trust and credibility it offers to investors. Unlike ICOs, which were largely unregulated and faced significant trust issues, IEOs operate under the purview of established cryptocurrency exchanges. This means that projects looking to raise capital through an IEO must pass through the due diligence procedures set by the exchange. These procedures serve to vet the project's legitimacy, reducing the risk of fraud – a pervasive problem in the world of ICOs. Consequently, investors can take confidence in the fact that the project has undergone rigorous scrutiny and is held accountable to the exchange's standards, significantly bolstering the trust and credibility of the token offering.

Moreover, IEOs offer a much more streamlined process for investor onboarding. Since exchanges take the responsibility of managing KYC and AML procedures, the friction for both projects and investors is considerably reduced. This leads to a smoother, more efficient transaction process, a stark contrast to the often cumbersome and complex procedures seen in ICOs. Another key advantage that distinguishes IEOs from their ICO or STO counterparts is the immediate liquidity they provide. Once the IEO concludes, the tokens are typically listed for trading on the same exchange, facilitating price discovery and offering immediate liquidity for investors. This feature is particularly attractive as it eliminates the uncertain waiting period often associated with ICOs before a token gets listed on an exchange.

Lastly, the role of exchanges in an IEO extends beyond merely facilitating the token offering. Often, exchanges also provide extensive marketing support to projects conducting an IEO. This partnership with a well-known exchange can help increase awareness of the project, attracting a larger pool of potential investors, and potentially increasing the overall success of the token sale.

The evolution of ICOs into IEOs signifies a natural progression in the blockchain startup financing world. Given the multitude of benefits of IEOs, it is not surprising that they have effectively replaced ICOs. From 2021 onwards, traditional ICOs have become a rarity, with only sporadic campaigns claiming (often without tangible confirmation) to have raised significant funds. The shift towards IEOs has been marked and decisive. By addressing the pitfalls that were inherent to ICOs, IEOs have crafted a more trustworthy and user-friendly landscape for both projects seeking to raise capital and investors eager to participate in the expanding realm of digital asset investments. Nevertheless, despite their popularity, it is worth noting that the frequency and volumes of IEOs have not reached the heady heights of the ICO boom in 2017–2018.

While the advantages of IEOs are numerous, they are not without their limitations and drawbacks. These disadvantages must be considered alongside the benefits to present a comprehensive view of the current state of startup blockchain financing. Among these, one of the most considerable is the cost associated with hosting an IEO. Exchanges typically charge a substantial fee for this service, and these fees can significantly increase the cost of fundraising, especially for smaller projects. The price is so high that not all projects can afford it, which brings into question the cost-effectiveness of using IEOs as a fundraising method.

Another notable concern is the degree of centralization that comes with conducting an IEO. Since the process relies heavily on a single exchange, it introduces a level of centralization that may not sit well with the decentralized ethos championed by many projects and investors in the blockchain space.

This centralization is a stark contrast to the principle of decentralization, which forms the bedrock of the blockchain ecosystem.

A significant limitation of IEOs is their potential to restrict investor access. Participation in IEOs is generally confined to the users of the hosting exchange, thereby possibly reducing the pool of potential investors. This is in stark contrast to ICOs, which are typically open to the public. Moreover, popular exchanges, faced with high demand for IEO tokens, often resort to rationing investor participation or mandating the possession of exchange tokens for participation. Due to the high demand for buying coins in an IEO, exchanges often hold a lottery to decide who gets to buy and how much they can purchase. This practice results in investor rationing, which can be a point of frustration for many participants. Moreover, transaction fees incurred during participation add to the costs for the investors.

This requirement to hold exchange tokens in order to participate introduces an added layer of risk associated with market volatility. To join an IEO, investors are frequently required to lock in the principal token of the exchange for a specific duration. This lock-in period can leave investors exposed to market risks if there are substantial market fluctuations, which could potentially lead to significant losses.

Lastly, the quality of cryptocurrency exchange platforms varies significantly. While some are stringent in conducting due diligence and enforcing regulations, others may not uphold the same standards. As such, the reputation of the exchange platform becomes a vital factor in the success of hosting an IEO. If an exchange encounters any security or operational issues, it could negatively impact the IEO, further emphasizing the importance of due diligence and careful selection of the exchange platform for hosting an IEO.

Notable IEO Examples

Some noteworthy examples of successful IEOs underscore the potential benefits of this fundraising approach. Take BitTorrent Token (BTT), for example. In January 2019, BitTorrent launched its IEO on the Binance Launchpad, managing to raise $7.2 million in just 15 minutes. The BTT serves an integral function within the BitTorrent ecosystem, facilitating faster download speeds and access to premium features for its users. This IEO was not the first on the Binance Launchpad, but its speedy fundraising success drew significant attention to this novel form of fundraising on cryptocurrency exchanges, particularly in light of the concurrent decline in traditional ICOs.

In response to this growing interest, numerous other cryptocurrency exchanges set up their own launchpads, offering their services to blockchain startups that either lacked the capability to run independent ICOs or were too small to finance an STO. By mid-2019, around 40 exchanges had hosted at least one IEO, and approximately 180 projects had secured funding through this channel.[1]

Another successful example is the Matic Network, which held an IEO on the Binance Launchpad in April 2019, raising $5 million to develop a scalable blockchain platform. The MATIC tokens serve as the native currency of the Matic Network, powering transactions and securing the network. Elrond followed suit in July 2019, conducting its own IEO on the Binance Launchpad and raising $3.25 million to build a scalable, high throughput blockchain platform. ERD tokens are used for governance, staking, and transactions within the Elrond ecosystem.

However, the IEO landscape was, and continues to be, dominated by a small number of reputable exchanges. For instance, only 28 IEOs were hosted by just six prominent exchanges by mid-2019, with the majority listed on smaller venues often accused of manipulating trading volumes or orchestrating pump-and-dump schemes. Once again, the significance of the intermediary's role in IEO success was highlighted, with most of the biggest and most successful IEOs listed on Binance, the world's largest crypto exchange.

While there have been many successful IEOs, there have also been instances where IEOs failed to meet expectations or encountered difficulties. One such example is Raid (RAID). Scheduled to launch its IEO on Bittrex International in March 2019, the exchange decided to cancel the offering mere hours before it was set to begin. This sudden cancellation was due to the discovery of fraudulent claims made by the founders regarding partnerships between RAID and gaming data companies, OP.GG, and Riot Games.

Another case of an underperforming IEO was Ocean Protocol (OCEAN). Despite launching on Bittrex International in April 2019, it only raised about $6 million of its intended $8 million hard cap. Following the IEO, the price of the OCEAN token dropped significantly, causing losses for investors. The Ocean Protocol project focuses on building a decentralized data exchange platform, but despite its ambitious goals, the IEO's underperformance and subsequent token price decline raised concerns among investors.

THE ROLE OF CRYPTO EXCHANGES

As was already mentioned above, cryptocurrency exchanges have played a critical role in the evolution of digital asset fundraising methods, emerging as key intermediaries in the process. This section will explore the role of crypto exchanges in the IEO and STO landscape, highlighting the similarities and differences between exchanges and traditional crowdfunding platforms.

Crypto Exchanges as New Intermediaries

In the landscape of digital asset offerings, the reputation of a cryptocurrency exchange has proved to be a critical factor in determining the success of an IEO. This reputation factor resembles the dynamics of traditional financial markets, where the credibility of an investment bank can significantly influence the outcome of an IPO. Similarly, in the crypto ecosystem, the standing of an exchange can carry substantial weight for projects choosing a platform for their IEO.

Drawing parallels between cryptocurrency exchanges hosting IEOs and traditional crowdfunding platforms unveils both commonalities and critical differences. Both mediums operate as intermediaries, facilitating the process of fundraising for projects while simultaneously serving as platforms for investors to discover and support these initiatives. Yet, the nuances distinguishing these two models span across the types of assets offered, the regulatory frameworks they function under, their targeted investor base, and the liquidity they provide.

In terms of the assets on offer, crowdfunding platforms traditionally facilitate fundraising by offering rewards, services, or equity to their backers in return for financial support. These platforms might support creative projects, new product developments, or early-stage startups looking for equity financing. Contrastingly, cryptocurrency exchanges host token sales, such as IEOs and STOs. In these scenarios, backers are offered digital tokens that might serve various roles within the project's ecosystem, such as providing access to a service, granting governance rights, or serving as a form of currency.

The regulatory landscapes of these two mediums are strikingly different. Cryptocurrency exchanges functioning in the domain of digital assets navigate a relatively nascent and complex regulatory framework. The laws governing digital asset fundraising methods like IEOs and STOs vary by jurisdiction and continue to evolve rapidly. Crypto exchanges must ensure compliance with a diverse array of regulations, such as securities laws, and KYC and AML requirements. In contrast, crowdfunding platforms operate under a more established and predictable set of regulations, although these can also vary significantly between jurisdictions.

When it comes to the investor base, crowdfunding platforms are typically designed to attract a wide spectrum of backers, ranging from average individuals to institutional investors. These platforms can cater to different levels of financial sophistication and often emphasize the story or mission behind a project, making it appealing to a broad audience. On the other hand, cryptocurrency exchanges cater to a more specialized audience. Participants in IEOs or STOs are generally individuals with a deeper understanding of blockchain technology, cryptocurrency markets, and digital assets. They are investors who are often comfortable with the associated risks and volatility of the crypto world.

Finally, the liquidity provided by these two mediums is vastly different. Digital tokens sold through IEOs or STOs on crypto exchanges typically offer immediate liquidity to investors. The tokens are often listed for trading on the exchange shortly after the token sale concludes, allowing investors to buy or sell these assets freely. This dynamic creates an active secondary market, which is a major draw for investors looking for flexibility and the opportunity for short-term gains. Crowdfunding platforms, in contrast, may not provide a secondary market for the assets or rewards they offer. Whether it is a reward-based perk or equity in a startup, these investments are typically less liquid and often require a long-term commitment from backers.

In the early days of IEOs, some projects were hosted on lesser-known, smaller exchanges. These venues were often accused of unethical practices such as price manipulation and pump-and-dump schemes, where prices were artificially inflated to attract investors before being abruptly sold off for profit. Such unsavoury incidents created a climate of mistrust and uncertainty, deterring potential investors and projects from participating in IEOs. However, with time, the scenario began to change. Certain exchanges started to set themselves apart with their stringent due diligence processes, regulatory compliance, robust security measures, and strong commitment to investor protection. These platforms gained prominence and became the preferred choice for conducting IEOs, thereby reinforcing the importance of exchange reputation in this fundraising model.

Among these, a few exchanges including Binance, Huobi, and OKEx, have managed to secure strong footholds in the IEO domain. Binance, in particular, has become a standout leader. Its dominance can be attributed to its expansive global presence, a broad and diverse investor base, and an impressive trading volume. Furthermore, Binance's stringent vetting process for projects, coupled with a robust infrastructure for conducting IEOs, has significantly contributed to its reputation and success. Binance's role in the IEO ecosystem has grown so prominent that its Launchpad platform is often the first choice for blockchain startups looking to raise capital. The Launchpad's successful track record has boosted investor confidence, which in turn has drawn more projects to it, creating a virtuous cycle that has further reinforced Binance's standing in the IEO space.

In the following section, we delve deeper into Binance's role in the IEO ecosystem, exploring how it has used its global presence, technological prowess, and reputation to become a pivotal player in the world of IEOs.

Binance

Binance, one of the largest and most influential cryptocurrency exchanges, has played a leading role in the IEO market through its Binance Launchpad platform. While Binance has primarily focused on IEOs, the exchange also expressed interest in the STO market. In 2019, Binance announced the acquisition of the token issuance platform, TokenSoft, which specializes in STOs. This acquisition signalled Binance's intent to expand into the STO market and leverage its position as a leading exchange, providing comprehensive token fundraising services to issuers. However, Binance's plans appear to have changed later on, and as of mid-2023, there are no signs of its involvement in STO offerings.

Binance has instead focused on IEOs, through its introduction of Binance Launchpad, the exclusive token launch platform for transformative blockchain projects (Aysan 2021). Before Launchpad, blockchain projects staged their own ICOs to raise crypto funds for their own growth and development. Results have varied under this old approach, with each success story being matched by cautionary tales of failures and frauds, and crypto users who lacked necessary protections were left on their own. The introduction of IEOs on Binance Launchpad spurred a new paradigm under which projects can raise funds and users can support these projects in a more convenient and safer way.

While IEO campaigns on Binance Launchpad do resemble ICOs by nature, they have some specific peculiarities. To begin, interested participants must first create an account on Binance. This acts as the primary step towards engaging in the wide range of services and offerings provided by the platform, including its renowned IEOs. Signing up is a simple process, typically requiring only a valid email address and a secure password. However, if an investor wants to have access to a wider range of services and products, the next crucial step involves the completion of KYC and AML procedures. This phase ensures regulatory compliance, a key component of Binance's operations, and bolsters the security of all transactions on the platform. During this procedure, Binance users will need to provide identification documents such as a passport or an ID card, along with proof of address. However, it is important to remember that due to varying regulatory landscapes, residents of certain countries might be restricted from participating in IEOs.

After fulfilling the KYC/AML requirements, users are then required to hold Binance Coin (BNB) in their accounts. BNB plays a significant role in the Binance ecosystem, enabling users to participate in Binance Launchpad projects. The specific holding period and amount of BNB required can vary with each project, with details typically announced by Binance ahead of each IEO. In general, the greater the quantity of BNB a user holds for a predetermined period before the IEO, the higher their chances of securing more tokens offered. This requirement has created an intriguing pattern for BNB prices, whereby they often increase, sometimes by up to 5–7 per cent, at the time of the announcement of the next IEO. This occurs as investors accumulate their BNB holdings, and then the price tends to drop somewhat once the BNB Holding Calculation Period is nearing its end. This pattern is well known and serves as a nice opportunity for arbitrage for savvy investors.

After encountering issues with the first-come-first-served basis of IEO token distributions – where sales were concluded within minutes – Binance revised its Launchpad Token Sale Format. Since March 2019, Binance has adopted a lottery system for most of its IEOs. This serves as the primary mechanism by which users can purchase tokens. The number of lottery tickets a user can claim directly correlates to the amount of BNB held in their account. After the specified holding period, users can claim their lottery tickets and then wait for the lottery draw. If a user's ticket is drawn, an equivalent amount of BNB is deducted from their account in exchange for the tokens. The final stage of this process is the receipt of tokens. For lottery winners, IEO tokens are directly distributed into their accounts. These tokens can then be freely traded once they are listed on Binance, usually one to two days after the token distribution.

IEOs run on Binance have proven to be quite successful. First, IEOs trigger enormous interest because the coins launched through them begin trading on Binance almost immediately. So far, nearly every single token launched through an IEO on Binance Launchpad has seen its price skyrocket immediately after it was listed for trading on the exchange, from 2019 up to the first half of 2023. Typically, the initial average daily trading price is at least ten times higher than the offering price. Naturally, this attracts a lot of attention from investors. In a way, Binance IEOs represent a form of *free lunch* for its customers who maintain BNB balances in their cryptocurrency portfolios. However, given the high demand, the final token allocations to retail customers typically represent only 1–2 per cent of their BNB holdings, measured at the first-day trading prices.

From its inception until the start of the second half of 2023, Binance Launchpad conducted 36 IEOs, raising more than $60 million with over 4 million total unique participants. The number of campaigns is below the once per month target set by Binance at the launch of the platform. However, considering the challenges posed by the COVID-19 pandemic and the significant price correction of Bitcoin and other cryptocurrencies in recent times, this is still notable progress.

CONCLUSION

Previously, we emphasized one of the most significant drawbacks of IEOs – their high cost for founders. This hefty expense has left many teams merely dreaming about the possibility of being listed on a reputable exchange, explaining the relatively low number of IEOs conducted in recent years. However, the relentless advance of innovation propels the industry forward, always seeking solutions to current challenges. One such breakthrough in response to the high costs associated with IEOs has been the emergence of Decentralized Exchange Offerings. Additionally, the introduction of Non-Fungible Tokens has expanded the scope of blockchain financing, predominantly serving the art industry.

Although these mechanisms do not strictly conform to the traditional ICO format, their significant impact and potential to shape the future of blockchain financing are undeniable. Consequently, we dedicate the final chapter of our book to these two innovative fundraising methods, aiming to illuminate their role in the evolution of the blockchain financing landscape.

NOTES

1   staging.bitcoinist.com/just-64-of-legitimate-ieos-were-profitable-new-data
-shows.

REFERENCES

Anson, M. (2021) 'Initial exchange offerings: The next evolution in cryptocurrencies', *The Journal of Alternative Investments*, 23(4), pp. 110–121.
Aysan, A.F., Khan, A.U.I., Topuz, H., and Tunali, A.S. (2021) 'Survival of the fittest: A natural experiment from crypto exchanges', *The Singapore Economic Review*, https://doi.org/10.1142/S0217590821470020.
Boreiko, D., Ferrarini, G., and Giudici, P. (2019) 'Blockchain startups and prospectus regulation', *European Business Organization Law Review*, 20, pp. 665–694.
Chaisse, J. and Kirkwood, J. (2022) 'Tokenised funding and initial litigation offerings: The new kids putting third-party funding on the block', *Law and Financial Markets Review*, 16(1), pp. 20–42.
Henker, R., Atzberger, D., Scheibel, W., and Doellner, J. (2023) 'Real estate tokenization in Germany: Market analysis and concept of a regulatory and technical solution', in 2023 IEEE International Conference on Blockchain and Cryptocurrency (ICBC) (pp. 1–5). IEEE.
Kondova, G. and Simonella, G. (2019) 'Blockchain in startup financing: ICOs and STOs in Switzerland', *Journal of Strategic Innovation and Sustainability*, 14(6), pp. 43–48.
Lambert, T., Liebau, D., and Roosenboom, P. (2022) 'Security token offerings', *Small Business Economics*, 59, pp. 299–325.
Maas, T. (2019) 'Initial Coin Offerings: When are tokens securities in the EU and US?', SSRN. Available at: https://ssrn.com/abstract=3337514 (accessed: 1 July 2023).
Mendelson, M. (2019) 'From Initial Coin Offerings to security tokens: A US Federal Securities law analysis', *Stanford Technology Law Review*, 22(1). Available at: law.stanford.edu/publications/from-initial-coin-offerings-to-security-tokens-a-u-s
-federal-securities-law-analysis (accessed: 1 July 2023).

Momtaz, P.P. (2023) 'Security tokens'. In H. Kent Baker, H. Benedetti, E. Nikbakht, and S. Stein Smith (eds.), *The Emerald Handbook on Cryptoassets: Investment Opportunities and Challenges*. Leeds, UK: Emerald Publishing Limited, pp. 61–78.

Takahashi, K. (2019) 'Prescriptive jurisdiction in securities regulations: Transformation from the ICO (Initial Coin Offering) to the STO (Security Token Offering) and the IEO (Initial Exchange Offering)', SSRN. Available at: https://ssrn.com/abstract= 3566663 (accessed: 1 July 2023).

Wang, C. (2023) 'Trading securities as digital tokens', SSRN. Available at: https://ssrn .com/abstract=4341289 (accessed: 1 July 2023).

11. Decentralized finance and Non-Fungible Tokens

The emergence of blockchain technology has paved the way for new forms of finance and digital assets. Two of the most prominent examples are Decentralized Finance (DeFi) and Non-Fungible Tokens (NFTs). While they differ from previous blockchain financing models such as Initial Coin Offerings (ICOs), Simple Agreements for Future Tokens (SAFTs), Security Token Offerings (STOs), and Initial Exchange Offerings (IEOs), they share a similar spirit of innovation. DeFi introduced Decentralized Exchanges (DEXs) – platforms that facilitate token trading and other financial operations without a middleman. These platforms have proven extremely valuable as they allow for direct token listing, enabling project founders to finance their ventures almost cost-free. The so-called Initial DEX offerings represent a new form of blockchain financing that is a follower of ICOs and a direct competitor of IEOs. Conversely, NFTs have emerged as a popular method for financing ventures in the arts industry.

In this final chapter, we will begin with an overview of DeFi. We will define what it is, contrast it with traditional finance, and delve into the key components of the DeFi ecosystem. This section explores a variety of DeFi platforms and protocols, including lending and borrowing platforms, DEXs, asset management platforms, prediction markets, and insurance services. Subsequently, we shift our focus to NFTs, providing an explanation of what they are, their use cases, and key characteristics. We will discuss how NFTs, which originated in digital art, have evolved to cover a broad range of applications in gaming, collectibles, and real-world assets.

Next, we examine the evolution from ICOs and IEOs to IDOs and NFTs. We will highlight the lessons learned from the ICO boom and how IDOs and NFTs have addressed some of the previous model's shortcomings. We will also explore the advantages IDOs and NFTs have over ICOs in terms of security, transparency, and flexibility. In the following section, we delve into the risks and challenges associated with IDOs and NFTs.

Finally, we will look towards the future of DeFi, IDOs, and NFTs, exploring the trends shaping the DeFi ecosystem and the potential impact of NFTs on the global financial system. We will examine the prospects for the adoption and mainstream integration of NFTs and the potential for DEX offerings to transform the financial landscape, fulfilling the financing needs of funds-hungry startups, in the blockchain industry and beyond.

DeFi

DeFi, short for Decentralized Finance, is an emerging financial system built on top of blockchain technology. It seeks to offer an alternative to traditional finance by creating a more open, transparent, and accessible financial system that is not dependent on centralized intermediaries, such as banks or financial institutions (Schueffel 2021). Generally speaking, it is both a large-scale vision for a new way of conducting financial transactions – free from intermediaries, central authorities, and done exclusively in a peer-to-peer modality – as well as an umbrella term for scores of non-custodial financial products and services known as protocols. DeFi is inextricably linked to the rise of cryptocurrencies, but it is not solely about crypto tokens. In this section, we will provide an overview of DeFi, including its definition, how it compares to traditional finance, and the key components of the DeFi ecosystem.

Definition and Overview of DeFi

DeFi represents a broad financial system operating on decentralized networks such as Ethereum. Utilizing open-source software, smart contracts, and blockchain technology, DeFi applications are created that are accessible to anyone with an internet connection. They operate in a permissionless environment, meaning anyone can participate without the need for approval from a central authority (Chen and Bellavitis 2020).

In the early 2010s, it became evident that the Bitcoin blockchain required upgrading or replacement by a more advanced, flexible network capable of accommodating the expanding needs of the crypto industry. Early projects, dubbed *coloured coins*, greatly enhanced Bitcoin's functionality (Rosenfeld 2012). The Mastercoin project (later rebranded as Omni) was a pioneering ICO that introduced Mastercoins as a digital currency and communications protocol built on the Bitcoin blockchain. It promised features such as a DEX, but due to limited functionality and traction, it did not become a standard.

Notable successors, like BitShares and Waves, were launched in 2014 and 2016, respectively. BitShares, founded by Dan Larimer, who also co-founded blockchain projects Steemit and EOS, aimed to improve financial market efficiency and accessibility using blockchain technology. It allowed users to trade digital assets directly without a centralized third party. Waves, a blockchain platform, included a DEX as a key feature. The Waves DEX enables users to trade their tokens, including Waves-based custom tokens, directly from their wallets. It is designed to facilitate the issuance, trading, and management of digital assets and has been utilized by many projects to issue, distribute, and exchange their custom cryptocurrencies.

However, it was the Ethereum project, with its innovative smart contract functionality, that was instrumental in fostering the development of DeFi on a large scale. Ethereum introduced a new approach to blockchain technology (Chen et al. 2020). Unlike Bitcoin, which uses its blockchain primarily for peer-to-peer money transfer, Ethereum is designed to serve as a platform for running complex applications known as smart contracts. A smart contract is a self-executing contract with the terms of the agreement directly written into lines of code. The code and the agreements contained therein exist across a distributed, decentralized blockchain network.

Smart contracts automate the execution of an agreement, eliminating the need for a trusted intermediary and thus making transactions trustless, transparent, and secure. This functionality enabled a whole new array of decentralized applications (dApps), many of which fall under the DeFi umbrella. DeFi and dApps offer a range of financial services, including borrowing and lending, trading, asset management, and insurance. These services are built on top of decentralized protocols and operate without intermediaries. Users can interact with the DeFi ecosystem using digital wallets, such as MetaMask, and can transact with a variety of cryptocurrencies. Flexibility and versatility have been key factors that have allowed DeFi to proliferate and gain popularity.

Contrasting Traditional Finance and DeFi

The evolution of the financial industry has always been marked by the pursuit of more efficient, secure, and accessible ways of managing and transferring wealth. Traditional finance systems are largely centralized, with established financial institutions such as banks, insurance companies, and stock exchanges acting as intermediaries, playing a critical role in the financial ecosystem. These intermediaries serve various functions, including risk assessment, transaction validation, settlement processes, and regulatory compliance. They ensure the integrity and security of the financial system, facilitating trust between parties who may not have direct relationships. However, this traditional model often comes with drawbacks such as high transaction costs, limited accessibility for unbanked or underbanked populations, inefficiencies due to reliance on manual processes, and susceptibility to centralized points of failure.

Crypto exchanges emerged as a new type of intermediary within the blockchain ecosystem, offering a platform for users to trade cryptocurrencies. Even though these platforms utilized the innovative blockchain technology, their operational model was still based on conventional principles of financial intermediation. They acted as custodians of users' assets, maintained order books, matched buyers and sellers, and charged transaction fees, much like traditional stock exchanges. However, the ideal of a fully decentralized financial system, devoid of intermediaries, continued to inspire many within the blockchain industry. Early attempts, such as the ICO market, revealed the challenges of this vision, underscoring the need for certain oversight and control mechanisms to ensure system resilience and safety.

In contrast to the traditional and crypto exchange models, DeFi operates on a blockchain network, primarily Ethereum, utilizing smart contracts to automate financial transactions. This decentralized approach allows users to interact directly with protocols, bypassing intermediaries entirely. This shift can be described as a transition from a *user-to-user* model to a *user-to-contract* model, where users engage with smart contracts that automatically execute transactions based on pre-set rules (Wieandt and Heppding 2023).

DeFi offers several potential advantages over traditional finance. It could reduce costs by automating processes that are typically performed manually in traditional finance. It could also improve transparency since transactions on the blockchain are publicly visible, and smart contracts' code can be audited. Additionally, DeFi may offer greater financial inclusion by providing access to financial services for unbanked or underbanked populations, who may find the costs of traditional financial services prohibitive.

Nevertheless, even in developed countries like the US, a substantial unbanked population exists, primarily due to lack of funds. Traditional financial services often come with high costs, including account setup fees, transaction fees, and periodic charges such as credit card membership fees. Consequently, these services can be unattainable for individuals with low incomes, rendering them financially excluded. DeFi, by virtue of its decentralized and accessible nature, is viewed as a potential solution to this issue, enabling the provision of affordable, efficient, and secure financial services to a broader population.

Key Components of DeFi

DeFi has emerged as a transformative force in the financial landscape, fuelled by a combination of blockchain technology and the advent of smart contracts. Its value proposition lies in its ability to democratize access to financial services, eliminate intermediaries, and foster a more inclusive and efficient financial system. However, to fully comprehend its potential, one must delve into the core components that constitute the DeFi ecosystem (Ozili 2022).

At the foundation of DeFi lie blockchain networks. The most popular among them, Ethereum, serves as the bedrock for most DeFi applications. These networks are characterized by their decentralization, meaning no central authority governs their operation. Instead, their operation is distributed across multiple nodes worldwide. This global network of computers forms the infrastructure that upholds DeFi applications, providing a platform for the creation and execution of smart contracts.

Smart contracts are the neural synapses that bind and animate the DeFi world, creating a complex and interconnected network of automated financial services. These are essentially programmable contracts that automate the execution of agreements without the need for an intermediary. The terms of the contract are written in code and are executed automatically once the conditions specified in the contract are met. This automation reduces the need for trust between parties and eliminates the need for middlemen, thereby potentially reducing costs and increasing efficiency (John et al. 2022).

Built on these smart contracts are dApps. Unlike traditional applications, DApps operate within a decentralized environment and do not rely on a single entity for their operation. They leverage the transparency, security, and global accessibility of the blockchain. DeFi DApps are tailored specifically to offer financial services, such as lending, borrowing, or trading assets, mirroring the functions of traditional financial institutions but in a more open and inclusive manner (Metcalfe 2020).

A critical type of dApp in the DeFi space is DEX. These platforms provide users with a place to trade cryptocurrencies directly with each other, bypassing the need for an intermediary. DEXs operate through smart contracts, making them open and accessible to anyone with an internet connection. By doing away with central control, dApps and DEXs confer users with unprecedented control over their assets and transactions.

Stablecoins are another integral component of the DeFi ecosystem, providing much-needed stability in the otherwise volatile crypto market. They are cryptocurrencies designed to maintain a stable value, typically pegged to a reserve of stable assets like the US dollar or a commodity such as gold. They serve as a reliable medium of exchange, a stable store of value, and a unit of account within the DeFi ecosystem, enhancing its usability and utility.

Finally, oracles serve as the bridge between the on-chain world of blockchain and the off-chain real world. They relay off-chain data to smart contracts on the blockchain. As smart contracts are confined to the information within the blockchain, they rely on oracles for external data, like real-world events or price feeds, enabling DeFi applications to interact with the world outside their blockchain.

Together, these components work symbiotically to create the DeFi ecosystem. Their interaction facilitates a system that is transparent, open, and accessible, revolutionizing the way we interact with financial services. Nevertheless, each component presents its own set of challenges and vulnerabilities that need to be addressed for DeFi to realize its full potential and become a mainstay of the global financial system.

DeFi PROTOCOLS AND PLATFORMS

The core components mentioned above have facilitated the realization of various financial services within the DeFi ecosystem. These services include lending and borrowing, trading, asset management, and insurance, all of which are built on top of decentralized protocols and platforms. In this section, we will delve into some of these key DeFi protocols and platforms, which encompass lending and borrowing platforms, DEXs, asset management and tokenization platforms, prediction markets, and insurance providers.

To gauge the scale of the DeFi market, one can consider the total market capitalization of the tokens used by lending protocols, a method similar to those employed to compare the relative importance of conventional financial markets. However, it is crucial to note that in the context of DeFi, the market cap does not necessarily reflect the Total Value Locked (TVL) in the protocol. TVL includes all the assets that are currently staked, lent, or otherwise utilized within the platform.

According to data from the DeFi portal Stelareum.io, as of June 2023, the total TVL across all DeFi sectors stands at around $66 billion, with 175 active protocols (each having a TVL above $1 million) spread across eight major segments.[1] This is far below the peak values of $250 billion that the market saw in November 2021. Nonetheless, the resilience and survival of DeFi amidst crypto market fluctuations indicate that the DeFi ecosystem is likely to continue evolving in the future.

Lending and Borrowing Platforms

DeFi lending and borrowing platforms have revolutionized the traditional finance sector by allowing users to lend and borrow cryptocurrencies directly, eliminating the need for intermediaries like banks. By utilizing smart contracts, these platforms facilitate lending and borrowing agreements that are executed on the blockchain, providing users with enhanced control over their assets and often reducing fees and interest rates.

In essence, DeFi lending involves offering crypto loans on a decentralized platform. Among all the dApps, DeFi leads in global growth rate for lending services. DeFi has become one of the primary platforms for locking crypto assets due to its unique approach to lending. Unlike traditional banks' loan processing systems, DeFi lending empowers individuals to act as lenders, akin to the role traditionally played by banks. Individuals can lend their assets to others directly and earn interest on these loans. Rather than depending on loan officers found in traditional banks, DeFi lending relies on lending pools. Users can add their assets to these pools, facilitating efficient loan distribution among borrowers through smart contracts.

Savings

The DeFi dApps development services are now coming up with innovative ways of savings management through the DeFi lending apps. By plugging into different lending platforms, users can maximize their earnings and avail the services of interest-bearing accounts.

Some notable lending and borrowing platforms include Aave, a prominent DeFi platform, that empowers users to lend and borrow cryptocurrencies, eliminating intermediaries by leveraging smart contracts to establish lending and borrowing agreements. Users have the flexibility to choose between fixed and variable interest rates. As of June 2023, Aave commands a dominant market position, holding 77 per cent of the sector's market share, significantly ahead of its nearest competitor, Compound, which holds a 10 per cent share.

Compound is another renowned DeFi lending platform that employs smart contracts to facilitate the lending and borrowing of cryptocurrencies. It uses an algorithmic model to determine interest rates based on supply and demand, enabling users to earn interest on their deposited assets. The platform gained significant backing in 2018 when eminent venture capital firms, Andreessen Horowitz and Bain Capital Ventures, contributed $8.2 million to Compound's investment round. In the cryptocurrency ecosystem, security is crucial, and Compound prioritizes this aspect. The platform has undergone numerous security audits by renowned auditors, including Trail of Bits and Open Zeppelin, which have confirmed the reliability of the platform's coding and its capacity to secure network demands.

Asset Management and Tokenization Platforms

DeFi asset management and tokenization platforms allow users to manage their cryptocurrency assets and create new digital assets on the blockchain. These platforms use smart contracts to automate asset management and enable the creation of new tokens. The key advantage of these platforms is that they provide users with greater control over their assets and enable the creation of new digital assets. Some notable asset management and tokenization platforms include Yearn Finance, Nexus Mutual, and Polymath.

Yearn Finance is a DeFi platform that automates yield farming by automatically moving funds between different DeFi protocols. The platform is designed to maximize returns on deposited assets and is accessible to anyone with an internet connection. Nexus Mutual is a DeFi insurance platform that uses smart contracts to provide coverage against smart contract bugs and hacks. The platform allows users to pool their funds and collectively underwrite insurance policies. Polymath is a platform that allows users to create and manage digital assets on the blockchain. The platform enables the creation of security tokens, which are digital tokens that represent ownership in real-world assets, such as stocks, bonds, and real estate.

Prediction Markets and Insurance

DeFi prediction markets and insurance platforms allow users to bet on the outcome of real-world events and hedge against risks, such as smart contract bugs and hacks. These platforms use smart contracts to create markets and enable users to trade in real-time. The key advantage of these platforms is that they provide users with greater control over their assets and enable more efficient risk management.

Some notable prediction markets and insurance platforms include Augur, Opyn, and UMA. Augur is a decentralized prediction market platform that allows users to bet on the outcome of real-world events. The platform uses a decentralized oracle system to determine the outcome of events, and users can earn fees for reporting on the outcome of such events. Opyn is a DeFi insurance platform that allows users to hedge against risks, such as smart contract bugs and hacks. The platform uses smart contracts to create insurance policies and enables users to buy and sell insurance on a secondary market. UMA is a DeFi platform that enables the creation of synthetic assets and pre-diction markets. The platform uses a unique synthetic token system to enable the creation of new digital assets and prediction markets.

DEXs

DEXs are platforms that enable the trading of cryptocurrencies without inter-mediaries, such as centralized exchanges. These platforms use smart contracts to execute trades and are accessible to anyone with an internet connection. The key advantage of DEXs is that they provide users with greater control over their assets, as well as increased privacy and security. They are instead dis-tributed across the blockchain, making them more resilient to hacks and thefts. Additionally, DEXs offer users greater privacy since they do not require Know Your Customer (KYC) checks or personal information to trade. DEX liquidity can be higher than some centralized exchanges, as the platform can draw from multiple liquidity sources.

In the context of this book on ICOs, DEXs play an integral role, ushering in a new form of blockchain financing known as IDOs. IDOs have democratized access to capital for many smaller companies within the crypto sphere. These offerings enable companies to list their tokens directly on a DEX, providing immediate liquidity and accessibility to investors. In an IDO, founders do not always raise capital by selling tokens directly to investors. Instead, founders generate a liquidity pool on the DEX, consisting of their native tokens representing the project and an equivalent value in another, often more established, cryptocurrency such as Ethereum or Binance Coin. As investors purchase these tokens, they add a corresponding value of the second cryptocurrency to the pool, thereby raising funds for the project.

The price of the tokens is dictated by their ratio to the second cryptocurrency in the pool – increasing demand drives up the token price and vice versa. However, the decentralized nature of this fundraising method also carries inherent risks. A significant drop in the token's price can reduce the value of the liquidity pool and the funds raised, necessitating careful management of the liquidity pool by projects. To ensure long-term project commitment and to protect investors, projects typically implement a vesting schedule in an IDO to gradually release funds over time. This schedule is encoded in the token's smart contract and is transparently available to all participants.

By providing a platform for direct, peer-to-peer trading, IDOs can eliminate many of the inefficiencies and inequities associated with traditional fundraising models. They lower the barriers to entry for both investors and projects, democratizing access to capital, and fostering a more inclusive and equitable financial ecosystem.

The TVL in DEXs stood at $20 billion as of June 2023, with competition fierce among new players. Notable DEXs include Uniswap, SushiSwap, Balancer, and Curve Finance. Uniswap and SushiSwap use an automated market maker (AMM) system to determine prices, incentivizing users to provide liquidity. Balancer uses a unique weighting system to balance asset supply in its pools, reducing price slippage. As of 2023, Curve Finance has risen to prominence in this sector. Designed for extremely efficient stablecoin trading, Curve allows users to trade between stablecoins with low slippage and fees. Despite not currently having a native token, Curve plans to release one in the future.

It is worth noting that the popularity of DEX offerings has led some crypto exchanges to organize decentralized liquidity pools for various tokens. For instance, Binance Launchpool allows new projects to list their tokens in a decentralized manner, aligning with the spirit of DEX offerings and bypassing traditional IEOs. As the DeFi sector evolves, platforms like these will likely continue to play a crucial role.

Future of DeFi

In summary, DeFi protocols and platforms are revolutionizing the financial industry by providing users with greater control over their assets and more efficient access to financial services. These platforms are built on top of decentralized technologies, such as blockchain and smart contracts, and offer a range of financial services, including lending and borrowing, trading, asset management, and insurance. While DeFi offers many advantages over traditional finance, there are also risks and challenges, such as smart contract vulnerabilities, liquidity and market risks, scalability and interoperability, and environmental concerns. As DeFi continues to evolve, it has the potential to transform the global financial system and bring financial services to those who are currently underserved or excluded.

US regulators have been stepping up their scrutiny of DeFi, a burgeoning marketplace for crypto assets that operates without meaningful regulatory oversight. The Securities and Exchange Commission (SEC) issued a revised proposal in May 2023 clarifying that DeFi crypto trading systems should be regulated like stock exchanges.[2] In addition, the US Treasury issued a paper in April 2023 that pointed out the illicit finance risks in DeFi.[3]

NFTs

NFTs have gained significant attention in recent years, but the concept can be traced back to 2017 with the launch of CryptoKitties, a blockchain-based virtual game developed by Axiom Zen on the Ethereum blockchain. CryptoKitties is often credited as the first successful use case for NFTs. It allowed users to adopt, raise, and trade virtual cats, with each cat represented as a unique token on Ethereum's blockchain. Each CryptoKitty was a non-fungible, unique asset that a user could truly own (i.e., have exclusive ownership rights that could be verified on the blockchain).

CryptoKitties' significance lay not just in its popularity, but also in the way it demonstrated the potential of blockchain beyond just financial transactions. It showcased how Ethereum's smart contract functionality could be used to create digital assets, each with its own set of unique attributes, thus giving each token a distinct value. The success of CryptoKitties sparked a wave of interest in NFTs, leading to the diverse array of use cases we see today, including digital art, virtual real estate, and even intellectual property rights. Despite the game's relative simplicity, it was innovative in that it highlighted the potential of NFTs for representing ownership of unique digital items. The notion of scarcity in the digital world, hitherto almost non-existent due to the ease of replication in the digital space, was also brought to the fore by CryptoKitties.

This marked the beginning of the NFT trend, which has since grown and evolved to include not just games but a wide variety of digital content, including artwork, music, virtual real estate, and more, each uniquely represented on the blockchain as an NFT. In the years since NFTs exploded in popularity, the situation has only gotten more complicated. Pictures of apes have sold for tens of millions of dollars, there has been an endless supply of headlines about million-dollar hacks of NFT projects, and corporate cash grabs have only gotten worse. Indeed, the general public have been puzzled by media reports of simplistic icons of various forms being sold for millions of dollars.

NFTs are a type of digital asset that represents ownership or proof of authenticity of a unique item, such as art, collectibles, and other rare or one-of-a-kind items. NFTs are built on top of blockchain technology, which provides a secure and transparent way to prove ownership and authenticity of the underlying asset. In this section, we will explore the definition and overview of NFTs, as well as their use cases.

Definition and Overview of NFTs

NFTs represent a significant evolution in the world of digital assets. They are unique tokens stored on a blockchain, and unlike cryptocurrencies such as Bitcoin or Ethereum, they cannot be exchanged on a like-for-like basis. Each NFT is distinct, carrying a unique identifier that sets it apart from any other NFT, thereby making it a truly unique digital asset. At the heart of this uniqueness is the immutable nature of blockchain technology that NFTs leverage. This technology provides a secure, transparent, and tamper-resistant ledger, thereby ensuring the provenance and authenticity of each NFT. When an NFT is bought or sold, the transaction is recorded on the blockchain, providing an unforgeable record of ownership that is publicly verifiable. This is a crucial feature of NFTs, as it gives them property rights, something that has been traditionally lacking in digital assets (Chalmers et al. 2022).

NFTs can represent a vast array of tangible and intangible items, including digital art, music, virtual real estate, virtual goods in video games, collectibles, and intellectual property rights. The concept of digital ownership has taken on new significance in recent years, and NFTs have been at the forefront of this shift.

The surge in popularity of NFTs has been fuelled by several high-profile sales. One of the most famous is the sale of digital artist Beeple's work *Everydays: The First 5000 Days*, which was sold as an NFT at a Christie's auction for a staggering $69 million.[4] Other high-profile sales include NBA Top Shot collectibles and virtual real estate parcels in Decentraland. Indeed, the market for NFTs has grown exponentially. In 2021 alone, sales of NFTs reached $2.5 billion, up from just $13.7 million in the first half of 2020. This explosive growth shows the widespread interest and investment in these unique digital assets. However, as with any rapidly expanding market, it is crucial for both creators and buyers to understand the potential risks and rewards associated with NFTs.

Use Cases for NFTs

Looking to the future, the potential applications of NFTs are vast. From tokenizing real-world assets to creating new forms of digital identity, NFTs could significantly transform many industries and practices. Despite the challenges and uncertainties, there is no denying the disruptive potential of NFTs, and their role in reshaping our understanding of digital ownership and value.

NFTs have sparked a revolution in numerous domains, expanding their significance far beyond the crypto world. One of the prominent fields affected by this disruption is art and collectibles. The conventional art realm has been astoundingly revitalized by the infusion of blockchain technology. With the advent of NFTs, artists can authenticate and sell digital art, which was once deemed of lesser value than physical pieces. NFTs help artists preserve the uniqueness and exclusivity of their work while providing the buyer with a verifiable proof of ownership. Similarly, tangible collectibles such as sports memorabilia and rare trading cards can be tokenized, adding an additional layer of security and traceability.

In the sphere of digital gaming, NFTs have opened up new horizons. In-game items can be represented by NFTs, adding real-world value to them. Players can now truly own, buy, sell, and trade these items in a secure and transparent environment. This functionality breathes life into the virtual economy, encouraging gamers to invest more time and resources into their virtual pursuits. The music and media industry also finds NFTs quite valuable. Musicians and artists can use NFTs to represent ownership of their work, allowing them to bypass traditional intermediaries. This direct sale of unique copies to fans provides artists with more control over their creative output as well as their earnings.

Furthermore, the influence of NFTs has also extended to the realm of real estate. They can be used to represent ownership of property, adding a new level of transparency and security to real estate transactions. This usage is transforming the way we think about property ownership, making it more accessible and efficient. Thus, NFTs, by providing an immutable record of ownership and the capability to tokenize nearly any asset, have opened up a wealth of opportunities across diverse sectors, promising to further blur the lines between the physical and the digital worlds.

EVOLUTION FROM ICOs TO IDOs AND NFTs

The advent of IDOs and NFTs represents a significant evolution in the world of blockchain and cryptocurrency, an evolution characterized by adaptability and innovation. This shift was prompted by a series of challenges and shortcomings associated with the traditional ICO fundraising model. Between

2015 and 2018, ICOs were the standard method for raising funds within the cryptocurrency space. However, despite their widespread use and the bustling marketplace of projects that they gave rise to, ICOs were inherently flawed in three major areas: their lack of regulatory oversight, their proliferation of fraudulent projects, and their disproportionate emphasis on rapid profitability over sustainable development.

The absence of regulatory oversight meant that ICOs often operated in a grey area, leading to a lack of trust and inhibiting widespread adoption. ICOs also attracted many fraudulent ventures looking to capitalize on the hype and potential for quick returns, which led to numerous high-profile scams. This situation eroded the credibility of ICOs as a funding mechanism and made investors wary. Moreover, ICOs were often driven by short-term profitability rather than the sustainable development of the project, which undermined the long-term success of many ventures.

This realization led to the emergence of IDOs and NFTs as alternatives that aimed to mitigate these issues. IDOs, facilitated on DEXs, offered a novel approach that prioritized transparency and security. The decentralized nature of DEXs allows for peer-to-peer transactions without intermediaries, resulting in a more open and inclusive process. Furthermore, IDOs introduced liquidity pools, creating an ecosystem where projects could raise capital indirectly, thereby providing immediate liquidity and access to investors. This structure addressed the challenges of sustainability and long-term development that often plagued ICOs.

On the other hand, NFTs introduced a unique approach to tokenizing assets on the blockchain. Unlike cryptocurrencies, which are fungible and identical to each other, NFTs are unique and cannot be interchanged on a like-for-like basis. This characteristic opened up new possibilities for tokenization, particularly in the creative and entertainment sectors, where artists could monetize their work in a decentralized and direct manner.

In essence, the shift from ICOs to IDOs and NFTs represents a response to the former's challenges and a progression towards more secure, transparent, and sustainable practices. By offering a broader range of assets and democratizing the financial landscape, these new methodologies present promising advancements in the realm of digital finance, and they also hold the potential to redefine our understanding of financial systems and services. The adaptability and innovation inherent in these developments reaffirm the transformative potential of blockchain technology, illustrating its capacity to constantly evolve in response to the evolving needs and challenges.

FUTURE OF DeFi AND NFTs

Despite the potential risks and challenges associated with DeFi in general, and NFTs in particular, their future prospects appear promising. Several key trends are defining the trajectory of the DeFi ecosystem. One of these is the burgeoning use of cross-chain interoperability, which allows different blockchain networks to interact and transact with one another, thus increasing efficiency and promoting innovation. Furthermore, the development of more advanced financial instruments like derivatives, often characterized by increased complexity and risk management capabilities, marks an important progression within the DeFi landscape. Additionally, DeFi's growing integration with traditional finance, often termed as 'CeFi' or centralized finance, indicates a gradual blurring of lines between the traditional and crypto financial systems, with both leveraging the strengths of the other.

On the NFT front, we are still in the relatively early stages of acceptance and adoption. However, with an increasing number of artists, creators, and innovators gravitating towards NFTs and creating more diverse use cases, there is potential for a substantial uptick in the use and adoption of NFTs in the near future. As discussed in this chapter, this adoption is not limited to the artistic community.

The recent decline in the NFT market as described in several recent studies[5] can be attributed to a multitude of factors, including market saturation, regulatory uncertainty, and perhaps most significantly, a decline in the speculative hype that initially fuelled its meteoric rise. However, a bear market in the short term does not necessarily spell doom for the technology in the long term. The lower trading volume could signify market stabilization, as lower-quality projects fail, and more promising ones emerge. While the era of *white whales* making million-dollar purchases may be less frequent, this could lead to a more balanced ecosystem where utility and innovation are prioritized over speculation.

Looking forward, NFTs still have significant room for development and integration into broader digital and economic systems. The technology is still in its nascent stages, and its potential for enabling digital ownership, provenance, and asset interoperability across platforms is largely untapped. As blockchain technology itself matures and finds more mainstream adoption, NFTs could evolve into a more stable and useful tool. In addition, as scalability solutions for blockchain improve, the environmental concerns that cloud NFTs could be mitigated, making them more palatable to a wider audience. So, while the explosive growth seen in 2021 may not return in the same form, dismissing NFTs as a fad could be premature. The future of NFTs is not just about trading value but about the new kinds of digital interactions and ownership they could enable.

Both DeFi and NFTs have the potential to profoundly influence the global financial system by democratizing access to financial services, reducing reliance on conventional intermediaries, and fostering new, more sustainable financial models. While these emerging models do come with their own set of risks and challenges – from technological vulnerabilities to regulatory uncertainties – the prospective benefits they offer are substantial (Momtaz 2022). By facilitating more inclusive and sustainable financial practices, DeFi and NFTs could be instrumental in shaping the financial system of the future.

CONCLUSION

The contemporary era is marked by a transition from centralized finance to a more democratic, agile, and autonomous financial system. The initial incarnation of ICOs demonstrated certain inefficiencies and became overshadowed by rampant fraudulent activities, which in turn discredited the concept of blockchain-based fundraising. This was especially evident considering the early use cases of cryptocurrencies, which were often associated with illicit activities such as money laundering and black-market transactions. Regulatory bodies were slow to respond, but their growing wariness eventually helped curtail fraudulent activities. However, the very process that reined in the scams also effectively stifled the ICO market.

The industry's answer to this predicament came in the form of SAFTs and, later, STOs. Yet these alternatives were unable to completely sway regulators, who remained sceptical and often viewed all crypto tokens as disguised securities. The continuous need for financing from blockchain startups, however, led to the evolution of token sales into IEOs. In these offerings, the process seemingly reverted to the traditional system of involving an intermediary to run the token sale, thus instilling trust and efficiency in the process. Simultaneously, smaller projects sought financing through IDOs, and the arts sector began experimenting with NFTs.

What we are witnessing now is the rapid evolution of the blockchain ecosystem, marked by an ongoing tussle between market participants and regulatory bodies. Gradually, the perception that all cryptocurrencies are inherently securities is changing, and using almost century-old criteria like the Howey Test to provide a framework for innovative and complex products is increasingly seen as an outdated and stifling approach. The recent legal decision that the trading of Ripple's token on crypto exchanges does not constitute the sale of securities is a promising development for the industry.

As such, the task that lies ahead for us, as researchers, is to remain vigilant and tuned in to these rapid developments, keeping our fingers on the pulse of the crypto world. The pace of innovation has never been this fast and pervasive. As a blockchain enthusiast, I am heartened that we are living in such transformative times.

Welcome to the blockchain future.

NOTES

1 www.stelareum.io/defi-tvl.html.
2 www.ft.com/content/7bf570af-8507-4919-a23f-0269047b102f.
3 home.treasury.gov/system/files/136/DeFi-Risk-Full-Review.pdf.
4 www .theverge .com/ 2021/ 3/ 11/ 22325054/ beeple -christies -nft -sale -cost -everydays-69-million.
5 www.marketplacefairness.org/cryptocurrency/are-nfts-dead/ or dappgambl.com/ nfts/dead-nfts/ to name a few references to the point.

REFERENCES

Chalmers, D., Fisch, C., Matthews, R., Quinn, W., and Recker, J. (2022) 'Beyond the bubble: Will NFTs and digital proof of ownership empower creative industry entrepreneurs?', *Journal of Business Venturing Insights*, 17, e00309.

Chen, Y. and Bellavitis, C. (2020) 'Blockchain disruption and decentralized finance: The rise of decentralized business models', *Journal of Business Venturing Insights*, 13, e00151.

Chen, W., Zhang, T., Chen, Z., Zheng, Z., and Lu, Y. (2020) 'Traveling the token world: A graph analysis of Ethereum erc20 token ecosystem', in Proceedings of the Web conference 2020, pp. 1411–1421.

John, K., Kogan, L., and Saleh, F. (2022) 'Smart contracts and decentralized finance', SSRN. Available at: https://ssrn.com/abstract=4222528 (accessed: 1 July 2023).

Metcalfe, W. (2020) 'Ethereum, smart contracts, dApps'. In M. Yano, C. Dai, K. Masuda, and Y. Kishimoto (eds.), *Blockchain and Crypto Currency. Economics, Law, and Institutions in Asia Pacific*. Singapore: Springer, pp. 77–93.

Momtaz, P.P. (2022) 'Is decentralized finance (DeFi) efficient?', SSRN. Available at: https://ssrn.com/abstract=4095397 (accessed: 1 July 2023).

Ozili, P.K. (2022) 'Decentralized finance research and developments around the world', *Journal of Banking and Financial Technology*, 6(2), pp. 117–133.

Rosenfeld, M. (2012) 'Overview of colored coins', White Paper. Available at: http://diyhpl.us/~bryan/papers2/bitcoin/Overview%20of%20colored%20coins%20-%202012-12-04.pdf (accessed: 1 July 2023).

Schueffel, P. (2021) 'DeFi: Decentralized finance – an introduction and overview', *Journal of Innovation Management*, 9(3), pp. I–XI.

Wieandt, A. and Heppding, L. (2023) 'Centralized and decentralized finance: Coexistence or convergence?' In T. Walker, E. Nikbakht, and M. Kooli (eds.), *The Fintech Disruption: How Financial Innovation Is Transforming the Banking Industry*. Cham, Switzerland: Springer International Publishing, pp. 11–51.

Index

academic knowledge 5
ACChain 192
active community engagement 187
adequate financing 14
advisers and industry experts 107, 125–6
aggressive marketing 79
aggressive promotional campaigns 78
aggressive promotional strategies 78
Agrawal, A. 20, 110
Ahlers, G.K. 109
allocated tokens, distribution of 95
Alshater, M.M. 159, 163, 172
alternative blockchains 45, 92
alternative financing (AF) 14, 20, 30
alternative fundraising methods 55, 222
alternative fundraising models 33
alternative trading system (ATS) 134
Amsden, R. 96
Amsterdam Stock Exchange 202
anecdotal evidence 119
anonymity 2, 28, 60, 70, 111, 112, 114,
        115, 119, 182, 186
anti-money laundering (AML) 4, 54,
        130, 208, 223, 224, 227, 229
anti-touting provisions 128
Application Programming Interfaces
        (APIs) 146, 148, 153–5
Archive.is 144
artificial intelligence (AI) 115, 173
ArtistShare 19
Asia, ICO regulation in 212
asset management 12, 121, 132, 133
        digital 48
        and tokenization platforms 239–40
auditors/security firms 108
Augur 102, 105, 151, 152, 166, 167, 239,
        240
        token sale 45
automated distribution 102
automated market maker (AMM) 96
        platform 59
        system 241

automate financial transactions 236
Avalanche 55

Bahamas Test 160
balanced regulatory framework 3
Balancer 241
Balina, I. 128
Bancor Network Token (BNT) 50, 167,
        197–9
bank-based financial systems 15
bank loans 15
Bankman-Fried, S. 133
Barsan, I.M. 162
Basic Attention Token (BAT) project
        74, 165
Bayus, B.L. 109
Beaconcha 153
Belitski, M. 76, 96, 164
Bernard L. Madoff Investment Securities
        LLC 181
Bezos, J. 1
BigQuery 74
Binance 50, 58, 92, 94, 134, 167, 184,
        208, 211, 213, 226, 228, 229–30
Binance Coin (BNB) 50, 94, 229, 230
Binance Launchpad 58, 222, 225, 226,
        228–30
Binance Launchpool 241
Binance Smart Chain (BSC) 92, 104
BitAngels 36
Bitbond 219
Bitcoin 1, 8, 33, 36, 53, 60, 90, 93, 147,
        193, 211, 230, 235
        analysis of 148–52
        blockchain 37, 38, 98, 101, 148,
                149, 152, 234
        coloured coins 29
        contribution 149
        crowdfunding 152
        and illicit transactions 28–9
        in nutshell 27–8